# Political Science and Political Behaviour

By the same author:

*Constituency Electioneering in Britain*
*Political Culture*
*The British General Election of February 1974* (with David Butler)
*The British General Election of October 1974* (with David Butler)
*The British General Election of 1979* (with David Butler)
*British Politics Today* (with W. Jones)
*New Trends in British Politics* (editor with Richard Rose)
*The Politics of the Labour Party* (editor)

# Political Science and Political Behaviour

Dennis Kavanagh

*Professor of Politics, University of Nottingham*

London
GEORGE ALLEN & UNWIN
Boston Sydney

**George Allen & Unwin (Publishers) Ltd,
40 Museum Street, London WC1A 1LU, UK**

George Allen & Unwin (Publishers) Ltd,
Park Lane, Hemel Hempstead, Herts HP2 4TE, UK

Allen & Unwin, Inc.,
9 Winchester Terrace, Winchester, Mass. 01890, USA

George Allen & Unwin Australia Pty Ltd,
8 Napier Street, North Sydney, NSW 2060, Australia

First published in 1983
Second impression 1984

---

**British Library Cataloguing in Publication Data**

Kavanagh, Dennis
Political science and political behaviour.
1. Political psychology
I. Title
306'.2 JA74.5
ISBN 0-04-322008-8
ISBN 0-04-322009-6 Pbk

---

**Library of Congress Cataloging in Publication Data**

Kavanagh, Dennis.
Political science and political behaviour.
Bibliography: p.
Includes index.
1. Political sociology. 2. Political participation.
3. Political science. I. Title.
JA76.K362 1983 306'.2 83-9978
ISBN 0-04-322008-8
ISBN 0-04-322009-6 (pbk.)

---

Set in 10 on 11 point Times by Grove Graphics, Tring, Hertfordshire
and printed in Great Britain by
Redwood Burn Limited, Trowbridge, Wiltshire

# Contents

*To . . .*

Jane, David, Catherine and Helen

# Preface

My interest in the subject of political behaviour dates back to a seminar which I attended on the subject at the University of Manchester in 1964/5. The class was given by Richard Rose (now of Strathclyde University) and I was a graduate student at the time. I remember that one prescribed book was *Political Behaviour* by David Butler of Nuffield College, Oxford. Eventually I taught the subject at Manchester, after Rose's translation to Strathclyde. In the intervening years both David Butler and Richard Rose have provided me with friendship and intellectual stimulus. Indeed, I have jointly authored journal articles and books with each of them.

This book was conceived and written while I was a member of the Government Department at the University of Manchester. Like so many other past and present members I owe much to the department's tolerant and stimulating atmosphere. I also owe particular thanks to Hugh Berrington and Frank Castles for comments on early drafts of chapters.

I have dedicated the book to my children, including Helen who arrived as I was completing it. My greatest debt, as ever, is to my wife who creates the conditions in which I can study and write.

Dennis Kavanagh

# Introduction

My purpose in *Political Science and Political Behaviour* is to offer a critical but sympathetic assessment of the behavioural approach to the study of politics. For many of its advocates and its opponents, behaviouralism has appeared to be either a promise or a threat of a revolution to established methods of studying politics. The former welcomed it as a catching-up of politics with other social sciences, a major step towards a scientific study of behaviour and the application to politics of the methods of the natural sciences. For the critics it appeared to be a misguided pursuit of science and a quite inappropriate approach to the study of behaviour. My main concern is not to decide whether behaviouralism is a scientific approach and whether its findings constitute a body of scientifically founded statements. That would involve going over yet again what is by now familiar and rather inconclusive ground. If my own answer to both questions is negative, that does not mean that behaviouralism has not resulted in an improved understanding of the political process and a more rigorous approach to study.

What I regard as more useful is to look at a number of areas in political science which have been most studied by behavioural methods. The term 'political behaviour' refers as often to a set of methods or research perspectives as to a subject of study, that is, human behaviour in a political context. It is fair to judge the approach by its works. The findings represent the claims of behaviouralism to provide a new or improved political science; some represent additions to knowledge, some are confirmations or specifications of what was widely known through other approaches, intuition and personal impressions, and some are so inconclusive as not to deserve the title 'findings'. They are a mixed bag.

If we date the actual development of behaviouralism in political science in a significant way from the early 1950s, then the approach has been with us now for about a generation. The time is ripe for an assessment, not least because a second stage is under way. This includes the emergence of new theoretical models, more sophisticated techniques and methods, and revised interpretations. These have combined with changes in the real world to encourage students to ask new questions of their subject matter and to challenge many of the early findings. In addition, there has developed a powerful critique of behaviouralism, of both its assumptions and its findings.

This book presents chapters on a number of topics. For each topic I have tried to present the major substantive findings, comment on how they challenged traditional assumptions, and then discuss their contributions to a new science of politics. Most of the topics covered here have by now acquired their own special literature of articles, textbooks, volumes of readings, and controversies; some, indeed, are sub-fields in their own right. Inevitably, the need for compression and selectivity will give rise to objections about my choice of contents and omissions – let alone my interpretations and assessments.

I should make it clear that I think there has been a major improvement in the political science literature over the past two decades. There has developed a useful literature in almost every topic of research. In most fields the increase in our knowledge over these twenty years or so is impressive. In that respect, the potential is there for a more cumulative political science, even though its failure to achieve the status of an actual discipline or science (except in a loose sense) or acquire a general theory is quite marked.

Chapter 1

# The Study of Political Behaviour

In the postwar era the major growth area in the study of politics has undoubtedly been within the segment designated political behaviour. Political behaviour is something of a canopy term, referring both to a particular approach, a set of methods for the study of politics, and to a field, the study of human behaviour in politics. In large measure the growth is associated with a scientific study of politics, itself a part of the wider quest for the scientific study of social behaviour. The purpose of this opening chapter is to describe the behavioural treatment of politics and the circumstances surrounding its emergence.

On many counts the so-called scientific revolution in the study of politics during the 1950s had, by the late 1960s, already been absorbed so successfully into the discipline that, some might argue, there is little that is now distinctive about it. Some students became so convinced of the case for many of the behaviouralists' claims that, in 1961, Robert Dahl could write an 'Epitaph for a Monument to a Successful Protest' (Dahl, 1961a). By this, Dahl meant that the 'behavioural mood' could be expected to disappear not because it had failed, but because it had succeeded in so many of its aims and been incorporated into the discipline.

Behaviouralism represented a critical reaction against certain features of political science in the interwar years, particularly the fashionable concentration on formal political institutions and constitutions, and the relative neglect of actual political behaviour and informal political processes. During the 1950s this concern was joined to an impatience with the failure to employ quantitative methods to the same extent as the other social sciences and to a search for an over-arching theory or conceptual framework in which disparate research findings could be integrated.

It is easy to associate the behavioural approach with the Americanisation of political science. Given that some three-quarters of political scientists today are working in the United States, it is understandable that the dominant 'ethos' of contemporary political science is identified with activity in that country. It is also tempting to associate the approach with those fields in which it has been most evident, for example, the study of electoral behaviour, public opinion, political socialisation and policy outputs. Although these subjects have certainly attracted much of the research endeavour, it is incorrect to associate the approach exclusively with a particular field. Behaviouralism is an orientation which has affected research in most fields, including public administration, comparative government, political development and international relations. One spokesman has claimed that there is no sphere of political behaviour which is *per se* unamenable to the approach. Other advocates have argued that it is only a matter of time and the development of more sophisticated techniques and further research before the study of politics is able to rival the 'hard' sciences.

## Traditional Political Science

A major reason why the behavioural approach attracted controversy from the outset was that it arose out of dissatisfaction with the current state of the discipline; it was a 'protest' against the methods and substantive concerns which were dominant up to the end of the Second World War. Its more ambitious spokesmen saw it not as a development of current trends but as an overthrow, a revolution. In this, they have certainly exaggerated the degree of discontinuity between the old and 'new' political sciences. Before 1950, to set an arbitrary date, there were two dominant approaches in traditional political science: those of political theory and political institutions.

### History of Political Theory

Much traditional political theory was heavily normative or prescriptive, as much concerned with questions of the desirable forms of government, relations between man and society, and so on, as with analysis and description (Easton, 1953, ch. 10). Other theorists were concerned with the clarification of concepts, such as democracy, justice, or representation. Obviously Hobbes, Locke, Rousseau, or Bentham based their classic theories of political conduct on a view of human nature. Yet the behaviouralists' complaint about these political theories or philosophies was that human nature was so often taken for granted and rarely studied. By a process of deductive reasoning these writers appeared to move from a general premise (e.g. a person's quest for security) to conclusions about political behaviour, forms of government, 'justification' of authority, and so on. Traditionally, the study of theory had been a means of understanding the moral frame of reference or values of the theorists. By the opening decades of the twentieth century, however, what passed as political theory, far from dealing with great moral questions, as in the past, seemed to have declined into antiquarianism. This encompassed a historical treatment of ideas, and a relativistic view of values, as the writer concerned himself with relating ideas to past events and placing theories and theorists in their historical context.

A second charge concerned the low status of the discipline, particularly its vague and careless use of concepts (usually employed both normatively and descriptively), neglect of crucial topics, and disagreement on a central core in the study of politics. What followed from these shortcomings was a lack of cumulation in political studies. Other social sciences appeared to be better provided with systematic theories and to have developed the marks of being a discipline.

Easton, apart from mourning the decline of moral theory, wanted to advance a different kind of theory, which he called *causal* or *general* theory. This, he claimed, would elucidate significant areas for research, identify relationships between variables and enable us to integrate data. Armed with such a general theory the student of politics would be able to derive narrow generalisations and specific empirical conclusions which could be tested against the general theory.

## Legal-Institutional Approach

The institutional approach involved a concentration on the formal apparatus of politics – government; institutions, constitutions and states. There is a ready litany of critical adjectives to describe this approach: 'formal', 'sterile', 'lifeless'. It is a fair complaint that the approach often lost sight of the actor and ran the risk of mistaking the prescribed institutions and roles and the formal powers for reality. Indeed, politics was hardly seen as an *activity* or *process*. The emphasis on institutions had the effect of restricting the field of study both in time – to the modern period – and in area – to Western societies. It was difficult to study other societies which did not have analogous institutions or patterns of behaviour.

The legal-institutional approach, because of its assumptions about the importance of circumstances or environment in shaping behaviour, may usefully be placed in a larger perspective. As the study of politics emerged as an autonomous field so it sought its own subject matter. Social behaviour, including the political dimension, was already being studied by other social sciences. Students of politics could fasten on to the formal laws and institutions as 'their' own data. Eckstein (1963, pp. 10–11) has claimed that the positivist outlook, with its search for a value-free analysis and the accumulation of hard facts, also encouraged a focus on institutions. The emphasis on such 'situational' data was later extended by 'realists' to include non-government bodies such as elites, pressure groups, political parties and the mass media.

The most extreme example of the 'situational' approach to the study of behaviour was found in the behaviourist school of psychology associated with J. B. Watson, Pavlov and B. F. Skinner. Easton (1953, p. 174) notes that situational factors include:

(*a*) the physical environment;
(*b*) the non-human organic environment;
(*c*) the social environment.

These are 'given' or contextual factors and the key assumption made is that it is these factors and not the orientations of the actors themselves which substantially determine behaviour. In behaviourist psychological experiments these environmental factors may be controlled and observed. The process is neatly summarised in the S–R paradigm, whereby similar environments or *stimuli* are expected to produce similar *responses,* regardless of the subjective state of the respondent. In the hands of the behaviourist, of course, this is a scientific approach in the sense that he is solely concerned with the observable phenomena, that is, the stimuli and the responses, and discounts the subjective elements.

## Reactions

In the study of politics the situational approach was reflected in an emphasis on the impact of laws and institutions on political behaviour. It was later challenged by studies which emphasised the values and motives of the actors. The S–R paradigm was replaced by an S–O–R one, in which O refers to the *organism* or the actors' predispositions. In this model the actor independently affects both the stimuli and the outputs; hence the interest in attitudes, motives, perceptions, culture and 'operational codes' of the actors.[1] What was required was an appreciation of how the context and individuals interact, and of the relation between situational and psychological data. The way incumbents define their situations in an institution, for example, is an important factor in how they behave and how the institution works (e.g. studies of the different styles of politicians). As a careful scholar has noted, behaviour is a function of both the environmental situation in which actors find themselves and the psychological predispositions they bring to these situations (Greenstein, 1969).

The criticism, in summary, made against both the political theory and legal approaches was that they lost sight of political activity, particularly that which was taking place outside the formal political institutions. Many significant problems were also neglected –

bureaucracy, groups, mass movements, political apathy, the breakdown of political institutions and charismatic leadership, for example (Eulau, 1969).

A separate complaint was that students lacked a theory of politics in the shape of a conceptual framework which would provide orienting concepts, criteria for the selection of crucial variables, and connections between different phenomena. A more empirical political science, it was claimed, that would tackle these subjects by enlarging the scope of relevant and observable data and responding to the need for testing hypotheses. Somit and Tanenhaus summarise and evaluate the work of the opening two decades of the twentieth century as follows: the political science . . . tended to be legalistic, descriptive, formalistic, conceptually barren and largely devoid of what today would be called empirical data' (1967, p. 69).

A few scholars broke out of these confines. Graham Wallas and Walter Lippmann drew on personal experience and the infant study of psychology in their studies of public opinion. Like Walter Bagehot, they attacked what Wallas termed 'the intellectual fallacy', or the assumption that 'political action is necessarily the result of inferences as to means and ends [and] that all inferences are of the same "rational type" ' (1921, pp. 18, 45). A. F. Bentley's idea of a science of politics was based on a ruthless concentration on observable data. His approach was to observe and measure the influence of groups, which he regarded as the manifest 'reality' of politics. Speculation about the role of motives and ideology, was so much 'soul stuff' (as he scornfully described Dicey's famous essay, *Law and Opinion in England During the Nineteenth Century*, first published in 1905). Instead, students should concentrate on the observable end-results of these factors:

> If we can get our social life stated in terms of activity, and of nothing else, we have not indeed succeeded in measuring it, but we have at least reached a foundation upon which a coherent system of measurements can be built up. Our technique may be very poor at the start, and the amount of labor we must employ to get scanty results will be huge. But we shall cease to be blocked by the intervention of unmeasurable elements, which claim to be themselves the real causes of all that is happening, and which by their spook-like arbitrariness make impossible any progress toward dependable knowledge. (Lippmann, 1922, p. 202)

In the interwar years other scholars like Jennings, Herman Finer, Friedrich and Laski were sensitive to the new developments. The 'school' of elitists, Mosca, Pareto and Michels, writing at the turn of the century, also saw themselves as fashioning a genuinely neutral or scientific study of politics. Previous social theorists, they claimed, had confused prescription with description. They now wanted to go behind the 'fictions' embodied in constitutions, ideologies and intellectualist assumptions in search of the forces which shaped politics. They claimed to find rule by elites, regardless of different ideologies and political institutions. They were, of course, aware of the important differences between the natural and social sciences. Their own claims to be scientific rested on their avowed objective study of 'the facts of society' and its tendencies, and their disregard of normative questions as to what was desirable or how things might be different (Parry, 1969, ch. 1). In addition to challenging the optimistic outlook of many liberal writers, their work was also an important counter to another scientific interpretation: that of Marxism. In contrast to Marx, they claimed that there was a permanent ruling class and that no classless society would be possible in the future.

The search for a more empirical, scientific study of politics was encouraged by other factors in the interwar period. There was a growing awareness of the importance of informal – as opposed to institutional – politics, and of social and economic factors. The experiences of the Soviet Union, Nazi Germany and Italy were rude reminders that 'progress' to liberal democracy was not inevitable. After 1945 newly independent states in Africa and Asia ensured that the subject matter had to take account of non-Western experiences. Subsequent events in these states again pointed to the difficulty of 'exporting' Western-type political institutions. Developments in concepts and research methods, in sociology, anthropology and social psychology, also had implication for the study of behaviour in politics, particularly in the realm of political culture. Finally, there was a quest for a general theory of politics, which was most felt in comparative politics (Almond and Powell, 1966).

## Towards a Science

The development towards a political science went through different stages. The first stage was the break-up of philosophy, or the general body of knowledge, into distinct specialisms. A broad division evolved in the eighteenth century between the natural and the social sciences, and the latter gradually fragmented into various social science disciplines. Politics, though able to trace its lineage back to Aristotle, was perhaps the last of the social sciences to carve out a separate sphere for itself.

In the nineteenth century the study of society made important strides towards achieving a scientific status. St Simon, Herbert Spencer, Karl

Marx and Auguste Comte were prominent 'system' theorists. All claimed to be scientific in that they could explain the causes of social phenomena and, on the basis of this knowledge, make predictions. Comte, for example, claimed to have introduced into his work the 'positive' methods of the natural sciences. Human knowledge, he wrote, had passed through three stages, the 'theological', 'metaphysical' and 'positive', and now the knowledge of the third stage was to be applied to the study of man. As a rule, these writers were also interested in applying the new knowledge to the reconstruction of society. The successors of Comte were the Logical Positivists, a group of philosophers working in the 1930s. They claimed that valid knowledge was that which could be perceived or experienced by an observer, and rejected the validity of value judgements on the ground that such statements could not be tested by experience. Applied to the social sciences, such an approach held that the procedures of the natural sciences could be applied to the study of society, that there was a unity of the sciences, and that one could arrive at law-like generalisations.

The American context has undoubtedly shaped the notion of a science of politics. The debates about the constitution in the 1780s and the outlook of many of the Founding Fathers reflected an Enlightenment belief in a 'science of politics'. The United States was also sympathetic to pragmatism, the experimental method, and knowledge which could be observed and tested. A general regard for an engineering approach to society was joined to an optimism that new techniques and forms of knowledge could be applied for the improvement of society. The twin pillars of science as a method and moral progress as a goal were joined in the Progressive temper. Landau notes that the pragmatic side and the scientific temper favoured not only the development of formal theory and 'hard' science, but also 'a search for veridical knowledge, for fact and of cause–effect relations – goals which exhibit a cardinal property of the scientific situation' (1972, p. 19).

The outstanding figure associated with this development in the United States was Charles Merriam, the pioneer of the so-called Chicago School. His *New Aspects of Politics* (1925) articulated the concern that politics was not keeping pace with developments in other social sciences, particularly economics and psychology, and that there was a need for a more scientific and quantitative observation of human behaviour (Crick, 1959, ch. 8). Merriam unashamedly believed that this new science should help in the formation of citizens and the building of a democratic society. The challenge to a scientific politics, he claimed, was to solve problems, prevent war, reduce class conflict and remove the causes of revolution. A similarly therapeutic thrust lay behind the growing interest in a science of public administration (ibid., p. 81). David Easton's (1967) view is that the social sciences have been going through a third phase, as behavioural sciences, and that the study of politics might have been alienated from the other social sciences if it had not embraced behaviouralism.

## The Quest for Theory

The emphasis on more empirical work was coupled with the search for theories which would orientate research, in the shape of hypotheses which could be tested in the real world, and integrate findings. Gabriel Almond (1967, p. 8) noted that the search for 'comprehensiveness, for realism, and for precision' strained existing frameworks and vocabularies. Easton (1953) was probably the most systematic critic of the neglect of over-arching theory and lack of analytic rigour, compared with most other sciences. The result was 'hyperfactionalism', and the collection of data with little attention being paid to their significance or interrelationships. He claimed that a body of theory would provide a tool for organising the material. A second use of theory was that it provided a means of separating political science from political ideology. The new theory would be empirical and descriptive rather than normative. Easton's own distinctive contribution was the notion of the *political system* as a set of interrelated processes and structures, which is concerned with 'the authoritative allocation of values in society'. The polity consists of *inputs* (demands and support) and *outputs* (authoritative allocations of policies, regulations, decisions and laws). The polity is separate from and bounded by an environment which includes such external conditions as the culture, economy, its international position, and so on. The system both influences and is influenced by the environment.

Gabriel Almond's attempt to break out from an institutional and Western-dominated framework took the form of a functional approach to political analysis. In this he was influenced by Talcott Parsons's idea of a social system, which Parsons in turn derived from Pareto and Weber. Almond suggested that certain input and output functions were common to all societies, even though they might be performed by different structures and institutions. A focus on functions enabled one to compare both primitive and advanced systems in terms of which structures performed certain common functions. Yet his set of output functions (rule-making, rule application and rule adjudication) was borrowed from the traditional legal-institutional approach with its distinction between legislative, executive and judicial tasks. As Almond admits, his terms were an attempt to codify and systematise ideas which had been in currency for a long time. System functionalism was not, however, a theory dealing with causation but rather a framework or approach for analysing and ordering findings.

It is now fashionable to write of 'the failure' of such general approaches as systems, structural functionalism, or communications. Critics have fairly pointed to logical weaknesses in the concept of 'systems' (Finer, 1969), the difficulties of basing empirical research on such general and abstract theories (La Palombara, 1968), and the problem of separating function from structure (Sartori, 1970). The influence of these theories is now more reflected in the vocabulary of the contemporary political scientist, as seen in such terms as political socialisation, political culture, inputs and outputs, and so on. And the notion of 'system' reminds one of the interrelatedness of the parts of the political system. By and large, much 'grand' theory has taken the form of models which attempt to identify important phenomena, provide categories for organising information, and suggest questions and relationships between political and other phenomena.

## The Behavioural Approach

Most behaviouralists have avoided a precise and limiting definition of behaviouralism. They have variously spoken of an 'approach', 'tendency', 'mood', 'stance', 'orientation' and 'persuasion'. These terms direct our attention more to the style and method than to the substance of the research. It is these features associated with research techniques which, we are told, mark out the behavioural scholar. Behaviouralism has been praised as the means of making the study of politics truly scientific, by reducing the subjective element in research, by testing hypotheses, by avoiding prescriptive statements and by providing quantifiable statements about relationships between variables. On the other hand, critics have condemned it as mere methodism, which produces brute empiricism and is hostile to the imaginative, speculative and critical spirit. Much contemporary critical comment, it is worth noting, is found among the ranks of behaviouralists themselves (Dahl, 1967; Easton, 1969; Almond and Genco, 1977).

What are some of the salient features of the approach (Somit and Tannenhaus, ch. 12; Easton, 1967, pp. 16–17)? It is, first of all, an orientation or disposition to collect, analyse and interpret evidence according to the canons of scientific research. This has depended on developments in research techniques, such as sample surveys and multivariate statistical analyses and the availability of computers able to process large quantities of data. Obviously the social scientist's basic data – the acts and orientations of individuals and groups – do not enable him to rival the 'hardness' of the physical scientist's material;

the respective experimental conditions which face the two are hardly comparable. The main emphasis has been on a recognition of the difference between facts and value judgements. A descriptive statement may be subject to empirical tests in contrast to a statement of value preferences. It also requires that other researchers can check the methods of collection and analysis of data; where this is achieved we say that the statement is amenable to the tests of inter-subjective validity. Data should be collected along systematic lines and subject to classification, measurement and replication. Again, philosophers have asked awkward questions about this 'positive' stance, about the analogies with the natural sciences, and about the possibility of separating 'ought' from 'is' questions in studying politics (see Chapter 10).

The focus is on *behaviour,* in large part because this is observable. According to Heinz Eulau, the approach 'is concerned with what man does politically and the meanings he attaches to his behaviour' (1963, p. 5). For example, we study institutions not only through their formal rules and procedures, but also through the actual behaviour and orientations of individuals who operate in the institutions. If we say of the electorate's mood that it has moved in a particular direction, we transform this into statements about the motives of individual voters, the policies of particular parties, the appeals of candidates and the interaction between them. If we want to study a legislature, then the legislator is our unit of analysis and the legislative system the object of analysis. In itself, this approach is not incompatible with legal or institutional analysis. Clearly, constitutions and institutional procedures, and the set of expectations and rules which they embody, all affect behaviour. A bureaucracy, for example, may attract and also shape recruits with 'appropriate' personalities. But if there are limits to the impact of personality on a person's formal political role and its demands on him, then there are also limits to the extent of this institutional engineering.

Behaviouralism reflects the close relationships between political science and the other social sciences. Politics has long been a borrowing discipline. In its early (nineteenth-century) stages as an academic subject it was closely tied to the study of law, philosophy and history. One may still discern the legacy of these historical roots on it. The impact of behaviouralism, with its emphasis on observable behaviour, made the study of politics more open to developments in other social sciences, particularly those in social psychology in the 1920s. These influences on the behavioural study of politics arose in large part because they met a felt need. It is often claimed that an understanding of a person's political behaviour will usually be advanced by studying it in a broader context. A person's political activity may well be closely linked to, say, his social class, his religion, or even his personality. In studying social structure or political culture, we have to reach out to other disciplines for modes of explanation which are primarily psychological, sociological, or anthropological. In comparative politics the structural functional approach, for example, drew heavily on sociology and anthropology to develop a new vocabulary and set of concepts that replaced those which were institutional, legalistic and manifestly Western-oriented.

The assumptions (*a*) that the political should be seen as part of a wider pattern of behaviour, and (*b*) that the political act is probably derivative, because politics is a peripheral activity for most people, have led to the complaint of reductionism. As each social science has tried to expand its own sphere of competence, so it has tended to explain the political in terms of its 'own' variables. This has been particularly true of approaches of sociology and economics. Sartori's question about the role or influence allowed to the political factors in political sociology is apposite for much behaviouralism: on what terms do the two disciplines combine in the hybrid? Is it, as he complains, a sociology of politics rather than a genuine political sociology?

Finally, behaviouralism is concerned to develop hypotheses which are testable. The goal is to build up empirical political theory, to interrelate substantiated research findings and to explain political behaviour. In other words, can our statements stand the test of objective assessment? According to Moon: 'Theories are genuinely explanatory only if one can use them deductively to infer statements cast in observational terms, which can then be seen to be true or false' (1975, p.146). Developing hypotheses which are amenable to verification or falsification requires that definitions and concepts be operational, or that they be so framed that we can develop empirical referents or indicators for them and transform them into variables. Once this is done, we may proceed with empirical research, examine relationships between variables and, hopefully, make probability statements and conditional predictions of the 'if . . . then . . .' kind. Do the findings confirm or disconfirm the theory? Falsifiability is the essence of the scientific approach. As Popper (1959) points out, we can never finally 'prove' a hypothesis. We can eliminate hypotheses where the expected consequences are not confirmed in a test, whereas successive confirmations provide at best corroboration though not final proof of the hypothesis.

Political scientists have developed indicators for several concepts; political culture, political efficacy, ideology, alienation, partisanship, power, and so on. We may measure a person's partisanship or party identification by asking him which party he supports, or feels closest to. We may assign a person to a social class on the basis of his occupation (objective class) or his own rating of his class (subjective class). We can also move to a richer set of indicators for a more complex definition of social class, adding education, home-ownership, and so on, to the above questions. In making the concepts operational we look for two features:

(*a*) validity – does the item measure what it purports to?
(*b*) reliability – does the item give similar results under similar conditions? (cf. Rosenburg, 1968).

But conceptualisation is prior to and more important than operationalisation. And it has to be admitted that many concepts in popular usage among political scientists leave a great deal to be desired. Terms like democracy, power, political development and party system have different meanings for different scholars. The lack of agreed, precise and consistent definitions results in the terms covering so many cases that they become imprecise. There is a 'stretching' of the concepts (Sartori, 1970).

The remaining chapters of this book examine the findings of political behaviour research in such various fields as public opinion, political culture, political socialisation, electoral behaviour, political leadership, policy outputs, and the relationships between political structure and social and economic factors. These chapters do not amount to a comprehensive list of the areas in which the behavioural approach has been applied. But they do constitute a substantial enough body of research to permit some assessment of the approach. The final two chapters examine the influence of the studies on theorising about democracy and then assess the impact of the behavioural approach in the light of the new post-behavioural reaction to it.

## Note: Chapter 1

1 Some critics might now complain that the stage has been reached when the contextual or institutional factors have become under-valued. A good example is the plethora of studies of electoral behaviour, which make hardly any reference to the role of party and electoral systems or the activities of candidates and voters. (See Chapter 5 below.)

Chapter 2

# Public Opinion

The term 'public opinion' suffers from being used in everyday discourse as well as being used by academic students of politics. It is therefore a prey to different meanings and interpretations. In recent years the academic study of public opinion has been transformed by the development of sample surveys. Such surveys, which scientifically draw a representative sample from a population and systematically question it, provide a more reliable guide to the views of the public than those provided by hunch, letters to a newspaper, ordinary conversation, or the claims of pressure groups. The explosion of survey research has produced a mass of data on public opinion and electoral behaviour. Surveys can now provide us with information on the balance of opinion on a question and distribution of opinion across groups in a population. In Britain a representative sample of 1,500 people will have a margin of error of ± 3 per cent in 95 per cent of cases. This means that in nineteen out of twenty cases our results will be within 3 percentage points of the actual result. Thus, a finding that the electorate supports one party over another by 55:45 per cent means that the party's support may range between 52 and 58 per cent and that of the opposition may range between 42 and 48 per cent. The larger the sample, the smaller the margin of error. Most surveys are prepared to work at 95 per cent levels of confidence.

## Qualities of Public Opinion

As usual, it is important to be clear and consistent in one's use of terms. It is easy to confuse 'the public' with a particular *group* (defined by age, occupation, residence, interest, religion, or whatever), or with the most *informed*. In the nineteenth century, indeed, the terms 'public opinion' and 'the people' were equated with the educated middle class. Opinion pollsters frequently encounter people who are prepared to express a view without having the slightest knowledge about the subject. It is also useful to distinguish between an *opinion* , or an expressed view on an issue; an *attitude,* which refers to a more general stance or disposition; and a *belief,* or an attitude which is deeply held. An opinion may vary in its intensity, its informational context and its stability. Generally speaking, the more intense, informed and stable an opinion is, the more likely a person is to act on it.

We also need to distinguish statements of opinion on an issue according to whether they are cognitive (concerning knowledge about it), affective (whether it is liked or disliked), or evaluative (judgements about it). The term public opinion, for better or worse, usually refers to the aggregate of such diverse opinions. We have already noted that people are willing to express views, regardless of whether they have even heard of the subject. Slight differences in question-wording elicit different responses (e.g. 'devolution' or 'an independent Scottish Assembly'; the 'Common Market' or the 'EEC'). Philip Converse's (1964) replication of identical questions to a panel of respondents over a period of four years in the United States found great inconsistency in the opinions expressed on issues. On average in only thirteen out of twenty cases did people choose the same side on an issue position at both interviews. In Britain, Butler and Stokes found that, out of a panel of voters interviewed in 1963, 1964 and 1966, only 39 per cent expressed the same view on nationalisation on all three occasions (1969, ch. 8).[1] But this volatility among individuals masked great stability at the aggregate level. Such instability is a crude indicator of the low salience of an issue to a person.

Another example is the marked swings of opinion regarding support for entry to membership of the Common Market between 1961, when the first moves were made by a British government to join the Community, and 1973 when Britain became a member. Until 1966 Gallup found that the balance of opinion was favourable to entry; between 1967 and 1971 opinion gradually turned against entry; and opinion was evenly divided in 1972–3. The shifts have continued since (King, 1976, p. 20). Until 1970 there was little polarisation of opinion on partisan grounds, for the two main parties did not present clear and opposing lines on the issue. Since early 1971, however, the opinions of most Labour voters on the issue have shifted in response to that party's changes of line on the EEC. According to one survey: 'through the various stages of the EEC issue, the voters were willing to endorse the standpoints chosen by the party they generally supported, in particular if that party was in government' (Sarlvik *et al.*, 1976, p. 97). Some part of the shift is to be explained by changes in Britain's relations with the Common Market, by events, and by the lead set by the parties. But a good part is also explained by the low salience of the issue; most people simply did not have settled views on the EEC.

The intensity of a person's opinion on an issue depends on such factors as the salience of the issue for him, and his perception that it affects his own interest or a group with which he identifies. For example, teachers, civil servants and other members of the public services are likely to be very concerned about parties' proposals about levels of public expenditure in general, and plans for their particular services. Intensity often accompanies stability of opinion on an issue. In Ulster, for example, political and religious loyalties are so entwined and opinions so strongly held that political compromises between rival Catholics and Protestants are difficult to achieve. One Ulsterman, when asked to account for his political beliefs, referred back to the Battle of the Boyne, fought in 1690! Intensity of opinion-holding may also be related to personality structure; authoritarianism and anti-semitism, for example, appear to be part of a personality pattern (see below). Katz (1960) has emphasised the psychological functions of opinions for a person. They may serve to organise his environment, provide a self-image or self-identity, and allow the projection of attitudes on to an external object. Festinger's work on cognitive dissonance (1957) has shown how the centrality of a belief to a person's outlook affects the likelihood of his resistance to changing it and the strategies people have for coping with apparently divergent messages. An example of dissonance or contradictory views is where one is in sharp disagreement with the issue position(s) of a favoured political party or candidate. An early study of such 'cross-pressured' voters showed that they coped with dissonance either by deciding how to vote very late in the campaign, or not voting at all, misperceiving the apparent divergences, moderating the intensity of their rival preferences, and so forth (Lazarsfeld *et al.*, 1948). The more central the belief is, the more reluctant a person is to change it, and the more likely he is to adopt various strategies to ward off information which challenges it.

A number of writers in the nineteenth century were optimistic about the individual's capacity to reason about politics. A belief in the potential rationality of citizens was one of the arguments advanced for the extension of the suffrage in the nineteenth century. Certainly many liberals had an ideal of the rational, issue-based voter, one who thought of the public interest, would seek out information on the issues of the day, compare the parties' stands and their likely effects on the public welfare, and then vote for the one nearest to his own position. This type of citizen was, of course, presented as an ideal to be promoted rather than one that was likely to be achieved in practice. But it was widely accepted as a goal worth striving for.

We now know that the ideal has not been realised. Even before 1914 some students of politics and psychologists were aware of the part that the non-rational elements of the subconscious, emotions and instinct played in political behaviour. Bagehot, writing about popular perceptions of the British monarchy, Michels on oligarchy in parties and organisations, Le Bon on crowds, or McDougall and Wallas on political behaviour, all reflected this awareness of irrationality in politics. Developments in the new studies of psychology and psychiatry further enhanced it. Wallas, in his aptly titled *Human Nature in Politics* (1921), criticised the common 'intellectualist fallacy' of many democratic theorists. Behaviour and attitudes, he suggested, emerged less from a process of reasoning than from prejudice, habit, stereotypes and symbols. Political behaviour, he noted, consists largely in the creation of opinion by the deliberate exploitation of sub-conscious non-rational inference. The political instability in Central Europe after 1919 and the emergence of dictatorships with mass appeal provided further evidence of the irrationality and suggestability of the mass electorate.

Recent empirical studies of electoral behaviour have shown that the votes of most individuals are decided less by specific issues and more by traditional party loyalty, perceptions of personal interest, the personality of candidates, a government's record, and so on. The general image of a political party provides a short cut for many people in deciding how to vote (Downs, 1957). Contemporary notions of rationality of opinions emphasise two features: first, that a person is open to new information on an issue, regardless of whether it reinforces or undermines his own position, and that he does not distort it; secondly, that he is able to relate his issue preferences in a logical manner, or make logical inferences between one preference and another. Lane and Sears (1964, p. 76) have suggested that certain issue areas are particularly prone to attract irrational opinion and prejudice. These include such topics as war, criminal punishment, immigration, and sexual matters. The general criteria for attracting irrationality, they suggest, are: 'The (*a*) more vague the refinements of an opinion, (*b*) more remote and difficult to assess its action consequences, and (*c*) more abstract the terms of debate.' Apart from the differences in the intensity, stability, informational context and structure of opinions, one may point to some other problems in interpreting an opinion. A 'paradox' is that many people hold opinions that appear at first sight to be incompatible. In Britain surveys show that people favour equality of educational opportunity and comprehensive schools as well as the retention of grammar or selective schools, or tax reductions and the expansion of welfare and educational programmes. In the United States there is majority support for the goals of equal opportunity and equal rights – but not for the affirmative action programmes which give preferential treatment to minorities. Well-conducted opinion polls which ask several questions on an issue are useful in elucidating the context (and meaning) of opinions.

One way of explaining this apparent paradox is that there are views which appear to be incompatible to the observer, but are logical to the opinion-holders. Many studies have noted how there is greater agreement on general or abstract propositions about politics and society but more disagreement when questions move to specific situations. The tendency is to 'stretch' the values, so that there is no apparent contradiction between the general and specific items. In turn, this disjunction between the general and specific values may be a form of 'false consciousness' (Mann, 1970). The responses to the specific and directly experienced problems are likely to be more 'real' than those dealing with remote matters.

Opinion surveys are useful for interpreting behaviour or evaluating a party's claim to have a mandate for its general programme or particular policy. In 1968 Senator Eugene McCarthy came close to defeating President Johnson in the New Hampshire presidential primary. McCarthy was a major spokesman for the opposition to the Vietnam War, and his impressive support was generally regarded as a 'peace' vote. In fact much of his support came from 'hawks' who were disaffected with Johnson and wanted a more vigorous prosecution of the war (Converse *et al.*, 1969). In Britain Labour won the two 1974 general elections, in spite, according to the surveys, of the unpopularity of a number of its left-wing policies.

Because surveys or other readings of public opinion may be interpreted in different ways, one may disagree about their implication for the political system. For example, Miller (1974) has presented data on the rise of mistrust and cynicism about American government between 1966 and 1970. His findings, based on questions repeated over these years, show a general increase in cynicism for both Democrats and Republicans and blacks and whites, and one that was particularly marked among those favouring opposing policies on the political left and right. Miller claims that his data show 'a pervasive and enduring distrust of government' (p. 1951). An alternative interpretation (Citrin, 1974) is that the attitudes were a reaction to the specific events and issues during these years, and that dissatisfaction with parties and leaders does not necessarily carry over to weaken the legitimacy of the regime.

## Attitude Change

We are interested in studying changes in attitude over time as a means of analysing causal relationships. A questionnaire is a static instrument that measures attitudes or behaviour at one point in time. A frequent complaint concerns the a-historical or non-dynamic quality of most survey research. We know that stability over time in aggregate data may disguise substantial variations among individuals. We are also aware of the dangers of extrapolating into the future from present or recent trends. There are, however, various ways of coping with this problem. They include the use of:

(*a*) *Panels*. By interviewing the same group of people at different points in time one may assess the extent and nature of changes in attitudes among individuals. Many major national voting surveys employ panels. The first edition (1969) of *Political Change in Britain*, for example, was based on interviews conducted in 1963, 1964 and 1966 with the same sample of voters. The problem with such panel surveys is not only that, compared to other surveys, they are expensive to conduct but that, over time, they risk becoming unrepresentative because of the loss of respondents through deaths, removals, and so on. They remain, however, the preferred research instrument for tackling this problem.

(*b*) *Cross-section studies*. One may make inferences about changes over time by analysing the responses of different age-groups, interviewed at one point in time. A good deal of *cohort* analysis takes this form. The idea of a cohort or *political generation* rests on the assumption that people of a particular age-group will be affected by certain large-scale events, e.g. the economic depression in the United States, or the experience of the 1939–45 war.

(*c*) *Replication*. As a variation on the panel approach one may re-interview respondents after a lengthy lapse of time. Newcomb (1943, 1967) re-interviewed his group of former Bennington female students some twenty years later when their roles had changed greatly, and Jennings and Niemi (1974, 1981) re-interviewed parents and their offspring after a gap of eight years.

(*d*) *Time-series data*. Major opinion polling organisations ask a limited number of key questions in their regular surveys. Since 1939, for example, Gallup in Britain has regularly asked voters for their party preferences, approval of the performance of the party leader and government of the day, and attitudes on issues. Such data, used carefully, are a useful guide to changes in political attitudes. Since the 1950s the Michigan series of election studies has asked American voters the same questions at different points in time.[2]

There are problems in analysing change in attitudes. Putman (1973), in his study of ideology among Italian and British politicians, has distinguished three different types of explanation (p. 76). One is a *life-cycle* explanation which holds that changes in attitudes are a function of a person's age. It is frequently claimed that as people become older, and assume occupational and family responsibilities, so they become more 'conservative' in terms of social attitudes, respect for traditions, and perhaps support for a right-of-centre political party. This interpretation assumes that people will in time adopt the attitudes older generations held when the latter were in their age-group. A *natural selection* explanation holds that changes in the attitudes of a group are a function of its changing composition, or the disproportionate withdrawal or removal of members with a particular view. It may be, for example, that the more radically minded members of a political party are more likely to become disillusioned over time and withdraw, so producing a change in the group's outlook. Alternatively, the withdrawal of the more weakly committed or 'moderate' supporters may shift the party in a more radical direction. In Chapter 5 we will see how the net effect of changes in arrivals and withdrawals in the electorate is another illustration of how political change may occur, without anybody actually changing his opinion. A *generational* explanation sees a person's attitude as a function of his age-group's situation and experiences at a particular time in history (cf. Inglehart, 1971). It assumes that during adolescence or early adulthood a person is particularly susceptible to new ideas and is likely to retain them in later years. A further possible source of change is *period effects,* in which events and trends affect the entire society. In practice it is not easy to separate these approaches to explaining change. A change in the political outlook from one generation to the next may be a product of both period and generational effects (i.e. influence by events). It may also have to do with the younger generation being better educated, for example.

## Consensus

There has been much debate among social theorists as to the importance of consensus for social order. For example, Rousseau wrote of the need for a 'General Will' and Parsons emphasised the need for common values to underpin stability in society. Marx, on the other hand, regarded these common values in a capitalist society as a form of ideological rule by the elite; in the absence of such agreement, the dominance of the elite is buttressed more openly by coercion. Other theorists (Dahrendorf, 1957; Mann, 1970), have argued for a 'mixed theory' of consensus and conflict, with agreement on some values and a mixture of disagreement and elite dominance on others. One school of political analysis explains the greater political stability of Britain and the United States, compared with Italy, France, and Germany, in terms of the greater consensus or agreement on basic political values in the former societies. A recurring theme in the literature of stable democracy is the importance of a general commitment to democratic values in the society. In contrast, Crick (1966) and Rustow (1970) have claimed that the essence of democracy arises out of disagreements and attempts to reconcile them – but not eliminate them. Agreement is an end-product, not a condition, of the democratic process, and consensus is not only irrelevant, but may be inimical to democracy.

The dictionary definition of consensus is agreement or unanimity. Political scientists have used the term in the following senses.

(1) *Agreement between political elites.* A number of surveys have found higher levels of agreement on the political 'rules of the game' among those who are more politically active and those with higher social status and education. In divided societies political stability has depended particularly on agreement between leaders of rival groups. In what Lijphart (1968b) calls *consociational* states, bitter antagonisms at grass-roots level have not been represented by the leaders and this helps the stability of the system (see Chapter 4).
(2) *Political style or political process.* Political parties, groups, legislatures, and so on, are said to be consensual if their demands are bargainable rather than zero-sum, and if political differences are resolved by a process of discussion, compromise and according to agreed procedures.
(3) *Agreement on political 'fundamentals'.* The fundamentals are often left vague, but usually they include such features as the nature of the system, (e.g. parliamentary, presidential, or monarchy), procedures for choosing a government, qualifications for citizenship and the location of political sovereignty.
(4) *Loyalty to cross-cutting groups.* This group theory hypothesises that a person's loyalty to various groups moderates the strength of his attachment to any one of them. On the other hand loyalty to reinforcing groups is conducive to the development of rival and conflicting sub-cultures (see below). The assumption is that group membership colours issue preferences. The implications of (4) for elites who want to promote stability is that, in contrast to (2) above, they should avoid making appeals which are exclusive to particular groups. Instead, policies should be general in appeal because of the lack of political sectionalism in the electorate (Lipset, 1959, pp. 77–8). The early voting studies showed that voters whose friends and reference groups belonged to different parties were likely to be moderate in their partisanship (e.g. Lazarsfeld *et al.*, 1948). In Britain, for example, the less working-class or middle-class

a person is in terms of possessing class-typical social characteristics, the more likely he is to defect from his class-typical party (Rose, 1980).[3] The only empirical study of the theory that multiple group membership dilutes partisanship is inconclusive (Verba, 1965).

There are subtle differences in the above formulations, even though they all share an emphasis on agreement. The first specifies agreement between elites on the main features of the system, or 'rules of the game'. The second assumes that differences exist but are not such as to lead to conflict, that politics is not a zero-sum game. The third refers to agreement among the public on 'the rules of the game' and/or that disagreements are only weakly held and not acted on. Finally, the fourth view sees attitudes as deriving from group loyalties and social pluralism as diluting the individual's strong or exclusive identification with any one group. In effect, the last two formulations regard consensus as the lack of sharp constitutional disagreements between clearly defined social groups.

Two well-known survey studies have tried to confront the question of the relations between consensus and democracy (Prothro and Grigg, 1960; McClosky *et al.*, 1960). The first study, conducted in the 1950s among two communities in the American South and Midwest, found virtually unanimous support for abstract statements about liberal democracy and associated principles of majority rule and minority rights. There was, however, a marked reduction in positive agreement when it came to applying those general precepts to specific cases and groups. By large majorities respondents agreed with the general right to free speech and of people with different views to run for political office; they did not accept, however, the rights of free speech for communists, or of blacks to run for public office. McClosky's sample was a two-tiered one, of political activists at the Democratic and Republican conventions in 1956, and the general public. He also found high levels of agreement on general propositions about 'the rules of the political game', the general values of free speech and equality, but disagreement when it came to specific cases. Both studies also found higher levels of consistency among the more politically active and the more educated. Similar patterns were found by Budge in his study of British politicians and voters (1970). The unwillingness or inability of many people to derive from general rules the appropriate specific applications suggested that consensus on democratic principles exists only at an abstract level.

These two studies have provided the empirical foundations for a number of claims about the place of values for democracy and the nature of political thinking. The first is that the absence of general agreement and the failure to apply many abstract values to specific cases shows that a deep or widespread attachment to democratic values is not a prerequisite for a functioning democracy. Instead, it is argued, the democratic system rests more on habit, or acquiescence in the principles, rather than an understanding of their implications. Secondly, the greater agreement and internal consistency in beliefs about abstract and procedural values among the more active and more educated has encouraged the claim that such people are 'the carriers of the [democratic] creed' (Prothro and Grigg, 1960, p. 205). The attitudes of such people are more integrated; they are also more likely to be involved in politics, and so they are likely to act on their (democratic) beliefs. The commitment of such people to the procedures, it is argued, ensures the working of the system in normal times. The authors suggest that the lower rates of political participation among those with a rudimentary understanding of democracy and a general lack of constraint in their views may be a blessing in disguise. Expansion of political participation carries the risk of involving the more illiberal groups in society, for 'those with most undemocratic values are also those least likely to act' (ibid., p. 294); hence 'the functional nature of apathy for the political system'.

## Belief Systems and Ideology

Other studies have also found that only a small minority of people appear to possess belief systems or political ideologies. Survey researchers, trying to cast these terms in a form suitable for empirical research, have emphasised two features: one is the consistency or stability of attitudes; the other is the constraint or intercorrelation of attitudes, that is, possession of attitudes that logically or commonly 'belong' together. For example, it is hardly logical to support simultaneously greater levels of government spending, a balanced budget and tax reductions, or to support, say, further nationalisation of industry and the practice of free enterprise. We may regard a person's beliefs as being constrained if, knowing his position on some issues, we are able to predict correctly his position on other issues. Instability is generally a sign that a belief is not salient or central for the person and often a warning sign of low constraint. We have already presented information on the inconsistency or instability of public opinion on many issues. Both British and American voting studies have also found that the 'expected' intercorrelations of opinions are limited, even among those having stable views. According to one study of British voters, 'when we confine our attention to the minority of people who have well-formed and enduring views, the actual association of attitudes is relatively feeble' (Butler and Stokes, 1975, p. 320). In the United States in the 1950s there was hardly any relationship between a person's support for an 'active' foreign policy and an 'active' role for the federal government on domestic policy, or between support for an 'isolationist' stand in foreign affairs and a limited role for government at home. The former sets of policies were regarded at the time as signifying a 'liberal' outlook on politics and the latter a 'conservative' one. Yet the American public possessed remarkably little in the way of an ideology, when viewed in these terms.

Another approach to the study of ideology has been to examine the extent to which voters actually use broad ideological terms or frames of reference to explain their choice of party. Is there any evidence that many people conceptualise politics in terms of 'left' and 'right', or talk in general terms about, say, the role of government or relations between the state and individual? To what extent do views derive from certain general principles? In Britain the political symbols of left and right have long been applied to the main parties, Labour and Conservative. But the terms appear to have little meaning for the majority of voters. A mere 25 per cent admitted that they thought of themselves in these terms and a further 20–25 per cent were able to link them correctly with the Labour and Conservative parties. Only a proportion of these were able to offer an elaborate explanation of the concepts; perhaps as few as a sixth of British voters actually think of parties and issues in these terms (Butler and Stokes, 1975, ch. 4). In the United States *The American Voter* (Campbell *et al.*, 1960, ch. 9) found that only 12 per cent could be regarded as *ideologues*, that is, as 'liberals' or 'conservatives', when it came to discussing candidates, parties and issues. The majority of Americans explained their votes in terms of group benefits or 'the nature of the times'. Broadly similar findings about French voters were found during the same period.

The research on political beliefs and consensus does cumulate in several respects. On the whole there is little in the way of structured thinking about politics among voters. An alternative formulation of the position is that the vast majority fail to relate issue positions, or general principles and specific applications, in a way that most students of politics or political activists would expect. One explanation has emphasised the cognitive limits of most people when it comes to the possession of the information and skills necessary to interpret the political world. If this claim is substantially correct, then these features might be expected to be permanent, regardless of differences across countries and situations. It is also clear that the data call into question the quality of many of the so-called 'opinions' tapped by surveys. Some of the responses (particularly where a 'don't know' response is not permitted) may be little more than artefacts of the questionnaire, reflecting more the respondent's wish to be co-operative than the expression of a viewpoint (Converse, 1964; Asher, 1976, p. 97).

Perhaps, however, we need to entertain the possibility of different levels of ideology so that a person may be ideological according to one criterion but not another. Free and Cantril (1968) find very different patterns of liberal and conservative outlooks, depending in part on how the terms are operationalised (see Table 2.1). On an 'operational spectrum' of ideology (which includes questions about the support for government programmes on welfare) most Americans are clearly liberal. Yet on an 'ideological spectrum' (which asks about what the government's role should be) the majority are clearly conservative. On a third measure, of 'self-identification' as liberal or conservative, they are evenly divided. One can only explain these inconsistencies by assuming that most people think about ideology in a different way from commentators.

Table 2.1 *Operational and Ideological Spectrums and Self-Identification as Liberal or Conservative*

| | *Operational* | *Self-Identification* | *Ideological* |
|---|---|---|---|
| Liberal | 65% | 29% | 16% |
| Middle-of-the-road | 21% | 38% | 34% |
| Conservative | 14% | 33% | 50% |

*Source:* Free and Cantril, 1968, p. 46.

## Revision

The above portrait of how the American public thinks about politics has been revised somewhat in recent years. There are three main planks to the revisionist case. First, there is a methodological objection to the quality of the original research, type of questions asked, analysis of data, and inconsistencies in the interpretations of findings. Secondly, it is claimed that too many commentators have too readily generalised from the findings about public opinion data collected in the 1950s and 1960s. Findings about low ideological awareness, for example, may have been a response to the relatively quiescent political context of the time. Finally, the recent collection of data has challenged the earlier research and its conclusions about public opinion.

## Methods

The surveys of Prothro and Grigg and of McClosky have been the subject of some sharp criticism by Femia (1979), particularly concerning the reliance on batteries of 'agree–disagree' questions to measure a person's belief in democracy. Many of McClosky's questions are ambiguous and open to diverse interpretations. (Perhaps the components of a democratic ideology are too subtle and complex to tap by means of mass questionnaires.) The claims that there is more authoritarianism and a generally weaker grasp of democratic values among the lower-status and less-educated groups rest largely on the failure of so many respondents to apply general democratic principles to specific groups and cases. The two American surveys do not, however, present any validation that the particular questions about groups and issues relate logically or subjectively to the general values. A person may, for example, have denied 'free speech' to communists in the 1950s and simply not seen this as a test of respect for minority rights. He may reject this specific application of the principle but accept many others which have not been studied. Lawrence (1976) has demonstrated that by 1971 compared with the 1950s there appeared to be appreciably higher levels of tolerance of the political activities (e.g. freedom to petition or demonstrate) of unpopular groups (e.g. militant blacks or radical students). It is also clear that such political tolerance is issue-related, that is, it depends on the respondent's sympathy to the goals of the group. Finally, one may question some of the operational definitions of ideology. Why, for example, should voters who provide a coherent explanation of their votes in terms of group benefits be excluded from the ranks of ideologues?

Political developments since the mid-1960s have certainly presented different stimuli to Americans. In 1964 the Republican presidential candidate, Barry Goldwater, took a more explicitly ideological stance than his predecessors. In the following years there were the divisive issues of Vietnam, race and urban violence. How did these events affect political attitudes? Qualitative analysis of voters' attitudes showed an increase in ideological orientations after 1964 (Pierce, 1970). Surveys repeating the original Michigan questions found that ideologues in the United States had grown from 2·5 to 7 per cent and near-ideologues from 9 to 15 per cent. The proportion of such ideologues was similarly around a fifth in West European electorates (Klingeman, 1972). Nie and Anderson (1974) also found a substantial growth of coherence (association between attitudes across issue areas) between 1956 and 1972.

The growth is not to be explained by the spread of further education among voters, for the increase in coherence was even more marked among the less well-educated. The most impressive gain was among those who were very interested in politics. But what could have occurred to promote a greater interest in politics? Nie, Verba and Petrocik (1976, p. 108) plausibly suggest that the growth occurred because the hopes and fears of many voters came to concentrate more on the problems and issues handled by the government between 1964 and 1974. Survey data showed some decline in these years in people's non-political hopes and fears, such as family and personal matters, health and happiness, but a rise in such issues as war, crime and inflation, issues about which the national government was expected to do something.

If there is more consistency and coherence in attitudes to politics it seems to stem from a heightened salience of politics and government. This salience has in turn encouraged a greater interest in, and exposure to, information about politics, which in turn has encouraged the consistency. The capacity and willingness of some voters to think in structured terms depends in some measure on the stimulus provided by parties and issues. This interpretation contradicts the early claims that voters' thinking is based on relatively permanent characteristics.

## Interpretation

Some commentators have employed these revisionist findings to attack the claims of pluralist and elitist theories of democracy. They suggest that if the original data are invalid then it cannot be demonstrated that elites are more democratic in outlook than the non-elites. Alternatively, they may claim that even if the original data are valid, then one is as justified in arguing for an extension of participation as for a limitation. Involvement and familiarity with the political system tend to make people more aware of the practical implications of liberal and democratic values (see Chapter 9).

Among the political elites different issues have been raised. There is still some debate around the theme of 'The End of Ideology'. The claim made by such writers as Lipset, Bell, Aron and Marcuse in the early 1960s was that the traditional sources of divisions between the parties of left and right and the social classes had declined in both range and intensity in the postwar era. In France and Italy the anti-system revolutionary parties of the left had lost their radicalism and there was a consensus around the mixed economy and the welfare state. In most Western states there prevailed, as Lipset expressed it, 'a conservative socialism'. Critics (usually on the political left) have claimed that the statement was not valid at the time and has been refuted by later events. But the original formulation by Lipset (1959) and Bell (1960) was both more subtle and more ambiguous than critics have allowed, and they certainly did not claim that conflict or disagreement had ended or that coherent political thinking had declined. A problem has been that the different uses of terms and the general dearth of relevant empirical data over time have made it difficult to take the discussion further (but see Putnam, 1973).

In the next chapter we shall see that adolescents and young adults are more prone to change their opinions than those who are older. But even among the latter there is more instability than has traditionally been recognised. Of course, changes of opinion on specific policy issues are more frequent than on party identification or underlying political orientations. One also has to allow for changes in question-wording; or for qualitative changes in the 'meaning' of the object which is being surveyed (e.g. being 'liberal' in Britain in the 1960s or 1980s); or for the opinion originally expressed on the issue being not the result of a considered view but an unthinking response to a question. These are all examples of changes of opinions which may be quite spurious (see Jennings and Niemi, 1981, ch. 12, for discussion of these points). Yet the amount of change among adults is impressive. Some changes are consistent with expectations regarding events, the person's life-style, generational effects, and so on, and can therefore be genuine. And a good part of this is because of the shallowness of most thinking about politics. It may also be that the continuity apparent in the orientations on basic beliefs is not so much a result of their internalisation as of the fact that they are so rarely challenged.

## Mass Media

Analysis of the effects of the mass media on the formation of attitudes has gone through three stages. The first, associated with the literature on mass society, emphasised the possibilities of shaping the values of large groups of people. The early psychological studies on the 'suggestibility' of crowds and the totalitarian nature of society in Nazi Germany and the USSR seemed to show the power of the mass media. But the first voting studies exploded ambitious claims about the power of the mass media and the malleability of individuals. Lazarsfeld *et al.*'s *The People's Choice,* contrary to its initial assumptions, found few changes in voting intentions which could actually be attributed to exposure to the media. Readers of the press and listeners to radio were *selective* in their *exposure* to political messages from the media; they sought a reinforcement of their existing position. Moreover, they were also likely to be selective in their *perception* and *retention* of political information. People therefore were not merely passive recipients of messages but were able to use information for their own purposes, screening out information which was not congruent with their established preferences. Since then, study of the avoidance of *cognitive dissonance* and 'the strain towards consistency' has been a major area of study (Festinger, 1957).

Another finding concerned the continued importance of personal contact and face-to-face groups as a source of information. Lazarsfeld *el al.* (1948) described the *two-step flow*: 'ideas flow from radio and print to opinion leaders and from them to the less active sectors of the population'. Moreover, this type of communication could be influential; it was found that respondents who decided how to vote late in the election campaign frequently mentioned personal contacts as an influence. In England, study of television in the 1959 general election showed that, while exposure to political television increased the amount of accurate information, there was no connection between campaign exposure and change in attitude or vote intention. Instead, there was '*a definite and consistent barrier between sources of communication and movements of attitude in the political field at the general election*' (Trenaman and McQuail, 1961, p. 192). This was further support for the reinforcement thesis, that while the media might help to create opinions where none previously existed, they failed to make conversions and largely confirmed existing attitudes and positions (Klapper, 1960).

A third stage has seen a shift from the hitherto unrewarding study of the 'aims' and 'effects' of the media to the 'needs' and 'uses' of the audience. This new focus is called 'the uses-and-gratifications approach'. It draws attention to the receiver's role in the interaction between himself and the medium, and the need, in assessing the effects of the media, to take account of the viewers' motives and expectations. The political role of television is of some interest here because, compared with the press, most independent Western broadcasting authorities are committed, formally or informally, to making a 'balanced' presentation of views and comments on politics, and also because viewers are less selective in exposure. Some idea of the diverse functions and uses of television can be gleaned from the Leeds study of political television in the 1964 British elections. It found that 15 per cent used television primarily for *vote guidance* (seeing what the parties will do, studying the leader), 23 per cent for *reinforcement* (appreciating their own party's own good points), 11 per cent had a *mixture* of both motives and 51 per cent of the sample did not fall into any category (Blumler and McQuail, 1968, pp. 68ff.). Something like a quarter of the electorate, uncertain how they would vote, seem to have turned to television as a source of guidance. The importance of the receiver's motive is suggested in the finding that the greatest gains in information were not made by those most exposed to television coverage of politics but by those who turned to television in search of information. Different viewers brought different expectations and orientations to television. Some were partisans, seeking reinforcements, some were spectators, seeking excitement, and some were monitors, seeking information.

While television does play a role in shaping attitudes, viewers still manage to cope with dissonant information to maintain existing positions. In the famous 1960 presidential television debates Vice-President Nixon's supporters reacted to the impressive showing of Senator Kennedy by down-grading the importance of debating skills and emphasising other attributes, on which they regarded Nixon as superior, or misperceiving Kennedy's position on issues, bringing these into line with their own preferences. In 1964 a number of British Conservatives acknowledged that their party's leader, Sir Alec Douglas Home, was less impressive on television than his Labour opponent, Harold Wilson, but they then tended to de-emphasise the importance of leadership as a reason for voting. Voters as viewers have various techniques for dealing with messages which challenge their established preferences. Devices for coping with dissonant information include distortion of the information, disbelief in it and re-evaluating the credibility of the source, as well as reorganising one's beliefs.

Television may now have a greater impact on political behaviour, largely because of changing political conditions. There is ample evidence, in a number of Western states, and in Britain and the United States particularly, of the decline of habit and traditional ties when it comes to voting for parties. As a smaller proportion of voters seeks reinforcement of party loyalties, so there is more scope for short-term events associated with the election campaigns, issues and personalities, as transmitted through the mass media, to influence voting behaviour (Sears and Friedman, 1967). One should not ignore, in this context, the probability that television, because it exposes more people to different viewpoints, may actually weaken partisanship. In France and Italy television may well have been significant in producing a moderation of the stands of left and right. At a time of 'bad news' it may also promote wider public awareness of the parties and politicians and so play a 'de-legitimising' role.[4] Most people in Britain and the United States now regard television as the main source of information about politics and the most impartial and trustworthy source (Blumler and McQuail, 1968, p. 43). There has been a tendency for the press, which traditionally has been partisan, to become more balanced in its treatment of politics (Seymour-Ure, 1974). There is also some speculation, but little hard evidence, that television is more important in actually setting the agenda of an election campaign and, in turn, the styles adopted by campaigners.

In explaining the genesis of opinions and attitudes, different disciplines and perspectives have emphasised different factors – social background, personality, or political context. An idea of the different emphases is seen in the study of working-class authoritarianism. Some writers have drawn on historical events (e.g. fascism in Germany), personal memoirs and opinion surveys to suggest that many manual workers are not well-disposed towards non-economic aspects of liberal democracy. Lipset (1959, ch. 4) explains this working-class authoritarianism in terms of the economic insecurities and instability of lower-class life, and the resultant preference for the short-term and concrete, for viewing issues as black or white, and the general dislike of complexity. All these features, he suggests, make it difficult for the lower class to grasp liberal values. In later work Lipset, with Raab (1970), has developed a sociological approach to present a theory of 'status politics' to explain the political protest by the radical right in the United States. Supporters of Joseph McCarthy, Wallace and the John Birch Society shared a number of values in common, and came disproportionately from upwardly mobile groups who were anxious about their social status.

A personality approach to working-class authoritarianism was advanced by Adorno *et al.* (1950). His F-scale of 'agree–disagree' questions purported to measure whether a person possessed an authoritarian personality. He found that the authoritarian outlook correlated strongly with his other scales for anti-semitism, political and economic conservatism (e.g. support for the status quo, for the interests of business against those of labour) and ethnocentrism (identification with 'in-groups' and rejection of 'out-groups' like immigrants and blacks). Authoritarian beliefs appear to be highly integrated and to be related to personality; by inference, such beliefs would be highly resistant to change. A later development was the perception of authoritarianism as a characteristic of the political left as well as of the right and of ideologies in general (Rokeach, 1960). Eysenck's conceptualisation of *tough* (authoritarian) and *tender-minded* (liberal) approaches to politics rested on distinctions between political ideas (left and right) and social class (1951). The two dimensions of left *v.* right and tough *v.* tender give four groups. Eysenck regarded social class as the best predictor of the political outlook, with the working class being disproportionately tough-minded and the middle class tender-minded, regardless of whether they were politically left or right.

Both of these psychological approaches have been criticised on grounds of faulty methodology. Agree-or-disagree questions are prone to elicit a response-set bias, particularly from lower-class voters. When researchers reversed the items on the scale there was little trace of the authoritarianism in the working class (Campbell *et al.*, 1960, pp. 512–15). Some of the values measured by the F-scale may tap values which are approved in certain milieux, for example, farms and small towns, and it may have been a form of 'farm authoritarianism' that was found among first-generation industrial workers in the United States and Western Europe (Hamilton, 1972, ch. 11). More recent research into support for McCarthyism in the 1950s in the United States rejects interpretations which stress personality and status politics factors. Rogin (1967) found that support for the senator's anti-communism sprang largely from concern among Republicans and Catholics for a more vigorous American policy in Korea and stronger opposition to communism. In a comparable study Douglas Schoen (1977, ch. 9) shows that support in Britain for the right-wing radical figure Enoch Powell has had more to do with political disillusionment and hostility towards coloured immigration and the Common Market than with the personality and social position of Powell's followers.

## Consequences

The primary interest for the student of political behaviour in the distribution and attributes of opinions on political issues lies in their impact on politics. In particular: what consequences do opinions have for political behaviour and for the working of the political system?

At a general level, attitudes towards the system are clearly important in determining the nature and level of political support, a factor which in turn may affect the effectiveness of the regime and of the political leadership. Much research into public opinion has been disillusioning for the rational-active model of the citizen and has shown that public opinion is often labile and latent. People are too busy with other things to pay much attention to politics (Wahlke, 1971). But the public can focus sharply in crises or on clear-cut issues, when it is usually reactive, responding to events or the initiatives of political actors (Mueller, 1973). Opinions are generally stronger – both at individual and aggregate levels – when the issue is salient and experienced directly. One is reminded of Lippmann's (1922) observation that the rationality of a person's opinion on an issue is likely to increase in line with his direct experience of it. 'Strong' opinions are also usually stable, firmly held and part of a structure of attitudes.

Talk of public opinion on an issue involves the aggregation of diverse states of mind. People who are interested in and well-informed about politics find it relatively easy to follow events and absorb new information. But for the poorly informed new information may mean little and fail to be absorbed. It is useful, therefore, to distinguish different tiers or levels of opinion-holders: a mass public whose views are for the most part poorly structured and which is not well-informed about or involved in the political process; an attentive public which is well-informed and whose views are well-structured; and the opinion-makers, who possess the same characteristics as the attentive public but also are in a position (e.g. a platform in the media) to shape public opinion. The first group may set very broad limits to what is accepted on the political agenda. Decision-makers, however, are more likely to be attentive to the mood of the last two groups (Key, 1961; Rosenau, 1961).

The strategic position of leaders as decision-makers heightens the potential impact which their views may have on the working of the system. We may see a person's political behaviour as emerging from two broad sets of factors:

(*a*) how structured the environment or situation is;
(*b*) the beliefs, personality, or predispositions of the individual or group.

Greenstein (1969) has suggested that we should see these two broad categories, the 'objective' and the 'subjective', as operating in a 'push-pull' manner. If a situation is highly structured in a particular direction, then it limits the scope for values to influence action. By contrast, the stronger the attitudinal pressure for a course of action, then the less need for situational stimuli. The impact of opinions, like that of such other subjective factors as an individual's personality or values, is a variable. We have also seen that individuals differ in their ability and willingness to draw specific issue preferences and behavioural consequences from general attitudes. The same constraints may affect the application of a politician's ideals or a party's ideology when he or it are in government. The 'real world' of government may look very different from that imagined before. Observers may regard the political actor's adjustment to the disjunction between the ideal and practice as opportunism, pragmatism, realism, or a mixture of all three.

If public opinion is so poorly structured for much of the time then it forces one to revise a view of the political system in which political decision-makers respond to messages from the public. Several agencies, including political parties, groups, the media, government and politicians themselves, claim to speak on behalf of the public or sections of it. But on many issues, on which public opinion has not developed a clear focus, then elites clearly have a good deal of room for manoeuvre in interpreting the state of public opinion and linking it to feasible courses of political action. One may, of course, have a broad correspondence between the policy decisions made by government and the preferences of the public without there being any overt communication from the latter to the former. Government leaders may frame policies in the light of anticipated reactions from the public, there may be a consensus shared by leaders and followers about lines of policy (Hewitt, 1974), or they may respond to public pressure, as British governments have done on immigration. What is clear is that in understanding the linkages between public opinion and government action a 'missing piece' of the puzzle is the 'activist stratum' (Key, 1961, p. 537). And we need to know, Key continues:

> How it works – the motives that activate the leadership echelon, the values that it holds, in the rules of the political game to which it adheres, in the expectations which it entertains about its own status in society, and perhaps in some of the objective circumstances, both material and institutional, in which it functions.

## Notes: Chapter 2

1 It may be, however, that the inclusion of five positions concerning the nationalisation of many industries was too stringent a test of stability.
2 Again, care is required in the analysis of such data. Even assuming that there are no differences in question-wording over time, there is the problem of changes in the meaning of a question. The terms 'liberal', 'conservative' and 'big government' have undergone such changes for many Americans (Nie *et al.,* 1976, p. 11).
3 See discussion of this point on page 85 below.
4 It has been claimed that television also promotes dissatisfaction with political leaders and institutions. In the United States supporters of Wallace in 1968 were more likely than supporters of other candidates to rely on the media for information, and such people were more likely to be pessimistic and misanthropic in their outlook. Coverage on television may have similar effects because of its 'de-romanticising' of politics (M. Robinson, 1976).

Chapter 3

# Political Socialisation

How do people learn about politics? How, for example, do they come to think of themselves as British, Russian, or Greek, or to identify themselves as Communists, Conservatives, or Democrats? Why do some people become interested and active in politics while others do not? Students of politics, even those who are interested in knowledge about attitudes or sources of attitudes as ends in themselves, also want to know the answers to such questions about national identity, party loyalty and political orientations. Political socialisation is the process by which individuals learn about politics. In turn it shapes the political culture, providing the cues for continuity and change in the culture. We want to know why people and groups have different attitudes towards political objects, as well as why they share common values. On a more practical note, political leaders in new or reforming regimes are often concerned to inculcate values which will enhance the legitimacy of, or popular support for, their institutions. In totalitarian regimes the schools, mass media and even art and sport have consciously been employed so that citizens acquire approved outlooks on political matters.

## Socialisation and the Study of Politics

The growing interest in the study of political socialisation and political culture reflects the change in the mood of the discipline and the influence of other approaches to the study of behaviour. One reason, the shift from the legal-institutional approach to an emphasis on behaviour and its sources, has already been mentioned in Chapter 1. The concept of socialisation was already in frequent use among sociologists, social psychologists and anthropologists before political scientists picked it up. Sociologists were more interested in how people related to groups and society, social psychologists in how individuals learned about and adjusted to the demands of groups and society, and anthropologists in how people learned about their culture. A second reason for interest in socialisation has been its relation to support for a regime. Rulers want to be obeyed, for reasons independent of their possession of superior force. As Rousseau stated: 'The strongest is never strong enough to be always the master, unless he transforms strength into right, and obedience into duty.' There has also been a practical interest in socialisation as a predictive or engineering device, a means of inducing political change and understanding the forces which might shape change in the future.

Paradoxically, these very interests have prompted criticisms of the work to date. Critics have suggested that such an emphasis on system maintenance has meant that socialisation is often seen as a conservative process and that its potential for changing the system has been neglected. Parsons, for example, regarded socialisation as a means of promoting the integration of values in society and providing an economical means for compliance to authority (1951, ch. 6). A second, more disciplinary objection is against the reductionism implicit in the approach, that is, that political behaviour is explained by a narrow range of primarily non-political factors. This is seen in the influence on the concept of psychologists and cultural anthropologists, and the greater emphasis on childhood experiences, the role of the family and the unconscious and latent aspects of socialisation as compared to the cognitive and manifestly political aspects (Almond and Verba, 1963, p. 323). There is some truth in the charge but in defence it can be claimed that a long line of writers, including Plato, Rousseau and Dewey, whose concern was primarily with the making of citizens, have emphasised the role of political socialisation.

Political socialisation may be conceptualised in a number of ways. One may think of it as a process of political education, involving the dissemination of information about the political system or training in citizenship. Or it may be regarded as the induction into a particular role, sub-culture or political culture, for example, the acquisition of a system's prevailing norms. According to William Mitchell, political socialisation is the 'attempt to train people to do what the system requires . . . in values, norms, information and skills considered desirable and useful in that society' (1962, p. 143). Thirdly, it may also be viewed as a developmental process, one which covers the acquisition of political beliefs and dispositions throughout life. Finally, political socialisation may be viewed as the means of legitimating inequalities in the allocation of power in society. Ralph Miliband, writing from a Marxist perspective, has described political socialisation as 'very largely a process of massive *indoctrination*', designed to produce a general acceptance of existing institutions in capitalist society (1969, p. 181). Plato, for example, argued that if different categories of men were to be fitted into their appropriate places in a hierarchical society, then men had to be socialised into accepting the moral correctness of their positions. His just Republic, modelled on the school, was designed to encourage an acceptance of the status quo.

The first approach sees socialisation as a process of cognitive learning; the second as a process of internalising those values and role expectations which support existing institutions; the third as the gradual acquisition of any values; and the fourth as a means of legitimating the dominance of an elite or social order.

## Political Support

An ambitious attempt to break out of the hyperfactualism of so many socialisation studies and to go beyond the emphasis on political continuity has come from David Easton (Easton, 1965; Easton and Dennis, 1969). His concept of political support refers to the attitudes people have to the regime and its leaders. Support itself is a neutral term and it may take a positive or a negative direction. Easton views the political system as a vast conversion process, with the political authorities responding to inputs or demands from citizens and the environment, and producing outputs in the form of policies, laws and decisions. The number and intensity of political demands and the nature of political support are affected in part by political socialisation. Easton acknowledges that the system maintenance bias of existing socialisation studies has been restrictive for theory and empirical research. Because hostilisation and change may occur, as well as idealisation and continuity, he prefers to talk about the 'persistence' of a system, a term which allows for change and diversity, along with underlying continuity. The quality of support affects the number and type of demands which are made and the willingness of people to comply with policy decisions and outputs. The support may be *specific*, that is, conditional on the citizens' satisfaction with the outputs, or *diffuse*, that is, unconditional and general, 'support that continues independently of the specific rewards' (1965, p. 124). The former is linked to and varies with perceived benefits and satisfactions, and is directed largely to the established authorities. The latter, in contrast, is largely determined by the process of political socialisation, is more durable and is directed towards the offices as well as their occupants.

The bulk of the socialisation literature has concentrated on childhood, on the assumption that this is the formative period for political learning. The sceptical question may be posed: how useful is it to study political socialisation among children? It has been suggested that study of an adult's political beliefs may have little relevance to his political behaviour and to the working of the political system, because only a minority of adults actually have political attitudes (see Chapter 2). Such a criticism applies even more to children, whose views are likely to be too poorly formed or articulated to be the subject of useful study. According to the child psychologist, Piaget, children under the age of 11 or so lack the conceptual skills (in terms of logical skills and abstract reasoning) to relate themselves to political phenomena, and they simply do not think about politics. Children are egocentric and do not conceptualise beyond the immediate, the concrete and the personal. The defence mounted by students of political socialisation is that children become politically aware by the process of *personalisation;* from an early age children are aware of authority figures like the local policeman, the Queen, or the American President, and personalise the system through these figures.

We may summarise the less controvertible of the findings of the extant literature along the following lines. Many children appear to have acquired some orientations to politics at an early age, around 10 or 11. They have already developed party loyalties, a sense of national identity and some awareness of their country's main political institutions. There is a sequence in the acquisition of these orientations, with the affective and evaluative orientations preceding the cognitive. Most American studies in the early 1960s suggested that children felt positively towards the nation's authority figures and the political system. But as children acquire greater knowledge and first-hand experience of politics in adolescence, so there is a decline in the rate of approval. During adolescence children are more able to differentiate their views about the personality of an incumbent from his formal role or office. (Later research suggests that this approval was largely confined to the period of study. Under Presidents Johnson and Nixon, 1964–73, there was a sharp decline in trust in the President.) What is interesting is the finding that the political system is viewed by young children in highly personal terms. In Britain, for example, the Queen is the most visible symbol of both political authority and the political world to young children. In the United States the local mayor, or the President, is perceived in similar terms. Over time there is both a filling out and a differentiation in the young person's perception of the political system; political authority is perceived as being exercised by various people rather than by a visible head of state, and political authority is regarded more as an impersonal and institutionalised than phenomenon as a personal one.

## Problems

The research into political socialisation has been extensive, amounting almost to a sub-field in its own right, and it has contributed many insights to several parts of the discipline. Yet it is fair to add that its contribution to our understanding of politics has hardly fulfilled the early promise. The research to date has been rather narrow in focus, being limited to studying the attitudes of children. Not surprisingly, the study of political socialisation has been vulnerable to the sceptical 'so what?' question. But recently political scientists have been willing to emphasise the role of events and political factors as influences on political attitudes – to regard socialisation as a continuous process – and there has been a shift in the discipline away from the input side of politics.

It is worth remembering the theoretical importance which Easton and Dennis originally attached to the topic. They wanted to relate their study of political socialisation to the support for a political system and in turn to understand the sources of stability and change in the system. There is, of course, a dauntingly large gap between a person's values in childhood and the particular political roles and values he has in adulthood. Ideally we need longitudinal studies which can trace the durability of attitudes from childhood into adulthood (Jennings and Niemi, 1981). As D. Marsh (1971) has forcefully observed, most of the assumptions about the relevance of youthful attitudes to adulthood and the political system are open to serious challenge. Two key assumptions are:

(*a*) Adult opinions are the end-product of youthful socialisation. This claim is derived from the basic personality school of psychology; it assumes that general orientations are formed early on, that these orientations persist, and that the general orientation shapes later views on specific issues and influences the individual's political behaviour.

(*b*) The sum of individual opinions affects the working of the political system.

The two propositions may be restated as: socialisation determines personality; personality determines political beliefs; beliefs in turn shape political behaviour; and, the final link, behaviour affects the operation of the political system.

The evidence for proposition *a*, however, is only mixed. Surveys on the orientations of boys and girls to political activity, for example, hardly correlate with the adult sexual roles in politics. Transmission of party loyalties in Britain and the United States between parents and children now seems to be less effective (Jennings and Niemi, 1974, 1981). But even if one showed the durability of the early attitudes then one would still have to demonstrate the strength of the connection between attitudes and behaviour, as implied in proposition *b*. All that we know about the lack of constraint in the views of many people and the fragility of many so-called opinions lead one to doubt the first proposition. Donald Searing has shown the rather poor fit between general orientations (presumably from childhood) and attitudes on specific issues (Searing *et al.*, 1973, p. 430). Finally, one has to remember that attitudes are only one stimulus for behaviour. It is not surprising therefore that current research has shown signs of adopting, appropriately enough, a less deterministic view of childhood orientations.

Another objection is to the ideological tenor of most socialisation studies. In the functional approach to politics, socialisation is seen as helping a system to persist; political socialisation builds support which, in childhood, is more diffuse than instrumental. Later studies, however, have been forced to take account of instability and a greater disillusion with political elites. The sharp rise in political distrust of the presidency and disillusion with American political institutions in the late 1960s and early 1970s, and the declining levels of attachment to the political parties in Britain and the United States, seem to be due to the impact of political events rather than to childhood socialisation (Miller, 1974).

Political socialisation is now seen more as a continuous process, going beyond childhood to cover adolescence and adulthood. Such a shift of attention accords a larger role to cognitive factors and to the impact of political events. It also accords more emphasis to socialisation as an interactive process, one in which the individual plays a creative role as a learner and user of information. For example, a study of the impact of civics courses in the United States (Dawson and Prewitt, 1969) found that it was only among the educationally deprived blacks that there was a notable increase in the level of information. For many other students, the authors suggest, the course content was redundant (p. 151).

There has been much debate over the extent to which there is generalisation from the overtly non-political sphere to the political. Harry Eckstein (1966) has suggested that democracy will be more stable where there is a congruence between authority patterns in society and those in politics. In the Weimar Republic a democratic political constitution – which assumed participant and egalitarian values – was imposed on a society which, for the most part, rejected these norms. Within the family, school, military, bureaucracy and trade unions, traditional hierarchical patterns of authority prevailed. A number of commentators have suggested that the incongruence between the authority relations demanded by the political institutions and those of society was politically destabilising.

It is where the boundaries between the social and political spheres are poorly defined that the behaviour and authority patterns found in the family do tend to be transferred. This is the case in the Philippines, according to Grossholtz (1964). Family and small group behaviour strongly affects popular expectations about government officials and politicians; politics, like the family, is seen as the provider of such basic needs as jobs, health treatment, and so on. Life tends to be seen in terms of power relationships; obligations to superiors are accepted on the understanding that the subordinate is able to claim certain rights. In politics the vote is regarded by electors and politicians alike as a *quid pro quo*, given in return for bribes and favours.

But the generalisation of social values to the political sphere is not confined to systems in which the political arena is poorly delimited. Almond and Verba have shown how, even in the well-defined political arenas of Britain and America, an individual's trust in other people affects his political values. Given the remoteness of politics for the vast majority of people even in such relatively 'participant' states as Britain and America, and the dominance of other roles such as spouse, worker, or parent, we are justified in assuming the importance for political socialisation of social attitudes. In Mexico, Almond and Verba found that the generally passive and resigned orientations to the social environment carry over to limit the sense of competence *vis-à-vis* the political system.

## Agents

There are numerous socialising agents, exercising different influences and varying in the degree to which they reinforce or contradict each other. In the early years of an individual's life the family plays a major role. But as the child attends school, becomes exposed to peer group influences in adolescence, and then takes up an occupation, he is exposed to and socialised by various agencies. A text on political socialisation covers practically all imaginable stimuli – the mass media, events, political parties and groups, as well as the family and the school. At times it may be difficult to acquire a sense of boundedness and to distinguish the origins of political socialisation from those of mere opinion formation.

Interest in the family as a socialising agent is based on its primacy and its diffuseness. It is in the family that the potential citizen first becomes aware of power relationships and experiences authority in several contexts. The studies of voting behaviour show how durable family influence can be. In Britain the best predictor of a person's vote since the war has been not his social class, but how his parents voted. Hyman (1959), drawing mainly on American evidence of twenty to thirty years ago, has shown the continuity of political outlooks and party preferences between parents and children (but see below).

The amount of schooling children receive and their experiences with teachers appear to be a major influence on the development of an individual's sense of political competence. Indeed, the authors of *The Civic Culture* found that the variables of childhood participation in making school decisions and higher education facilitated political participation and sense of competence across their five nations. The obvious amenability of schools to political direction has heightened their importance in many new states and in East European communist states which are engaged in remaking a political culture. In such cases the outcome is often a challenge to traditional authority patterns in the family; the younger children are socialised into the norms of the new regime more effectively than parents who may retain values associated with an earlier regime.

Within the Soviet Union there have been ambitious attempts to make a 'new Soviet man', in terms of distinctive Soviet values. The rulers have taken a purposeful view of socialisation or *respitanie*, regarding the relations between the individual and society as highly political. School instruction in the principles of Marxism-Leninism started in 1924 and was extended to the whole population two years later. Schoolchildren are also enrolled in the Octobrists, then the Pioneers and then the Komsomol to imbibe the Communist ideology. Theatre, cinema and the mass media also contribute to 'a political education programme of unusual scope and intensity' (White, 1979, p. 38). But White suggests that if the culture 'fits' the political system in the USSR it is due more to residues of traditional Russian culture than to the impact of the socialisation process; the results of the elaborate propaganda efforts have met with only limited success.

I have noted that the studies have shown that the majority of children are able to express a preference for a political party at an early age. The different contours of a country's history, political culture and party system give rise to distinctive patterns of partisanship in each country. Different party systems have different effects on the child's acquisition of party identification and produce different images of what the parties stand for. American children, for example, tend to think of elections in terms of voting for candidates, whereas English children think in terms of voting for institutionalised parties.

Until recently it was assumed that partisanship hardened throughout the life-cycle, with the renewal of party vote at each election making party loyalty firmer. Young or first-time voters were therefore less 'immunised' to contrasting political cues and more changeable in party loyalty. In recent elections, however, this volatility has spread to other age-groups in Britain and the United States.

Perhaps the main reason for the political importance attributed to the family is that children are particularly likely to inherit their political loyalties from their parents. Much depends, of course, on parents having loyalties to transmit in the first place and then actually communicating them to children. American parents are more willing to talk about politics and their party preferences in front of their children than are their counterparts in Britain and France (Caldeira and

Greenstein, 1978). In Britain in the 1960s children of parents who supported the same party, and the party was the 'natural' or dominant one for their social class (e.g. Labour for the working class), were likely in 90 per cent of cases to have started with the same party preferences as the parents (Butler and Stokes, 1975, p. 57). Where parents were split in their political allegiances, their offspring likewise divided almost evenly between the Labour and Conservative parties. British fathers are usually recalled as being more interested in politics and their party preferences were usually more apparent than those of mothers. Yet, paradoxically, when parents disagree about party choice, then in both countries the mother is more likely to influence the child's party choice (Butler and Stokes, 1975, p. 53; Jennings and Niemi, 1981). A caution is in order in assessing these claims. Not only were the correlations between parents' and child's reported party choice rather modest in the American studies, but they invariably relied on the respondent's recall of his/her parents' vote. This has been shown to result in a bias to greater consistency (Connell, 1972).

This scepticism about the influence of parents in shaping the political views of children is borne out in the major study by Jennings and Niemi (1974, 1981). The importance of this study is that it interviewed both adolescents and their parents and was a longitudinal survey. To repeat an earlier point, for similarity between parent and child to be regarded as a case of influence by the former depends on the parents actually having attitudes (i.e. stable views) and communicating them. Yet the authors found that many parents were indifferent to the political views of their offspring; some children were inaccurate in their perceptions of their parents' views; some adopted what they misperceived as their parents' partisanship; and both parents and children were prone to overestimate the extent of agreement. What this research shows is that the parent–child agreement varies across particular political items and that other agencies are important. The correlation scores between parents' and their children's views on items varied from 0·05 to 0·60; they were usually high where the item was concrete and specific (e.g. party loyalty) and usually low where it was diffuse (e.g. political trust and efficacy). For example, parents were relatively important in affecting the offspring's party identification and party and presidential vote, but on levels of political efficacy and on whether 18-year-olds should have the vote peer groups were more important. In England Dowse and Hughes (1971a, 1971b) have reported on the weakness of parents as influences, apart from party choice, on the values of children. The evidence on the whole encouraged the authors to minimise the role of the family as a political influence. Their own explanation stressed the low salience of politics as a focus of parent–child relationships as well as the role of other agents. The weakening of family life (in terms of rising divorce rates), the growth of the mass media, and the weakening of political allegiances may further limit the opportunity for transmission of values between generations.

Other research has indicated the scope for the influence of other agents, including peer groups, the political realm itself (in terms of events, issues and the activities of elites) and broad social and economic factors. Newcomb's famous study (1943) explained the liberal dispositions of his middle-class girl students at Bennington in terms of peer group pressure. In a follow-up study (Newcomb, 1967) he found that the women were still more 'liberal' than other middle-class women, and had chosen husbands and friends whose political and cultural views were similar.

Although Almond and Verba (1963) found that participation in the family, school and work-place correlated with higher levels of political participation, they also suggest that transfers from the family to the political system are the least likely in modern industrialised societies. In such states there are more sharply delineated boundaries between society and polity and more specialised political roles and structures. But even in less industrialised societies, Inkeles (1969) shows that experience of industrial work is important in developing a participant outlook. The organisation and creativity involved in industrial work make the factory 'a school for modernisation'. The process of economic development, with the creation of schools, mass media and factories, seems to leave in its wake a predisposition for greater activity among citizens. At more advanced levels of socio-economic development, Inglehart (1977) has presented persuasive evidence that a more participatory outlook is found among the younger generation. Experiences at places of work and in voluntary organisations are relevant because they are more contemporaneous with the individual's assumption of citizenship and closer in structure to the political system.

A clear statement of the importance of structural factors is offered by Dowse and Hughes (1971b, p. 64). Commenting on the unexpected lack of significant differences in many attitudes between girls and boys, they suggest

> that socialisation theory overstresses the importance of children's attitudinal predispositions to become involved as adults, since there may well be a whole range of 'accidental' structural features such as differential possibilities of trade union membership, the accidents of casual friendship, sudden issues which galvanise the previously politically inactive into action, the accident of living in a homogeneous political environment, etc. etc., which may cause people to become involved when otherwise they might have remained passive.

It is no simple matter to assess the relative influence of different agents. The effect of an agent depends in part on its 'fit' with other messages. The school may be less effective where parents present sharply different evaluations (Wylie, 1957). Children are more likely to follow a parental lead if both parents are of the same view, and if their views are broadly similar to those of peers, the media and teachers (Jennings and Niemi, 1974, 1981). Similarly, actual personal experience of the political system shapes perceptions and evaluations of the authorities and institutions. Widespread cynicism in Italy and Mexico about the police and bureaucrats has been derived from personal experience. Much early political learning is diffuse and detached from the experience of children and adolescents. The sense of political trust and efficacy, for example, will be based to some extent on personal experience of the system, which the young do not have.

## Recency *v.* Primacy

It is fairly obvious that some political learning occurs during most phases of people's life-cycle. Researchers have differed over which periods are the most important – childhood, adolescence, or adulthood – and different studies have advanced claims on behalf of each of them. The early studies stress the importance of the family, particularly in developing loyalty to a political party and acquiring political values (Hyman, 1959). Yet it is easy to overlook how membership of the family overlaps heavily with membership of a particular sub-culture or social class milieu. The study by Wolfenstein of crisis leaders (1967), on the other hand, stresses the basic family experiences as a formative influence on the personality of striking leaders like Lenin, Churchill and Gandhi. Other studies (Easton and Dennis, 1969; Greenstein, 1969) have focused on the school; and Almond and Verba (1963) emphasise the role of the workplace and experiences which are more contemporaneous with adulthood. Research on the outlooks of political elites has stressed the role demands of the job rather than earlier childhood experiences. More recently political scientists have been more sensitive to political events and social and economic trends as decisive shapers of orientations among the young generation (Inglehart, 1971, 1977).

These rival emphases are part of a lively debate between the competing schools of *recency* (or *Zeitgeist*) and *primacy*. On a simplified view the debate about the timing of learning is overlaid with claims on behalf of different disciplines and different agencies. The *primacy* emphasis stresses the durability of what is learnt early on and is usually advanced by psychologists who focus on the importance of the family and child-rearing. The 'basic' orientations are filled out in adolescence and adulthood, as a person acquires opinions on specific issues and personalities. It allows some scope for later learning and filling out, but not for *Zeitgeist* effects of later issues, personalities and events. A clear statement of this viewpoint is made by Greenstein *et al.* (1974, p. 285):

> Early learning in childhood appears to be consequential for later orientations and for behaviour in the adult years, in part because of its temporal priority. What enters the mind first remains there to provide lenses and categories for perceiving and sorting later perceptions. Furthermore, early learning occurs during the period of plasticity and openness: the assumptions acquired in childhood frequently appear to be absorbed in an unquestioned fashion. Such assumptions can become inarticulate major premises which then exercise a background effect on thought and overt behaviour precisely because they are not made sufficiently conscious to become open to challenge.

This view also underplays the role of specifically political factors. Attitudes to politics are viewed as side-effects of what is learned in non-political contexts.

The competing emphasis is on the *recency* aspect. According to this view socialisation experiences have a greater impact the closer in time and authority structure they are to the political context. Adulthood is associated with changes in membership of reference groups as well as of family, community and occupational roles. Studies of the role of elites, for example, pay greater attention to the actual demands of the role and recruitment practices. This approach can also be linked with the view of psychologists like Maslow and Erik Erikson. Both writers stress the importance of adolescence or early adulthood as a period when a person resolves his identity crisis and acquires values and a sense of personal identity.

A more qualified position is that a person's political views are structured by early experiences but that these can then be adapted and even changed drastically by later circumstances. I have already noted the several studies which have cast doubts on the claim that general orientations structure specific views (see Chapter 2). Moreover, the so-called general orientations, which are supposed to be very stable, are found to vary a good deal over time, and often change in response to what Searing *et al.* (1976) call '*Zeitgeist* effects', or the impact of the personalities, issues and events associated with a period. American study of changes in such general orientations as party identification, political trust and sense of political efficacy – and of the presumably derived issue beliefs and demands – shows that these have declined in recent years among all age-groups, which again is suggestive of '*Zeitgeist* effects' (ibid.). The importance of an orientation for adult behaviour and structuring other beliefs has to be demonstrated before we can justify concentration on its childhood origins. This is an important challenge to the theoretical relevance of political socialisation among children. The durability of the early impressions depends to some extent upon their usefulness in the new circumstances – particularly the political and social conditions – to which a person is exposed.

## Idealisation

An important aspect of the theory of political support lies in the idea of childhood idealisation of authority figures. Weber's discussion of the charismatic type of authority reminds us that the personality of political leaders may be a base for legitimacy for a regime – as in the case of de Gaulle, Lenin, or Washington. In Britain and the United States some significance may be attached to the monarchy and the presidency because they are the earliest political institutions of which the young child becomes aware. They do influence a child's affective and evaluative orientations towards the regime. It has been shown that among American and British children positive judgements of the incumbents of these roles precede actual knowledge about the President's party affiliation and the Queen's lack of effective political powers. In England some two-thirds (mainly in the working class) believe 'the Queen is more important than the Prime Minister in running Britain'. The Prime Minister is seen by most young children as her helper and the working-class child is slower to shed this unrealistic view than the middle-class child (Greenstein *et al.*, 1974). One may speculate that the favourable appraisal of the heads of state in Britain and the United States carries over to create reserves of support for the regime itself. For Britain, the more full-blown theory of the transfer of effect has been central to one idea of political deference. Shils and Young (1953) and Eckstein (1966) have speculated whether the traditional domination of government by monarchy and aristocracy has invested their mundane successors with a certain majesty, dignity and other deference-evoking qualities. The empirical evidence to date gives only slight support to the theory, among children at least. Subsequent studies in the United States of young blacks (Greenberg, 1970) and of children in the depressed Appalachian region (Jaros *et al.*, 1968) have uncovered more negative views about the President. In the wake of Vietnam and Watergate the perception of the President as a 'benevolent' figure has changed. In other countries such as Australia, France and Japan neither the Prime Minister nor the Emperor is seen as a benevolent or heroic figure (Massey, 1975; Roig and Billon-Grand, 1968). Japan, indeed, provides a case of 'the missing leader'. But a recent survey of adults by Rose and Kavanagh (1976) found that respondents who were favourably disposed to the British monarchy were much more likely to approve the regime and the political authorities than were anti-monarchists. Clearly, the childhood perceptions of political authority figures and the possible consequences for adult orientations to the system have to be related to the distinctive cultural and institutional milieu of each country.

## Conclusion

Political socialisation is a continuous process. For all the emphasis on childhood as a time of learning, we have to remind ourselves that socialisation continues through the life-cycle. We do know a lot more about the agencies of political socialisation and how people learn about politics and how they orientate themselves to the political world. A person's political outlook *may* be important in affecting his political behaviour – how important it is depends on other factors, not least the influence exercised by institutional and structural factors.

Chapter 4

# Political Culture

'Political culture' has become a vogue term in political science in recent years. There is even something called, rather grandly, a 'cultural approach' to politics. In this chapter I propose to examine the development and different meaning of the concept, assess some of its uses and, finally, comment on certain problems and difficulties associated with the approach.

Political culture is a rather new term for an old idea. The notion of a culture, spirit, mood, or set of values which shapes the conduct of politics of a nation or group has been around for as long as people have discussed politics. Aristotle wrote about a 'state of mind' which encouraged political stability or revolution, Burke praised the 'cake of custom' which affected the working of political institutions, and de Tocqueville, Dicey and Bagehot explicitly gave a place to political values and sentiments in their theories of political stability and change. Anthropologists and historians have, until very recently, written about the importance of a 'national character' or 'tradition' in shaping behaviour.

## The Concept of Political Culture

The systematic use of culture and political culture as social science concept dates only from the 1950s. Gabriel Almond (1980) has suggested that the concept emerged from the confluence at that time of three separate intellectual influences:

(1) *Social psychology and psychoanthropology*, stemming from the work of Freud and the insights of anthropologists like Malinowski and Benedict. Social psychologists wanted to study the factors which shaped the attitudes and behaviour of individuals; hence the growing interest in the phenomena of socialisation, group norms and loyalties, habit and tradition, and individual personality. Anthropologists developed the basic tools and concepts for studying the cultures of the combatant nations in the 1939–45 war. The early postwar surveys of voting behaviour

in the United States also reflected this approach to the study of attitudes.

(2) *European sociology,* represented in the work of Weber, Pareto and Durkheim. Weber had challenged Marx on 'cultural' grounds, by claiming that religion and values were important in affecting economic activity and political structures. Many of these writers' ideas, particularly those on the role of social norms and values, were in turn developed in the United States by Talcott Parsons (1951; Parsons and Shils, 1951). His notions of a social system and types of social action were important in orienting the study of culture.

(3) *Survey research,* and the development of more sophisticated techniques of sampling, interviewing and analysing data. Public opinion surveys enabled students to move beyond what had largely been speculative and impressionistic statements about a culture to collect data about a group's or a nation's psycho-cultural orientations to politics.

These intellectual developments and influences provided the inspiration for the concept of culture and the related concepts of socialisation, sub-culture and ideology. Yet appreciation of its importance was stimulated by actual events. Developments in continental Europe in the interwar years, particularly the collapse of constitutional regimes in Germany, Italy and Spain, had been disillusioning for those who had anticipated the gradual spread of liberal democratic regimes and enlightenment values. In the 1950s and 1960s the collapse of constitutions in many newly independent 'Third World' countries was again a forceful reminder of the complex relationships between political institutions, political behaviour and a nation's political culture. Explanations of stable democracy which rested heavily on institutional and socio-economic factors were clearly incomplete. Interest grew in the cultural bases of the functioning of political institutions. But the concept of political culture also met another need. The primary focus of behavioural studies has been on the individual actor; culture was a useful tool for describing the role of social aggregates and communities and providing a bridge from the micro-approach of social psychology to the macro-approach of sociology. The notion of culture suggests a pattern or a coherent set of values which 'fit together as a part of a meaningful whole and constitute an intelligible web of relations' (Pye, 1965, p. 7).

For our purposes we may regard the political culture as a shorthand expression to denote the set of values within which a political system operates. It is something between the state of public opinion and an individual's personality characteristics. According to Almond (1956), it is the 'particular pattern of orientations' to political objects in which a political system is embedded. Orientations are predispositions to political action and are determined by such factors as tradition, historical memories, motives, norms, emotions and symbols; the culture, therefore, represents a set of propensities. These orientations may be broken down into: cognitive orientations (knowledge and awareness of the political objects), affective orientations (emotions and feelings about the objects), and evaluative orientations (judgement about them) (Parsons and Shils, 1951, pp. 58ff.). The political objects of the orientations include such institutions as the executive, legislature and judiciary, the political parties and pressure groups, a person's view of himself as a political actor, and his view of other citizens.

The political culture, then, may be seen as the overall distribution of citizens' orientations to political objects. This interpretation, though largely derived from Talcott Parsons and not without shortcomings (see below), is an advance on previous global descriptions of such phenomena as a nation's 'national character'. We are now better able to think in terms of *what* kind of orientations are held by *which* people towards *which* political objects.

Culture is a variously used term and different definitions imply different conceptions of culture. One student (Patrick, 1976) has found more than thirty different definitions of political cultures. They appear to fall into one of four categories.

(*a*) *Psychological,* in which the culture is seen as a set of orientations to political objects (Parsons and Shils, 1951; Almond and Verba, 1963).
(*b*) *Comprehensive,* in which the culture includes both attitudes, as in (*a*), and overt or covert behaviour. For purposes of describing a culture this approach has obvious advantages; problems arise, however, if we wish to analyse the relationships between attitudes and behaviour (cf. Fagen, 1969; Tucker, 1973). There is a danger of circularity if we explain the French tendency to have revolutions in terms of a lack of consensus on political procedures, and the dissensus in terms of the revolutionary background.
(*c*) *Objective,* where the culture connotes 'the authoritative standards that define the range of acceptable behaviour for actors within any political system' (Patrick, 1976, p. 9). With this approach we are less interested in an individual's subjective state of mind than in the particular features of the system which shape a person's conduct. In communist societies the Marxist-Leninist ideology constitutes a set of goals or ideals for the population.
(*d*) *Heuristic,* in which the culture is a hypothetical construct and employed for analytical purposes. One might, for example, sketch

a type of political culture which is congruent with the way a system performs, and is, on certain dimensions, different from the existing culture. Almond and Verba (1963) suggest that a participatory political culture 'fits' a liberal democratic regime and a 'subject' or 'passive' culture 'fits' an authoritarian regime.

Patrick produces good reasons for preferring approach *c*. Anthropologists usually prefer approach *b*. The approach favoured here is *a*, as long as our main use of culture is to explain or understand behaviour. But a concentration on the psychological to the exclusion of action or behavioural variables does involve some disadvantages. Richard Fagen found that such an emphasis was of little help in his study of the transformation of Cuban political culture. The Castro political leadership was concerned to change not only the attitudes but also the manifest political behaviour of the masses; the leaders' vision of the new political culture consisted of newly transformed political values as well as political behaviour. Fagen, therefore, opted for an approach which encompassed behavioural as well as attitudinal factors. In some communist or radical regimes there may well be a gap between the 'official' or 'goal' culture and the 'operational' values or behaviour of people.

The relationships between data on the political culture and the working of a political system are discussed later in this chapter. But the linkages between values and behaviour of individuals and between these and the working of the system have to be demonstrated and not taken for granted. The main use of a good description of the political culture is to sensitise us to the limits of popular understanding and support within which the system is likely to operate. We have to be wary of making inferences from predispositions to actual behaviour. Some attitudes are more actionable than others. Attitude-holders vary both in the intensity of their beliefs and in their willingness to act on them; and, depending on the issue and the person concerned, the structural possibilities for action also differ. For example, Almond and Verba found that some three-quarters of Britons and Americans believed themselves able to influence their government, though only small proportions actually tried to exercise such influence.

Many of these problems were found in the 'national character' studies: there was, for example, a tendency to infer values from behaviour or institutions, and then use the behaviour to explain the values. One way to avoid this type of circularity is to infer beliefs *only from some types of political behaviour,* such as voting or group activity, and use these beliefs to explain *other behaviour,* such as compliance with laws. An alternative approach is to infer beliefs from behaviour during a certain time-period and draw on those beliefs to explain behaviour in a subsequent period. Much depends on the opportunities available in the political structure for acting on opinions. For example, in Cuba it appears that many workers have 'participated' in voluntary workforces without accepting the ideas of the regime as a response to peer group pressure and because there are few alternatives available to the workers. Another example of change occurring in political behaviour without there being a change in political values is seen in Northern Ireland. Attitudes of Catholics and Protestants to the regime have altered little, despite the *overt* displays of hostility to the regime by Catholics since the late 1960s.

## Methods[1]

Various techniques are used for describing and analysing political culture. The Almond and Verba survey was a landmark in survey research and in comparative politics. Data were collected by means of interviews with approximately a thousand respondents in each of the nations in 1959. As the first direct study of public opinion across the five nations, *The Civic Culture* resulted in a substantial enlargement of available empirical data on subjective aspects of the politics of the countries. There is no need here to discuss the problems involved in drawing up a questionnaire, locating representative samples, establishing the validity of the instrument – does it measure what it is supposed to? – and generally establishing a uniform or equivalent stimulus situation for all respondents. Such difficulties, familiar enough at the national level, were compounded five times over for such a comparative survey. Additional problems were posed by scheduling interviews, formulating questions, and conducting surveys in areas which were unfamiliar with such operations. In spite of these formidable difficulties, the comparative survey offers immense advantages in the study of political culture. The data present clear advantages in terms of their 'hardness', precision and replicability. Instead of crudely labelling a nation's political culture as 'participant' or 'deferential', one is able to suggest which groups disproportionately possess these features, the intensity of the features, whether they are changing and, if so, the rate of change.

Less direct is the method of content-analysis. In Cuba, Richard Fagen was not able to conduct survey research after Castro's rise to power. Instead, he chose to study two of the regime's action programmes which were designed to create 'a new Cuban man' – the Committees for the Defence of the Revolution, and the Schools of Revolutionary Instruction. He relied heavily on methods of content-analysis. David McClelland (1961) also employed content-analysis of children's stories and Greek funeral orations to develop measures of achievement-needs across different societies and different periods. Among political elites content-analysis of speeches and writings is a useful means of constructing an individual leader's 'operational code' or the belief system of a group of leaders (Leites, 1953). This approach is some advance on the old method of gathering facts about the social background of political elites and then making implicit inferences about their values.

The depth interview, inevitably with small samples, is another available strategy. Robert Lane (1962) conducted intensive interviews with sixteen residents in New Haven to collect material for *Political Ideology: Why the American Man Believes What He Does.* Pye's (1962) study of political elites in Burma and Solomon's (1971) study of Communist China also relied on intensive interviews coupled with Freudian techniques of interpretation. Such approaches, as conducted by Lane and Pye, gain in depth and richness, but pose problems of how representative the sample is of the wider universe. The depth interview would seem more applicable for small groups – for example, a Cabinet or Politburo, where a sample may be small but still representative – and for suggesting rather than testing hypotheses and insights.

Projective and semi-projective techniques have proved useful for exploring the orientation to politics of children, questioning respondents for whom politics is relatively remote, or dealing with potentially sensitive topics. These stimuli situations, because they are less structured than the fixed questions of formal interviews, are more likely to provide a rich picture of the individual's orientations and get behind those responses which are superficial or largely fabricated for the interviewer's questions. The study by Greenstein and Tarrow (1969) of children's orientations to their political systems in three nations employed semi-projective methods; one device they used to study images of political leaders was asking children to complete sentences about incidents describing the head of state being stopped by a policeman for a traffic offence. The children were then asked to imagine the conclusion to the incident. McClelland has measured achievement-levels among children by asking them to write stories after being shown blank or ambiguously marked picture cards. The stories were then scored for achievement-need levels. Finally Lipset's (1964) comparison of political cultures (or 'value systems') in Anglo-American states and France and Germany eclectically draws on opinion poll data, literature, symbols, behaviour and institutions to explain the different values.

Clearly, the most suitable method depends on the research focus. Doubtless, eclecticism in the use of source material and a willingness to appropriate insights from other disciplines will continue to be the order of the day in studying the political culture. For mapping a nation's political culture, the survey is the most appropriate; for reconstructing a past culture, content-analysis of available historical data; for exploring the orientations of the young or the less politically aware, projective techniques.

Because patterns of a group's political orientations only become distinctive when they differ from those of other groups, we may say that comparison is useful for the analysis of a group's political culture. For example, the frequent comparison of the political societies of Britain with those of France or the United States has led to (undue) emphasis being paid to the allegiant, consensual and deferential features of the former. In comparing their five national samples, Almond and Verba were impressed by the extent to which Britain and America contained the highest proportions of participant and competent citizens. However, when they later focused solely on these two cultures, they were led to define the British as a 'deferential political culture'. This was true, perhaps, as long as the comparative perspective was confined to Britain and the United States only; the broader five-nation perspective highlighted Britain as a 'participant political culture' (Kavanagh, 1971).

Clearly, what we compare is important. Britain and America, to return to the Almond and Verba example, were more *comparable* than any other two nations in that they were roughly similar along several dimensions (stability, liberal democracy, language, social and economic development), and this made it easier to trace the connections between the relatively fewer differing factors. In other words, broad similarities between the objects to be studied permit us to make statements like 'more or less', which are the essence of the comparative approach. As Lipset noted in his study of Anglo-American political and social systems: 'Only when we know what is unique on a comparative scale can we begin to ask significant questions about causal relationships within a country' (1964, p. 401).

Analysing and comparing political cultures on the basis of survey data across nations presents two immediate problems. The first is the *technical* one, involving the standardisation of questions and interview situations across the national groups, and has already been referred to. The second difficulty is a *conceptual* one of maximising the comparability of the cross-national data. Perhaps the most thorough attempt to deal with the problems of seeking equivalent indicators across nations was made in *The Civic Culture* (pp. 68–72). Included among the research strategies for increasing comparability were:

(1) Concentrating on the patterns of relations among variables within the nations. For example, analysis of amounts of political participation by level of education placed the differing national rates of participation in a new light. The more educated tended

to participate more frequently, regardless of nation. Of course, the content of a 'high' education differed in each country. But adopting ordinal measures of education within each nation heightened the validity of the comparison.

(2) Concentrating on the individual and his subjective outlook. Instead of comparing the institutions across countries, Almond and Verba compared the individual's subjective feelings towards the system.

(3) Selecting the least constrained or formal activities for constructing indicators of participation, competence, and so on. For example, as an indicator of political interest, comparison of exposure to politics in the mass media between Mexico and Britain is vitiated by the much greater penetration of the media in the latter country. The greater constraints placed on party membership or voting in the United States, compared with Britain, make these features invalid indicators of political participation. On the other hand, attending campaign speeches or talking about politics are less constrained and therefore more comparable as indicators.

## Uses

The utility of the political culture concept has been reflected, first, in schemes for mapping and describing political systems and, secondly, in causal analysis of political phenomena. It is worth noting that political culture is not a theory but rather 'a set of variables which may be used in the construction of theories' (Almond, 1980, p. 26). Almond's early (1956) typology of political systems was based on the following different types of political culture and role structure.

In *Anglo-American systems*, the political culture was homogeneous; citizens had shared values or managed to fuse different values; role structures such as parties, pressure groups and the communications media were relatively autonomous; and individuals belonged to a variety of overlapping groups. Consequently politics was conducted in a pragmatic or secular spirit, citizens were able to tolerate different loyalties and identities, and role structures were differentiated.

A second category was the fragmented *Continental European* culture. In France during the Third and Fourth Republics, and in Italy, the political culture was fragmented into rival sub-cultures and these were embedded in the various institutions. Group loyalties reinforced or paralleled each other. Catholics, for example, voted for Catholic-oriented parties, belonged to Catholic labour unions, read Catholic papers and restricted close friendships to co-religionists. Communists likewise restricted their contacts. The ability of interest groups, parties and the media to convert demands into bargainable policy alternatives was thus severely limited, as mutual reinforcements of social, religious and political loyalties into *familles spirituelles* increased antagonisms between sub-cultures. Politics in Northern Ireland reflects a similar division.

A third type was the mixed political culture in which there was a general lack of awareness of the regime and its norms, as found in *pre-industrial societies*. Finally, there was the synthetic homogeneous political culture in which apathy was combined with a general lack of commitment to regime norms. This was found in *totalitarian systems*.

The cultural homogeneity of the Anglo-American societies is related to their political stability, the fragmentation or polarisation of the Continental European societies to their political instability. This viewpoint has similarities to those group theories of democracy which stress the role of multiple cross-cutting memberships in producing a more consensual and stable society (Truman, 1951; Coser, 1956). In contrast, sharp and mutually reinforcing cleavages produces a deeply divided society, and threatens political instability.

The work of Arendt Lijphart (1968a, 1968b) and others on consociational democracies was a corrective to the Almond typology and highlights the dimension of (elite) culture which was neglected in earlier schemes. Lijphart suggests that 'centripetal' or consensual democracies correspond to Almond's homogeneous type. But his main qualification concerns the 'centrifugal' or fragmented democracies. The smaller European democracies of Austria, the Netherlands, Switzerland and Belgium are also fragmented, in that they possess mutually antagonistic sub-cultures, yet for most of the post-1945 period they have enjoyed political stability. For example, the Netherlands has, till recently, been a strongly segmented (*verzuiling*) society, consisting of three well-entrenched sub-cultures, the Catholic, Calvinist and secular. For the majority of citizens, party loyalty has been associated with membership of the 'appropriate' trade union, church, recreational group, and choice of schooling and newspaper. Looking at the distribution and intensity of attitudes, one was tempted to think of the Netherlands as 'several nations inhabiting the same country'. Yet compared with France and Italy the Dutch elites in Parliament were both willing and able to compromise and co-operate with one another in spite of hostility between the sub-cultures at the mass level.

Lijphart suggests another form of democracy, to refer to these divided but stable societies, which he terms 'consociational'. Antagonistic sub-cultures are not fatal for political stability, he states, if the relations between political elites do not reflect the bitterness felt at the mass level. In contrast to Italy and France, the political elites were often unable or unwilling to bridge the gap, and where there has been disagreement on the nature of the regime, the commitment of elites in the Netherlands to maintaining the system has prevented the cleavages from paralysing the government. In recent years that style of politics has been undermined, as the party system has fragmented and party leaders have been unable to 'deliver' the consent of their supporters.

Almond (with Verba) later developed a typology of *ideal* political cultures or citizen types (1963). Where most people are orientated to the input processes and see themselves as able to make demands and help to shape policies, then the political culture is *participant*;[2] the British, American and Scandinavian political systems best represent this ideal. Where most citizens assume a passive or obedient relationship to the system, only dimly perceiving themselves as influencing the input side, though being affected by the output structures, the political culture is a *subject* one; the East European and many new states approximate this type. Finally, where the individual hardly relates himself to the political system at all and has only a dim awareness and knowledge of its inputs and outputs, the political culture is *parochial*, a type found in many traditional societies. A political culture and its political structure may be said to be congruent when there is compatibility between the values and the institutions. This means that individuals have internalised the values appropriate to the operation of the system, their knowledge and understanding of the system are accurate, and the affective and evaluative orientations are positive.

It is worth stressing that these are ideal types. In fact, there are invariably mixes of these outlooks within individuals and within any political system. Moreover, individuals may shift their roles and self-perceptions according to circumstances. During elections or strikes, for example, they are participants, but when paying taxes or complying with laws and regulations they are subjects. Over time, with the extension of the suffrage and other citizenship rights and the diffusion of the notion that a democratic government should be responsive to the demands of citizens, the trend has been to a more participant culture. The crucial point about the culture is the individuals' perceptions of themselves as political actors.

Because so much of our description and analysis is conducted at the level of the nation-state, it is easy to overlook the non-coincidence of cultural and national boundaries. We need to appreciate the variations within a group or nation, even while characterising it under one label. In Canada many Quebecois, for various historical reasons, have looked to France for cultural identity. In Northern Ireland the legacy of history has led many Catholics to identify with Ireland south of the border, and not with the United Kingdom. There are a number of theoretical constructs which take account of cultural variations within nations. Marxist analyses of capitalist societies – starting from Marx's claim that 'the ideas of the ruling class are, in every age, the ruling ideas' –

state that such societies have a 'dominant' culture or set of values shaped by the upper class. In so far as the 'subordinate' class rejects these values, then it may develop a 'deviant' culture (Parkin, 1967). Brown (1977, p. 8) has usefully suggested the following possible configurations of political culture: (*a*) a unified political culture; (*b*) a dominant political culture which coexists with various political sub-cultures; (*c*) a dichotomous or divided political culture; (*d*) a fragmented political culture, one in which no statewide political culture has emerged to dominate the numerous political cultures or sub-cultures based upon tribe, locality, or social or national group. Brown suggests that in the communist states, in which political leaders are trying to 'remake' the culture, *a* is the goal, though *b* may be the present reality. In a multinational state, like Yugoslavia, or some of the culturally divided smaller European democracies, situation *d* is likely to prevail. Interwar Austria, divided between the 'blacks' and the 'reds', or the Catholic and Socialist sub-cultures, and Northern Ireland resemble *c*. Brown also draws a useful distinction between the 'official' or 'goal' culture – what *should* be – and the actual culture. The ideal of 'the new Soviet man' represents an aspiration, or ideal type of citizen.

## Explanations

Apart from using political culture for comparison and description, we may also use it as a tool for explaining political phenomena. Even the primarily descriptive studies also have an explanatory purpose. Almond's earlier (1956) typology was concerned to explain the greater political stability of Britain and the United States over France and Italy in terms of the cultural qualities. Political culture affects different patterns of political oppositions across political systems (Dahl, 1966). Whether or not political actors are pragmatic or rationalistic in their approaches to problems, co-operative or non-co-operative in their dealings with each other, allegiant to or alienated from the political system, trustful or not of other people, affects styles of opposition.

An early and most effective use of political culture has been to explain the propensity of the military to stage a *coup d'état*. The frequency of such a phenomenon has been well-documented. The existence of a strong military force, with its traditions, *esprit,* and sense even of being a state within a state, is one set of data. Clearly, a weak sense of the military's subordination to the civil power and the latter's dependence on it create a propensity for it to intervene. According to Finer (1962), whether or not the military intervenes depends on the popular support for the civil government. This in turn depends on two factors. First, is there a consensus about the procedures for assuming and transferring political power and is there general recognition of one sovereign power? This is the *legitimacy* factor; where legitimacy is well-established, then the government does not depend on the military for its existence and a military takeover would be widely rejected as 'unconstitutional'. The second factor is how *mobilised* the society is into various associations. Where the two factors are high then the political culture is a more reliable prop for the civil government.

As Finer emphasises, the two need not go together. Weimar Germany, the Fourth French Republic and Spain are examples of mobilised societies which were divided on major constitutional matters. The different types or levels of political culture (derived from the two variables) correlate with the likelihood and method of military intervention. In effect, Finer's use of the term 'political culture' is equivalent to the concept of legitimacy, long recognised to be a basis of support and of the stability of a regime. His advance on traditional usage is to link types of culture with one particular form of stability/breakdown, the *coup d'état*.

We shall now turn to an examination of some systematic applications of political culture as an explanation. Any summarisation runs the risk of doing an injustice to the subtlety and richness of these theories. However, their main elements are clear enough. The first two explanations, *congruence* and the *civic culture,* do not assume that the political culture is autonomous. They focus on it, for analytical purposes, as one element which interrelates with political institutions and political performance. The second two explanations, political *generations* and *hegemony*, regard the culture as a mediating factor and clearly see values as deriving from structural features. In this regard the culture factor may be seen as of secondary importance in explanations of political phenomena. *Hegemony* and *congruence* attempt to explain political stability and, by implication, provide explanations of political change. *Political generations* explicitly provides a theory of political change.

### (1) Congruence

A political culture is only a part of the larger culture of a society. It is for analytical purposes that we abstract from the larger culture those orientations relating to political objects. The two are, of course, often closely related. For example, the absence of a revolution in Britain for three centuries and the consensual, accommodative type of political culture is surely related to general cultural characteristics. The passive or subject political culture in the present-day USSR has been shaped by and is congruent with an authoritarian style of decision-making in society at large. In pre-revolutionary Russia few citizens had effective civil rights, there were no free interest groups, censorship was strict, and there were low levels of political participation and political understanding among the population. One can think of similar *linkages* between the general and the political culture in the case of Germans' traditional respect for authority, or the low level of interpersonal trust in France and Italy and its political counterpart, *incivisme*. At an individual level, we know that people who participate in politics are more likely to be active in other groups compared with those who do not participate, and that individuals who have a sense of political competence are more likely to be self-confident in other areas than persons who lack that sense of political competence. It is not surprising, therefore, that regimes which are engaged in remaking the political culture are careful not to neglect the general culture as well. Indeed, where there is a marked discontinuity between the two, then a regime is bound to face tensions. Another plausible notion is of there being a 'fit' between a culture and the political structure. A largely subject political culture 'fits' an authoritarian regime, or a parochial culture 'fits' a government that has hardly any relationship to its citizens.

Perhaps the boldest theoretical treatment of the relationship between the two has been proposed by Eckstein (1966). His main proposition is that the stability of a regime depends on the degree of congruence, or similarity, in authority relations found in the political and social spheres. Congruence (p. 239) means either *similarity,* or a *pattern of graduated resemblances,* or a similarity with those institutions *adjacent* to government. Similarity in the social relationships in the governmental and such non-governmental structures as the school, home and voluntary association reduces strains and helps to bring about appropriate role expectations. Eckstein illustrates his thesis by reference to England, where authority relations could be said to be broadly similar in both spheres (*congruence*) and Weimar Germany, where a highly democratic constitution had been imposed on an authoritarian society (*incongruence*). In England there were shared patterns of conduct, particularly in the parties, pressure groups and civil service structures, which were 'adjacent' or close to government.

To test the thesis, it needs to be recast in a form amenable to some sort of measurement. It is *amounts* of congruence and disparity that are crucial to establishing its validity. One might then measure the amounts of change in the regime. It is fairly obvious that the stability of a regime will be enhanced where the authority relations resemble rather than diverge from those in adjacent institutions. The major task, however, is to study the regimes in which the relations are neither highly similar (as probably has been the case in Britain) nor dissimilar (as probably was the case in Weimar Germany). It is fair to add that some of these criticisms have been met in a revised version of the theory by Eckstein and Gurr (1975), where the key variables of congruence, performance (instead of stable democracy) and adjacency are linked to indicators, and strategies for measurement are provided. For example, indicators of adjacency include *direct-boundary interchange*; such as sources of recruitment to government, and *cross-boundary interaction*, such as the frequency of meetings between members of the government and other groups.

As a cultural explanation, the congruence thesis is attractive on many counts. The claims advanced for the authority variable as explanation are explicit and there is no gainsaying the importance of authority in studies of politics. It links attitudes to the governmental and the social spheres, and utilises relevant research from social psychology on role strain and dissonance and their consequences for behaviour. By incorporating these approaches in an explicit framework it places the study of government and culture in a broad context. Moreover, Eckstein plausibly demonstrates how the factor of congruence in authority relations is able to encompass such other popular explanations of stable democracy as religious beliefs, rates of socio-economic development and strength of group membership. These, according to Eckstein, are important factors only in so far as they affect the congruence of the authority patterns (see p. 120). The notion of adjacency or relevance of values emphasises that the impact on the political system of values in the non-governmental institutions varies according to the likelihood that the institutions actually connect with the government. For example we would regard the major public schools as *adjacent* in Britain, because they are an important agency for recruitment into politics and the civil service.

## (2) Civic Culture

Almond and Verba justified undertaking a five-nation study on the grounds of its usefulness in explaining the structural-functional characteristics of the political systems under review. They hypothesised that a particular kind of culture, the 'civic culture', was the best 'fit' for a stable democracy. This 'civic culture' is a dualistic orientation to political authority, a balance of directive and acquiescent and of participant and passive attitudes. It is a mixed culture in which the subject orientations allow the elites the initiative and freedom to take decisions, while the participant orientations make the elites sensitive to popular preferences. For empirical purposes the authors regard the political culture as the sum of an individual's attitudes to the system, its parts, and himself as an actor in the system.

They suggest, in the light of each of their five countries' resemblance to the 'civic culture' model, that Britain and the United States best approximate the mix of the passive and participant outlooks. The balance in the British culture inclines slightly to the passive or deferential, while this quality is slightly less entrenched in the United States. The suspicion of active government in America is linked by the authors to the immobilism which periodically besets that country's political system. The deference-inclined mix in Britain is linked to the country's tradition of strong and effective government. Many Italians are alienated, both as participants and as subjects, from the political system. In Mexico citizens are often alienated from the particular policies and institutions of the government, but there is loyalty to the system because of its identification with the emotive symbol of the 1911 Mexican revolution. The political culture combines the cynicism and dissatisfaction of many Mexicans with present-day politics and their hopes and expectations that things will get better in the future. In Germany the citizens' subject political outlook is not matched by a set of participant attitudes which result in a 'civic culture' mix. Germans tend to be more impressed with the outputs of government than the system itself, and see their political participation as being rather formal and passive (e.g. voting), rather than informal (e.g. forming political groups and talking about politics). Specific or instrumental satisfaction with the performance and rewards ('ouput affect') of the government is not matched by a diffuse loyalty to the system itself ('system affect').

The distinction between attitudes to the system affecting its legitimacy and attitudes to the performance is a crucial one. The authors do allow that, over time, the outputs or rather public perceptions of a government's performance may spill over to affect attitudes to the regime itself. Indeed, since the 1959 survey Germans appear to have developed a high degree of attachment to their system (Conradt, 1980).

It is notoriously difficult to be sure that respondents are distinguishing between attitudes to the *regime* (the set of procedures and institutions), the *authorities* (the group of leaders who occupy the important positions at a particular time) and *outputs* (the policies or decisions). There is a temptation to conflate statements of desire for change in particular policies or incumbents into criticisms of the system as a whole. Yet satisfaction with government outputs or leaders may vary independently of attitudes to the system itself. In a recent reformulation of his notion of political support, David Easton distinguished between support which is either *diffuse* or *specific* (1975). The former is a general attachment to the system, largely independent of the varying performance or outputs of the system, and relatively enduring. Specific support, on the other hand, is contingent on the individual's perception of satisfactions and benefits of the system and may vary greatly even over short periods of time. The distinction (like that of Almond and Verba) is useful in spite of the difficulties involved in operationalising and measuring the motives on which an individual's support is based and the lack of research into the extent to which citizens actually distinguish the regime from the government.

Much of the dissatisfaction in Western states appears to be *specific*;

that is, it is directed at the political parties, their leaders and the performance of governments. For members of a political system to offer and withdraw this type of support depends on such criteria as their awareness of the authorities, particularly the party in government; their ability to associate the satisfaction and dissatisfaction of their needs and demands with the perceived behaviour of the authorities; and their attribution of responsibility to the authorities. In these conditions perceived performance actually influences levels of support (Easton, 1975, pp. 437–9). A good example of this specific support has been seen in recent years in the correlation between changes in the macro-economic measures of unemployment and price inflation and shifts in the popularity of governments (see below, Chapter 5).

Voters have regarded the policies of the government as a major influence on their standards of living, and changes in their evaluations of the government's economic performance are important in determining levels of party support. It is possible, however, that disappointment and consequent loss of specific support for the authorities, if maintained over time, will carry over and lead to general withdrawal of support (e.g. the Fourth French Republic and Weimar) or, alternatively, lower expectations.

The Almond and Verba study has been subject to many criticisms, some fair and some not so fair.[3] The main problem turns again on the causal connections between the political culture and the operation of the political system. It is not clear that any research design can actually demonstrate that a change in the culture produces a change in structure/performance, or vice versa. As Arendt Lijphart notes (1980, p. 53), predicting a relationship between the civic culture and democratic stability 'requires either a knack for predicting political changes or a lucky break'. As a second best, one could establish scales of democratic stability on which to rate the countries, so that there is some variance on the variable of the political system. The approach of Almond and Verba, however, is to assume that the two variables, 'civic culture' and 'democratic stability', 'fit' together largely because they are found in the United States and Britain. The problem is that in the absence of measures of the 'civic-ness' of the culture, or of stability or democracy, the two factors are not variables at all. Yet it is the case that the authors do find substantial and significant differences in national outlooks in the five countries, and that the differences do plausibly 'fit' many of the political system's characteristics.

## (3) Political Generations

The notion of 'political generations' assumes that as people are exposed to a shared set of experiences during a formative stage in their lives, so they acquire a common set of values. In explaining change in a society, it is easy to overlook the physical replacement of individuals, as older people die off and younger ones come of age politically. One wants to know if there is anything distinctive about the departing and arriving groups. Students of voting behaviour have employed a 'cohorts' theory to explain the changing political alignment of the electorate. The impressions about society and politics made on the voter when he first casts his vote are, it is suggested, likely to remain with him for life. He is exposed to a set of experiences and – because he is at a relatively impressionable stage – he acquires values which distinguish him from members of other age-groups. In Britain there was a pro-Labour generation which came of age in 1945; and in the United States a 'Depression generation', the young people maturing in the 1930s, who were more heavily Democratic than the generation before or since. These 'humps' in support for the Labour and Democratic parties are still seen in analyses of voting behaviour a generation later (see Chapter 5).[4]

Ronald Inglehart has argued that a combination of social and economic changes in Western societies has been producing a change in the culture via a distinctive set of values among the younger generation (1971, 1977). Inglehart draws on Maslow's theory of a hierarchy of human motivations or needs, particularly Maslow's suggestion that once a person's psychological safety and material needs are satisfied, so he accentuates the needs for affection, esteem and self-actualisation, in that order. One moves from material to expressive needs. Inglehart also accepts the common assumption that values are implanted during adolescence and are therefore relatively enduring. He hypothesises that the combined effects of peace and the growth of affluence in the post war period have satisfied the *material* or *acquisitive*[5] (material and security) needs of many of the younger generation. In contrast, their parents and grandparents who grew up at times of economic and physical insecurity would continue to regard these as priorities. As with the theory of marginal utility in economics, one places a higher value on goods which are scarce than on those which are plentiful. He hypothesises that:

(*a*) Younger people compared with the older generation would be more likely to share a *post-bourgeois* or *post-material* (stressing such values as the need for participation, affection and belonging) than an acquisitive outlook. Such people will accord a high priority to such participatory goals as 'seeing that people have more say in how things get decided at work and in their communities'. Similarly, the middle class and highly educated would be more *post-material* than the working-class and low-education groups, because their acquisitive needs would have been met.

(*b*) Because the stimulus for change in values was economic growth and affluence, so the rate of culture change across generations in countries would vary directly with the countries' rates of economic growth. On this assumption, Britain's relative economic strength before the war and (in comparison with its neighbours) poor postwar economic performance should produce a lower proportion of post-material types among the young generation and the lowest rate of cultural discontinuity between age-groups in comparison with other countries. The hypotheses concern differences between generations, social classes and nations.

These expectations were strikingly confirmed in the surveys conducted in 1970, 1973 and 1974. The *materialist* and *post-materialist* types do seem to provide valid categories; the attitudes of people on various issues do cohere as predicted. Individuals who chose material response on one issue were likely to choose such a response on other issues, and the same was true of the post-materialists. The 'pure' types are also very likely to give the 'expected' response on other attitude questions covering approval of student demonstrations, maintaining a strong army, and so on. The middle class and more educated have more *post-material* outlooks than manual workers and the less educated. Further support for the underlying logic of the theory is provided by an examination of the values of different national and socio-economic groups. Belgium and West Germany, countries which have experienced rapid economic growth in the postwar period, show more generational discontinuity than slow-growing Britain. Across the EEC countries the *post-materialists* are outnumbered about three to two by *materialists* in the young generation. But among the older generations they are outnumbered twenty to one. Further evidence for the generational difference is available in a five-nation study of political protest which showed that support for 'unconventional' political participation was a political protest markedly more prevalent among the young and those with a post-materialist outlook (Barnes and Kaase, 1979).

There is, therefore, evidence of a cultural transformation between generations and one that is related to social and economic change. Yet it is still worth remembering that the proportion of *post-materialists* across the West European states amounted to little more than a tenth of the adult population. Party systems are still based on socio-economic and religious cleavages and if sustained economic growth has been so important in shaping values, then the slowdown in growth in recent years should reduce even that small proportion of post-materialists.

A change in values has consequences for the conduct of politics, particularly for the political agenda, institutions and parties. According to the affluence post-material hypothesis, the younger generation has different issue priorities from the older generation, in particular being less interested in bread-and-butter economic issues and law and order. They are more international in outlook, dissatisfied with participatory opportunities in existing institutions and more willing to protest. Such persons are prone to think in more expressive and ideological terms. Because the *post-materialists* are gradually replacing the *materialists* in the populations of Western Europe, so present party alignments and political procedures may come under strain. The process of economic growth and associated growth in group membership, education and a 'civic' outlook had earlier been expected to promote support for these institutions. Instead, the process may give rise to demands for other, more direct forms of participation, and discontent. Politics in the post-industrial society may be less benign and government more difficult (Huntington, 1974) and it is among the more affluent, educated and high status that dissatisfaction is highest. On the other hand, if the theory is valid then a slowdown in economic growth (which has occurred since 1974) should lead to a decline in the level of economic well-being and to a reversal of the value priorities.

### (4) Hegemony

The study of political values has long been connected with an interest in the conditions of social order and the political stability of regimes. Regimes are maintained by a mixture of incentives, including force, legitimacy, tradition and the distribution of material benefits. Marx stressed the role of coercion in the persistence of regimes in capitalist societies, though he also acknowledged the place of values. On the other hand, some sociologists have stressed the primary importance of agreement on central values. Parsons, for example, talks of the need for internalised normative restraints based on 'a common system of values' (Parsons and Shils, 1951, p. 241) for the maintenance of social order. An attempt to interrelate the two emphases – *domination* via culture or values – has been made by writers on the hegemony of values.

There is a tradition, well expressed in the writings of Marx and Pareto, that the ideas of a society are those of its ruling class, and that they function as 'masks' of reality and 'legitimations' of elite domination. Gramsci later coined the now-fashionable term 'hegemony' to describe the process whereby the elite managed to impose its own view of society and its own system of values on the rest of society or the subordinate classes. Cultural cohesion is here explained through the broad process and content of political socialisation; it is claimed that the values presented in the mass media, the churches, schools, national symbols, and so forth, breed an acceptance among the non-elite of the status quo and the inequalities it institutionalises. In Britain this hegemonic or dominant model is often, though not solely, propounded by left-wing writers (Anderson, 1965; Miliband, 1969; Parkin, 1971) to explain such 'non-developments' as the failure of the Labour movement to be more radical, its inability to mobilise the working class more successfully at election time, or the lack of alienation in the lower classes from capitalist society.

This model acknowledges the cohesion of the culture and the value consensus but also asks: whose culture? whose consensus? It claims that integration is achieved by means of a 'dominant value system' which is so pervasive that it reconciles a substantial proportion of the working class to the contemporary social and political order and attenuates a distinctive and radical working-class sub-culture. 'Real' conflicts of interest and inequalities are muffled over by 'false consciousness', or the widespread inability by people to perceive the extent of their exploitation and its causes; and by their acceptance of a selectively defined version of the national interest which is advantageous to the elite. This hegemonic culture is not accidental but is the outcome of a manipulative process: socialisation is primarily a system-maintaining process in which people learn approved and integrating political roles. It stresses the superior normative and legitimating resources available to the defenders of the status quo over the proponents of change. According to Ralph Miliband (1969, p. 181), it is

> in very large part the result of a permanent and pervasive *effort,* conducted through a multitude of agencies, and deliberately intended to create what Talcott Parsons calls a 'national supra-party consensus' based on 'higher order solidarity'.

For these writers, the hegemony of elite values is found in all capitalist societies. Their mood reflects Marx's statements about the derivation of the 'superstructure', including cultural or ideational phenomena, from the material 'substructure'.

Parkin's interesting 'Working class conservatives' (1967), though more cautious in certain areas, deserves to be accommodated with the hegemonists. By arguing that 'the overall political culture and the normative system of the society [be] taken as a frame of reference' for explaining voting behaviour and socio-political values, he clearly suggests that an individual's values and party vote often depend on his location in the social structure. Dominant or hegemonic values are attached to major institutions like the aristocracy, monarchy, ancient universities, Established Church, public schools, private enterprise and the Conservative Party, and the deviant values to rejection of these institutions.

Moreover, because an individual's social location affects his exposure to it, this dominant value system is diffused unequally through society. The lower any given social stratum is in the hierarchies of prestige, power and wealth, the less complete is likely to be its acceptance of the dominant norms, and the greater the potential for deviant sub-systems and values to emerge. Parkin regards an individual's party vote as a measure of his commitment to dominant or deviant values, for 'political choice is an index of an individual's commitments not merely to party programmes but to a wide range of social values' (p. 279), and this allegiance is 'to an important extent a reflection of the values men subscribe to in areas of life outside of the realm of politics'. In other words, when we think of consistency in terms of alignment with the dominant norms in society, working-class Toryism may be regarded as consistency and Labour voting as deviance. Only if we assume a narrower class-determined view of party voting are we likely to see working-class Toryism as 'deviant'.

How might we evaluate these statements of hegemony? Is there evidence of apathy and passivity among the working class, as suggested by the model? The case is lent some support by the studies of working-class political and social deference, and by Runciman's (1966) demonstration of how many workers' acceptance of narrow reference groups limits their expectations and aspirations and thus produces acquiescence rather than resentment in the face of social inequalities. But the question remains; how much of this deference/withdrawal/working-class Conservatism is explained by the social structure and by 'dominant' values? Here one wishes that Parkin and others had provided a more elaborate inventory of these 'dominant' values, one which went further than associating them with elite institutions. We do know that features in the deference syndrome are concentrated among such groups as females, the retired, and workers in rural areas and small factories – those groups which are not well insulated against the dominant values. Dissent, or rejection of dominant values, on the other hand, is found among members of strongly working-class communities, active trade unionists, traditional proletarian occupations like docks and mining, and certain middle-class radical professions in which the individual is able to insulate himself from the core values. In this treatment, cultural and social structural factors are interrelated; theories of reference groups, deference and working-class Conservatism are all aspects of the *exposure to dominant conservative norms,* which in turn is affected by one's location in the social structure. But why assume that the values are necessarily derived from the structure. If the working-class deferential or Conservative lives in a middle-class area, works in a small factory, and so on, it is not outlandish to consider the possibility that a person's values have affected his choice of residence or employment.

There are various other difficulties associated with parts of the broad hegemonic statement. First, there are Miliband's charges that a ruling class manipulates lower-class values, regardless of their original sentiment (an assumption not made by Pareto incidentally), and gains from doing so. It is also not at all clear how one proceeds to test the statements that elites manipulate values and that the 'rules of the game' always operate to the benefit of the elite. No doubt elite values do have economic roots but it is a large, even arbitrary, assumption to make that economic interest is the *sole* or major explanation. If we point to inconsistencies in elite ideologies, or even to values or sections of the elite which seem to undermine their positions, we are confronted by the explanation that these are ruses or tactical concessions to mollify the masses. If the masses are not resentful, then this is proof positive of their blindness, of how their consciousness of their 'real' interest has been distorted. Now all this may be true, but no evidence can controvert it and data which, on the face of it, seem to weaken the theory, are actually taken to prove it! The conspiratorial strands in the model make it a self-fulfilling prophecy.

One might also question Parkin's crucial interpretation of the significance of the party vote: Conservative voting is seen as a symbolic acceptance of dominant values (and institutions), Labour voting as symbolic deviance. While it is plausible to see the long tradition of dissent in English life attaching itself recently to socialist ideas of equality and the brotherhood of man, Parkin seems to be placing too much interpretive weight on this very flimsy indicator of party vote. A general election, on this view, becomes a census on political values, in which votes for the two parties represent opposed value systems. Given the fairly even division over postwar general elections of the votes between Labour and Conservative parties, this suggests some massive dissensus. There is not, however, much evidence in the available survey research for this identification of party vote and sharply opposed systems of values. In fact much of the evidence suggests the opposite. Many workers vote Conservative for hard-headed, pragmatic, or instrumental reasons, or because they agree with that party's stand on issues.

A restatement of the hegemonic model would seem to strengthen it. A necessary major revision would make a distinction between those dominant and deviant values which have been internalised and those which are pragmatically accepted; all the above writings convey the impression of deeply held value systems. But there is, for example, ample evidence of the inconsistencies which exist between on the one hand a person's approval of general values and on the other the specific applications of them. When questioned about general or abstract issues the working-class respondent is more likely than not to proffer a consensual or deferential reply (i.e. one which is favourable to the status quo), while on more concrete issues, say, about work, the opportunity structure, or relations between social classes, he expresses more radical and class-conscious views. As Michael Mann (1970) has observed, it is important for empirical research to be clearer about the objects which the hegemonic or elite-favoured values relate to, and about the strength with which values are actually held. The failure of many people to bring their general or consensual beliefs and attitudes into accord with those which are interest-based or conflictual may suggest a degree of 'false consciousness'. Yet it may also be an example of a weak penetration of 'dominant' norms among the subordinate groups. One may point to the arena of industrial relations as a clear case of conflict; here successive governments have failed to achieve an incomes policy and a legal framework for collective bargaining acceptable to the unions, largely because of the absence of agreement on what a 'fair' policy is. A mixed model of cultural cohesion, as Mann would call this, would alert us to both the consensual elements (in the political sphere) and the conflictual (in the socio-economic sphere).

## Problems

Clearly there are a number of conceptual and technical difficulties involved in relating the political culture to other political phenomena in a causal sense. Such problems as imprecise hypotheses, poor operationalisation of concepts, and statements which are not expressed in a form amenable to disproof have been considered elsewhere (Barry, 1970; Kavanagh, 1972a). If we do find a relationship between culture and structure or performance,then how do we establish the link? The actual relationship may (is likely to) be one of mutual reinforcement over time, and the fact that they interact in this way makes it wellnigh impossible to separate the values from the performance of the political system.

Testing hypotheses about the effects of a change in values on political structure demands exacting experimental conditions – for example, controlling for extraneous factors such as wars and economic depressions, and developing criteria for measuring qualities such as civic culture and congruence at different points in time, and then waiting to see if and how a change in one factor affects change in the other. In other words, the culture and the system characteristics have to be variables. We would also require some idea of the proportion of the population who have particular values. No writer who has applied a label to the British/English political culture, for example, has been concerned to establish a 'threshold' for the frequency of particular attitudes. To what extent must there be such qualities as deference, congruence, 'civic culture', for there to be political stability and effectiveness?

These comments touch on the problem of analysing the survey material. While data collection is usually performed at the micro-level of the individual, culture is a collective phenomenon. The 'individualistic' fallacy involves a causal argument from the aggregated features of individuals to the global characteristics of a group of which the individuals are members. As Scheuch (1968) has observed, the proportion of respondents who express their support for, let us say, liberal democratic values does not tell us how 'democratic' the political system or political culture is. Where the political culture is seen as the aggregate of beliefs, emotions and values in society, the tendency is to overlook the problems of weighting the individual's values according to his amount of political influence. The political institutions, the weight they attach to the views of different groups, and the willingness and ability of individuals to act in support of their values determine the conversion of views into the culture and how the political system operates. The political culture is not the sum of its parts.

Such aggregate data are also likely to be misleading as a basis for making inferences about large-scale societies whose members are undergoing differential rates of change. John Lewis has suggested that in China 'the typical' peasant or worker may simply not exist, given the variations in the extent to which Mao managed to 'revolutionise' the political culture. According to Lewis (1966, p. 524):

> Aggregate data that may be used to identify ideal patterns lose their value for analysis of actual political orientations and attitudes. As elsewhere, the modernisation of China has begun to structure these orientations and attitudes along a broad continuum and has thereby rendered meaningless those simplistic interpretations of domestic Chinese politics based on general policy pronouncements and composite data.

One way of coping with the problem is to relate the broad distributions of values to characteristics of different political systems. As Verba (1980, p. 402) fairly comments, *The Civic Culture* did not move from individual data to the macro-level, but from one macro-characteristic (distribution of attitudes) to another (the working of the system).

Some of the imprecision in discussions of political culture results inevitably from the complex requirements of data collection, analysis and interpretation, and also from the political scientist's lack of a tradition of evaluating plausibility statements. In response to the question 'Can Plausibility become a Rigorous Concept?', Lucian Pye has argued (1972, p. 295):

> political scientists are able to be increasingly rigorous and precise with respect to measurement at the micro-analysis level, but our theories are not sensitive to the importance of quantitative differences in attitudes and sentiments, only to the necessity of 'appropriate' attitudes existing among the critical elements; on the other hand, it is at the *macro*-level that the critical hypotheses must be advanced and 'tested', but it is at this level that we lack capacity for rigour and precision.

Finally, one has to consider the argument implied in alternative historical and socio-economic approaches, that political culture may not be so crucial after all, that political values are not independent variables but 'are at best the last link in the chain of causation before behaviour itself' (Barry, 1970, p. 96). Such a devaluation of culture arises from a misguided attempt to place different explanatory factors in competition with each other rather than trying to explain the interrelations between them. Political values *may* be conditioned by history, social structure and the direct experience of people with the performance of the political system, yet the 'distal' historical and structural factors still have to be connected with the behaviour of groups and individuals. And it is here, even as an intervening variable, that values and attitudes have to be included in any strategy of explanation. In describing the context in which the values first developed, one need not be confined to economic factors as the sole or major determinant. Even if the political values are shown to be derivative at one point in time, they may, once established, be important thereafter in affecting political behaviour.

The concerns and efforts of many nation-building elites suggest that they regard the remaking of the political culture as being both important and within the realm of practical politics. This presents a paradox. On the one hand the effort invested in its reshaping is clearly a tribute to the importance of the culture. On the other hand, however, if the culture can be so readily shaped, then its importance as an explanation may be lessened for the student of politics. He would, it might be argued, be better employed studying the determinants of the culture. Attempts to change or transform a culture from 'above' usually occur in societies which are moving from a peasant to an industrialising society and/or follow a political revolution or rupture in political history. The new elites face the problem of how to handle the cultural inheritance of the adult population, while they try to bring the culture into conformity with the goals of the new system. A revolutionary 'vanguard' inevitably courts conflict and tension as it tries to eradicate the precursive influences and establish a new basis of legitimacy.

A useful test case of the extent to which the culture can be 'engineered' from above is afforded by the Communist regimes in East Europe and China, where the party has enjoyed a monopoly control over education, mass media and socialisation. These countries have also seen conscious and elaborate attempts to remake the political culture along socialist lines and to create a 'new' socialist man. In Communist China the 'thought reform' techniques and 'criticism – self-criticism' meetings were, according to one authority (Solomon, 1971, p. xiv), 'designed to exert continuing pressure against the traditional behavioural forms among Party cadres reared before "Liberation"'. Mao's concern to prevent the re-emergence of old values eventually culminated in the Cultural Revolution. Yet a recent study of political culture in these countries (Brown and Gray, 1977) emphasises the points of continuity and the tenacity of many old values regardless of change in the regime. The authors comment: 'our general conclusion must be that the results of political change so far in the Communist countries have been consonant with what we know of their previous political experience and political culture' (p. 267). In addition there are variations in the national political cultures, regardless of similar forms of regime: 'ruling Communist parties have been strongly influenced by the national political culture and have shown themselves to be capable of a creative response in terms of that culture, except where Russian force has dictated the lines and the limits of change' (p. 268).

Mao's stress on the need to 'remould' people's thinking reveals his belief that the basic factor shaping social action is the human personality (Solomon, 1971, p. 409), and was certainly a striking reversion of Marxist ideas. His awareness of the need for such a revolution in spite of years of party control is perhaps a reassurance 'that culture and personality are enduring influences shaping a political behaviour' (loc. cit.).

## Conclusion

One could certainly extend the litany of complaints about the way political culture has been and is used as an analytical tool. But we do not face a choice between dealing with political culture as the prime cause or ignoring it altogether; to ignore it is to miss out a crucial dimension of political behaviour. It is rather a question of how we use it. The positive case for the study of political culture rests on two planks.

First, it is clear that this part of the political system's 'environment' is worth getting at. The descriptive gains are an undoubted advance on the impressionism of previous studies and much of the crudity and 'reductionism' of the 'national character' type of analysis of the immediate postwar years has been avoided. On balance, the political culture approach provides us with more explicit, if still imperfect, tools for political analysis. On its own, however, it does not enable us to make predictions about political behaviour or even arrive at a set of testable propositions. For example, one may acknowledge the incongruence between the authoritarian political culture and the democratic political structure in Weimar Germany, but still accord due importance to the availability of Hitler, the miscalculations of defenders of Weimar and the economic and international pressures in causing the collapse of the regime. Similarly, in the Soviet Union one has to acknowledge the improved living standards and the country's international standing in explaining the legitimacy of the regime. Political culture is so often related to phenomena which have a number of other causes as well. In other words, culture alone will hardly provide a satisfactory explanation; a good strategy of explanation has to link the political culture with other variables. But appreciating the subjective environment in which political action takes place increases our understanding of why people behave as they do, and an awareness of the ways in which individuals are likely to structure and respond to situations helps us to narrow the range of possible outcomes.

Secondly, it may be that we have not been asking the most sensible questions about political culture. Complaints have usually come from political scientists who employ notions of determinacy and asymmetrical relations between variables. As Almond (1980) notes, it is the causal properties attributed to culture which have led to problems and dissatisfaction. It is the fact that the culture at some times shapes political structures, while in turn being affected by the structures, that makes it so difficult to isolate the political culture as an independent factor. The political culture, just because it relates to the context in which politics occurs, may contain a great deal of what we want to explain '*without explaining anything*' (Tucker, 1973, p. 179). It provides us with a handle on the propensities of a system, the sense in which, for example, one may talk about the opportunities of there being a *coup d'état*.

A large part of the difficulty arises out of the tendency to use culture as an explanation of macro-phenomena. We are now more aware of the problems involved in making cross-national generalisations about cultures, or even cultural statements at the level of the nation-state. It is the 'looseness' of cultural explanations that has resulted in the concept being less acceptable in a more hard-nosed discipline. The correct response is to reduce the focus and concentrate on more defined units. Other things being equal, such a unit is more likely to have a culture (i.e. a common set of values). Explanations of groups (such as elites) or sub-systems (as in consociational democracies) tend to be more successful, both because we are more able to get a better description and because we deal with something distinctive.

## Notes: Chapter 4

1 This section draws on Kavanagh (1972).
2 The input processes and institutions include, among others, elections, pressure groups and parties.
3 The best critical discussion is contained in Almond and Verba, 1980.
4 'Generation effects' may thus be distinguished from 'period effects', which are experiences which influence all age-groups, and 'life-cycle effects' in which change in outlook is associated with the process of ageing.
5 Respondents were allocated to the types on the basis of the relative importance they attached to two of the four following values: maintaining order in the nation; fighting rising prices; protecting freedom of speech; and giving people more say in important political decisions. Emphasis on the first two statements reflected the *acquisitive* outlook, on the last two a *post-material* outlook.

Chapter 5

# Elections and Voting Behaviour

Elections are such frequent events and the literature on voting behaviour is so massive that it would be understandable, if mistaken, for the political behaviour field to be identified with the exclusive study of voting. Study of electoral behaviour has blossomed, partly because the voting decision has been so amenable to sample survey techniques and partly because it lends itself to quantification. On the credit side there have been impressive gains in substantive knowledge, some cumulation in the research, and some genuinely theoretical developments. The subject and the empirical findings are important to any discussion about such topics as democracy, representation, political recruitment, the accountability of governments to voters and the context in which public policy is formed. Are the policies of governments in accord with public opinion? Do governments have 'mandates' for their programmes? Does a small group manipulate the agenda of politics and the policy outcomes? But, given the massive concentration of research resources in the field, some critics wonder if the final results represent an adequate return for their investment.

This chapter begins by looking at the role of elections today and at the different approaches to the study of electoral behaviour. It next examines the concept of partisanship or party identification, which generally plays a stabilising role in the individual's voting behaviour, and then at the potentially destabilising impact of short-term factors like the issues, personalities and economic conditions associated with each election. An election result is, it is now generally agreed, the outcome of the interaction of these two sorts of 'pushing' and 'pulling' influences. Finally, we will consider the consequences of elections for shaping the policy outputs of governments and promoting the accountability of governments to electorates.

## Election Rules

Elections take place according to established laws or rules of the game. An electoral system provides the framework on such matters as who is eligible to vote, how the votes are counted, frequency of elections, relation of votes to seats, finance, eligibility as a candidate, and so on. Election rules are important, not least in shaping voting behaviour, the agenda of policies, the number, electoral fortunes and behaviour of political parties, and the composition and stability of governments.[1] As Schattschneider commented on the importance of rules in general, *'Organisation is the mobilisation of bias.* Some issues are organised into politics, while others are organised out' (1960, p. 71, italics in original).

It is difficult to generalise about electoral systems because no two states have identical systems. Each state's electoral arrangements are the product of that country's particular configuration of culture, political history and party format. But one may offer some general comments on certain features (cf. Mackenzie, 1958).

An election outcome is determined by many factors. Explanation, therefore, is more than a matter of studying the sum of the individual votes for parties. Much study of electoral behaviour focuses on the social, psychological and political influences on the individual's voting decision. But electoral rules determine who votes and how the votes are counted. The factors that decide elections can be illustrated in the form of a flow chart, as in Figure 5.1.

In considering the relationship of seats to votes, a broad distinction may be made between the simple majority, first past the post, single-member system of most Anglo-American societies and the more proportional system of Western European states. The two systems represent a choice between different values – majoritarianism versus proportionality. The former tends to produce a 'clear' result, even if the strength of the parties in the legislature may be quite unrepresentative of their electoral support; the latter produces a more representative legislature, though this frequently entails the formation of coalition governments. The American, Canadian and British systems have produced results which are usually clear-cut and have forced the parties to make a broad appeal. Not since 1935 has a party in Britain formed a government with the support of 50 per cent or more of the voters and in October 1974 Labour gained more than half the seats with only 39 per cent of the votes. With two dominant parties, as in Britain, the former system tends to produce a clear electoral decision, a shift in votes between the parties is usually exaggerated in terms of seats, and the result is often unfair to minority parties, particularly if they do not concentrate their vote in a region.

Hence rules affecting the 'translation' of individual votes to legislature seats reflect different views about whether the election is primarily a device to represent public opinion or to produce a government. The proportional system satisfies the criteria of representativeness and

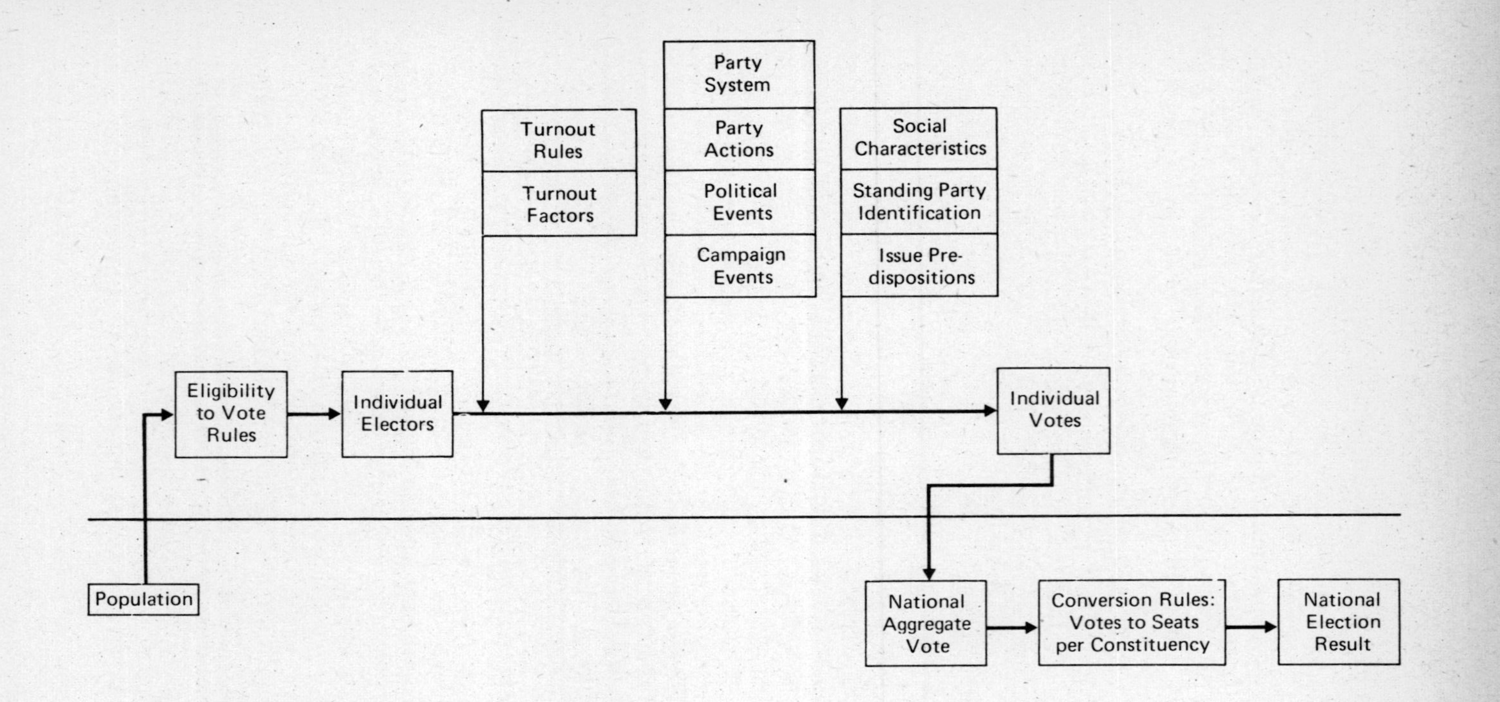


Figure 5.1 *How an election result is determined*

*Source:* Rose, 1974a, p. 9.

'fairness', allows the voter a more specific choice – though the weight of his preferences may be diluted in a coalition government which emerges – and it has tended to coincide with coalition governments. A prime example of 'proportionality' is provided by the Netherlands where a party needs only 0.67 per cent of the total vote to gain a seat in the 150–member Parliament. The political cost of the Dutch fragmented party system is seen in the crises and inordinate delays (up to six months) which attend the formation of a government. The idea of the simple relationship between type of party system and type of electoral system is far from perfect, however. The British electoral system has not forestalled some fragmentation of the party system since 1970, and in the 1970s in Italy, France and West Germany the trend in voting support has been to the two major parties or 'tendencies'.

Many examples of the important political consequences which stem from election rules may be found in American elections. The recent expansion of the primary system for the selection of delegates for nominating presidential candidates has further weakened the role of the quadrennial party conventions and party 'notables' in the selection of candidates for the presidency and meant an increase in the influence of the well-educated, middle-class, strong party identifiers and middle-aged: these are the groups who participate more frequently in the primaries (Ranney, 1972). These results were neither desired nor anticipated by the party reformers; most of them certainly did not want to weaken the party institutions.

Another example of the importance of rules is seen in registration. Most countries require a citizen to register before he is allowed to vote. In European countries registration is a government responsibility and is almost automatic; the electorate is effectively coterminous with the adult population. States in America, by contrast, require a person to register himself before he is eligible to vote. There seems little doubt that this rule has restricted the proportion of voters to adults ('the size of the political universe') in American elections. Average turnout in American presidential elections since 1960 is less than 60 per cent, compared with more than 90 per cent in Australia, West Germany, Italy and Belgium. But turnout among the *registered* electors in the United States is comparable to the average turnout of 75 per cent in British general elections. Historically, local control of registration was important in enabling local elites to exclude groups from voting and control the local political agenda. Indeed, there was a sharp fall in turnout between 1896 and 1924, when most states enacted their registration laws. In many Southern states, for example, literacy tests and poll taxes were used for many years to exclude blacks from the electoral register and, together with 'white' primaries, buttressed a policy of racial discrimination in the region. Similar tactics were used against groups of immigrants in the Northern states in late nineteenth century. In Britain before 1918, when semi-automatic registration was achieved, the emphasis on fixed residence and home-ownership for the suffrage effectively deprived many working men of the chance to vote.

## Types of Elections

Most states have elections. In some, however, the element of choice is so restricted as to provide elections without choice (Hermet *et al.*, 1978); voters have the opportunity to grant or withhold consent but not to choose between alternative programmes. About a third of contemporary states have competitive elections in the sense of providing a regular choice between competing teams of candidates. Voters may be variously asked to vote for measures (as in referenda), for a party list of candidates (as in the proportional list system), or to choose a candidate for a particular office. The range of effective choice may be wide, as in the Netherlands and Denmark, where the legislatures contain members from a dozen parties, or narrow, as in the United States, where all but one senator and all congressmen are Democrats or Republicans.

Although we have many typologies and classifications of electoral and party systems, we lack anything comparable for elections across countries. Of course, whether or not an effective choice between different parties is allowed at elections is a basic distinction between liberal democratic and authoritarian systems (cf. Dahl, 1971). The cyclical interpretations, such as the swing of the electoral pendulum in Britain or the changing tides of conservatism and liberalism in the United States, are terms of art rather than useful schemes of classification.

The most promising steps to building a typology have so far been applied to one country. Thus, we may distinguish movements of 'surge and decline' in levels of turnout and the support for the incumbent according to the stimulus or salience of the election (Campbell *et al.*, 1966). General elections, for example, are more salient than local, off-year, or by-elections. In the latter types of election the turnout is lower and tends to reflect the basic partisan loyalties of the smaller number who do vote. Where one party makes striking gains in a high-stimulus election (e.g. for the presidency) its extra support tends to come from independents and the weakly committed, most of whom vote on the basis of short-term factors. Such supporters are likely to fall away in subsequent low-stimulus by-elections or mid-term elections, or turn against the incumbent party because of dissatisfaction.

An interesting idea has been of a critical or watershed election, one which marks a sharp change in the electoral fortunes of the parties (Key, 1955). Change may include a reversal in electoral strength of the established majority and minority parties, or an important shift in the composition of a party's support. V. O. Key distinguished two types of electoral change: the *critical* election in which there occurs a sharp and durable realignment, and a *secular realignment* in which there occurs a gradual change in the strength of the parties. Key's analysis of the voting returns for the 1928 presidential election showed that, although the Democrats had temporarily lost their ascendancy in the South, they were making striking gains among the new immigrant voters in the big cities. In retrospect, the 1928 election was a forerunner of the New Deal coalition and the Democrats' electoral dominance which was established four years later. In the 1860 election the two main parties split into Northern and Southern factions. The new party system which followed the Civil War saw a rough balance established between the Republican and Democratic parties. This was upset in 1896, when the Democrats were largely confined to the South and West, and the Republicans gained a decisive advantage in the big cities and the Midwestern and Eastern states.

The concept of a 'normal' vote (see below) is crucial for developing a typology of elections and interpreting the quality of change at an election. If the change is durable rather than short-term, then we have a critical election. The classification in Figure 5.2 is based on two dimensions: (1) the victory or defeat of the normal majority party, and (2) whether the electoral cleavage is the product of short-term forces (i.e. the basic cleavage continues) or is more enduring. A *maintaining* election is one in which the great majority of voters follow their traditional party loyalties and the nominal majority party wins. A *deviating* election produces a victory for the usual minority party, though only in response to short-term forces associated with the campaign; it does not affect the enduring basis of partisanship. A *converting* election sees a greater-than-expected victory for the majority party, again because of short-term factors. Finally, there is a *realigning* or *critical* election, which produces a more permanent change in the balance of party strengths and may even presage the development of a new party system. These usually occur in response to a major event or crisis (e.g. the Civil War, or the economic depression of the 1930s).

Backed by careful analysis, the concept of a critical election is useful in assessing the 'meaning' of an election result. It increases our sense of historical perspective about a particular election or a series of elections, and provides a base for extrapolation from one point in time. It is when we try to hone the concept too finely, however, that problems emerge. In trying to identify a time at which an enduring change occurs, do we need to focus on one election or a period which covers more than

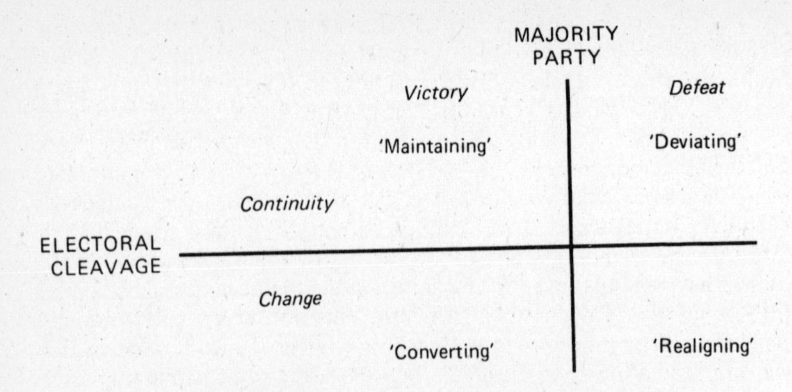


Figure 5.2 *A classification of presidential elections.*

*Source:* Pomper and Lederman, 1980, p. 86.

one election? Is it more plausible to regard the period 1928–36 in the United States as a realigning era, rather than selecting one of these three presidential elections as a realigning election? May the term be applied to a sub-system of the party system or electorate, such as the emergence of a minor party, or change in a region? In the American South, Republican presidential candidates have made sharp gains since 1960; and in Britain the Conservatives have had a minority of seats in Scotland since 1955. As a research concept, the critical election is probably more useful to the historian, for it is only after the passage of time (and further elections) that one learns whether there has been a realignment.

Historians have necessarily had to rely on aggregate data to interpret elections. The advantage of survey research, as a complement to this approach, is that one is able to collect information about the motives behind voting decisions and to assess whether the election outcome is likely to be a short-term or long-term change. Contemporary surveys showed that Republican landslide victories in the 1952 and 1956 presidential elections were short-term, a response to the personal popularity of Eisenhower till recently.

Because national party systems are linked to social, economic, constitutional and cultural features they may be thought to have a 'supporting' base. Parties also help to mould these forces (e.g. by shaping electoral systems, having access to the mass media and influencing political socialisation). As Lipset and Rokkan (1967) remind us, established parties have both the incentives and the resources to try to 'freeze' the system. The main parties in Western Europe today usually established their electoral foothold during a major stage in the country's history, or when there was an extension of the suffrage. But party systems are not immutable. In the United States and Britain there has been speculation about the possibility of a realignment in the party systems. Yet although there have been many symptoms of the decay of the established party systems in these countries, there are few signs of a new alignment taking hold. Electoral volatility and sharp short-term changes in the level of support for the parties may continue, but with many voters too detached from the parties to make a new alignment. Ivor Crewe *et al.* (1977) and Dean Burnham (1970) have suggested that the present trends in British and American voting behaviour and partisanship indicate that there is a dealignment rather than a realignment, that is, a change away from the established parties.

## Approaches

Voting is only one aspect of a person's political behaviour. The 'voter', as such, is an abstration. For most people, the role of voter is less important than that of student, wife, home-owner, or football supporter. Voting may plausibly be seen as the behaviour of ordinary individuals in electoral situations (Rose and Mossawir, 1967). Yet this limited activity – for the individual – has spawned a large literature. In this section we shall consider some of the alternative approaches to the study of voting. The approaches employ different models, as it were, of political man, make different assumptions about political behaviour, rely to some extent on different research methods and tools, and focus on different aspects of the voting decision.

### (1) Structural Approach

The structural approach emphasises the larger context in which the vote occurs – the social structure, party system, electoral rules, and so on. In most cases the voter enters an already established party system and often inherits from his parents a loyalty to a party. Many party systems in West European states are the product of cleavage lines of the past. The number of parties, the social bases of the party system and the type of appeals they make differ across countries because of distinctive patterns of history. Lipset and Rokkan (1967) have emphasised four social structure sources of political divisions: (*a*) social class or differences between employers and workers; (*b*) religion; (*c*) urban–rural contrasts; (*d*) language and nationalism. If we look at the social bases of voting support for Western political parties, then religion, perhaps surprisingly, is the most frequent source of differentiation between the parties (Rose and Urwin, 1969). But if we look at the content of their election appeals then the socio-economic division is the major division

(Lijphart, 1981). The range of possible party choices is, therefore, largely structured for the individual. Similarly, one may relate patterns of electoral behaviour to the nature of the political agenda. W. D. Burnham (1965) has argued that voting participation in the United States declined sharply between 1896 and 1924 partly because of the changed nature of the party system. The United States was divided into uncompetitive regions, a Democratic South and West and a Republican North-East and Midwest. The Republicans were based on industrial and capitalist interests and the Democrats under Bryan appealed to the farmers. Neither of the main parties was responsive to the social and economic concerns of the growing industrial working class. Other explanations emphasise the tighter registration laws which checked fraudulent voting and the extension of votes to women and immigrants in the 1920s as factors which depressed the rate of turnout.

### (2) Sociological Approach

This approach links the individual with the social structure, placing the vote in a social context. Most survey research still uses the standard demographic controls – sex, age, class, education – for analysis of responses. These factors have the advantages of being measurable and 'hard', that is, they are invariable. The development of sophisticated techniques such as 'tree analysis' even allows one to weigh the relative influence of different factors on a given dependent variable.

The early American voting surveys demonstrated a strong correlation between party support and social background factors. The authors of the Elmira study (Lazarsfeld *et al.*, 1948) formed an Index of Political Predisposition (IPP) from three factors: the voter's religion, residence in an urban or rural area, and socio-economic status. For example, a worker who was a Catholic and lived in an urban area, or a middle-class person who was Protestant and lived in a rural area, were each likely to vote Democrat and Republican respectively in over 80 per cent of cases. These features, it was argued, disposed a person to vote for his or her 'natural' party. It was a case of 'social characteristics determine political preferences' (p. 27). Where a person possessed 'contradictory' characteristics, then he was more likely to come to a voting decision late in the campaign, be wavering in his intentions, or abstain, or vote for the other party. The notion of such a person being 'cross-pressured' inferred a psychological state of mind from the social background factors, an extreme form of sociological determinism. Later attempts to apply the notion of this index to the national electorate proved much less successful (Janowitz and Miller, 1952). In more recent American elections the social bases of the old Democratic coalition have weakened still further.

A similar type of analysis has been applied to social class in Britain (Rose, 1980). If we think of the ideal manual worker as one who regards himself as working class, has received the minimum level of education, is not a home-owner and is a member of a trade union, then only a half of manual workers possess two or more of these characteristics. About a third of white-collar workers possess an opposite set of 'ideal' class characteristics. The more typical the person is of his social class, in terms of possessing these reinforcing attributes, the more likely he is to vote for the party typical of his class. This is demonstrated with reference to the 1979 election. Of the upper-middle class (in terms of occupation), 69 per cent of those who possessed four ideal-type class characteristics voted Conservative, compared with 31 per cent of those who possessed one. Of the working-class, 67 per cent of those with the four characteristics voted Labour, but only 34 per cent of those who had one.

### (3) Ecological Approach

The ecological or aggregate statistical approach relates aggregate votes to general features of an area, be it a constituency, housing estate, region, or country. The analysis depends on the availability of census data, which are broken down by the appropriate geographical unit such as ward or constituency. Campaign folklore traditionally relied on informal ecological methods for interpreting voting behaviour, for example, the religious basis for working-class Conservatism in Liverpool and Glasgow until the 1960s. The method is well established in France and the United States where census data on constituencies have long been available. They provided the basis for Siegfried's famous geographical division of France into areas of the political left and right (1913). For Britain, however, the data were only broken down at constituency level in 1966.

A problem with aggregate data for election analysis is that the findings are compatible with different explanations. Where there is a large turnover of voters in a constituency, we have no way of knowing whether changes in elections result from shifts in individual behaviour or from the physical replacement of voters between elections. The ecological fallacy (Robinson, 1950) invalidates our making inferences from the aggregate to the individual level. Correlations at the former level may be stronger than those at the individual level, for example. Yet the method is still useful for establishing correlations between large units and analysing aggregate changes over time. We may also use it to study the political behaviour of groups which are heavily concentrated in constituencies (e.g. miners, immigrants, students), for a representative sample survey will contain too few members of these groups for analysis (cf. Crewe and Payne, 1976, p. 434). And the more homogeneous the unit, the more confident we may be in offering explanations based on aggregate data. Crewe and Payne (1976) computed an expected or 'normal' vote for the Labour Party based on the proportion of manual workers in each constituency. 'Deviant' constituencies are those with markedly above or below the expected level of Labour voting.

### (4) Social Psychological Approach

An interpretation of the voting decision as the outcome of the voter's psychological predispositions or attitudes is associated with the Michigan School of election studies. The individual vote is studied within 'a funnel of causality', or a pattern of linked changes which occur over time. At the mouth of the funnel are the broad political context, the voter's social background and other distal environmental factors. As we move to the tip of the funnel (and the vote decision) we study a person's party identification and then the specific stimuli of candidates and issues associated with the election. The funnel concept represents a zone of time and as we move further back, so we go back to more distant factors. The final vote decision is interpreted as a product of the individual's attitudes to the candidates, foreign and domestic issues, groups and the records of the parties. These attitudes, it is assumed, immediately precede the voting decision.

The most famous concept associated with this research has been that of *party identification.* The concept refers to the voter's perceptions of which party he feels close to and it is assumed to be an enduring attachment. Party identification has been an essential tool for studying the nature of electoral change in America, and particularly in developing a 'normal vote' for the two main parties based on the popular distribution of party identification between the parties. Where the election outcome has differed from that expected simply on the basis of partisanship, then the deviation has been explained in terms of the short-term factors like the particular issues and personalities associated with the election. An election is an interplay between such stabilising forces as partisanship and social structure and those making for change. The concept of party identification has had a major impact on electoral studies, on cross-national research, and in stimulating research which links voting behaviour to childhood socialisation and develops a typology of elections (see above, p. 81).

### (5) Rational Choice Approach

This approach, borrowed from economics, relies on a few assumptions to make deductions about the instrumental and cost-effective behaviour of voters and campaigners. These assumptions include the voter's calculations about the costs of voting, the probability that his vote will affect the outcome, and the difference between the alternatives posed. These calculations determine, for the 'rational' voter, whether he should vote at all and, if so, for which party or candidate. A similar process of calculation affects the candidates who want to get elected; they present a package of policies and appeals designed to please a majority of voters. The theory can be used to explain the behaviour of both voters and candidates who want to minimise costs and maximise benefits. Where the Michigan use of party identification stressed the affective ties between voters and parties, the economic approach stresses the more instrumental aspects of the interactions.

Conditions assumed by the model are not always found in the real world. Many 'rational choice' theorists argue that the benefits of voting are negligible for the voter. The interesting question is not so much 'why do people not vote?' as 'why do so many bother to vote?'. In explanation, we have to fall back on psychological rewards, such as sense of civic duty or reaffirmation of group and party loyalties (Rose and Mossawir, 1967). Many voters, instead of being perfectly informed about parties' policies, rely on short cuts like tradition, ideology, or the party image for making decisions. Candidates and parties may be deliberately ambiguous about certain of their policies. Yet the landslide defeats of Senator Goldwater in 1964 and Senator McGovern in 1972 and Labour's defeat in 1979 demonstrate the validity of the main thrust of Downs's (1957) analysis; where a candidate is perceived as being at the minority end of a continuum of policy preferences, then his opponent is able to occupy much of the centre ground.

Thus voting behaviour may be studied through different analytic frameworks. For intellectual rigour there is much to be said for adhering to one model. However, one loses something in quality of explanation, for electoral change is then treated as the property of a 'closed' system. For, 'Only by cutting away huge segments of political reality would it be possible to apply a single, elegant model of change that was possible in its terms' (Butler and Stokes, 1975, p. 405). Apart from the structural approaches, the voting studies have been criticised for producing:

(1) *'Low-Level' or trivial relationships.* Establishing correlations between the vote and, say, class or party identification are, it is argued, a preliminary to rather than an explanation.
(2) *Tautological explanations.* Party identification, it is often claimed, is too 'close' psychologically to the voting decision to be useful as an independent explanation.
(3) *Apolitical explanations.* Both in neglecting the political context as

an influence on voting, and in selecting particular independent variables, these studies provide a form of sociological, psychological or economic determinism.

## Explaining Stability and Change

When we talk of an election outcome or verdict, we generally refer to which party (or set of parties) gains control of the government. Such an outcome is the result, first, of an aggregation of millions of individual voting decisions and secondly, of the electoral system, which translates the votes into seats. Our focus at this point is on the first of these processes.

It is from the Michigan School that we have developed the most useful approach to the analysis of electoral change. We may think of an election result and the individual voting decision as the product of factors which are disposed to produce stability and change. The major factor making for stability is the party identification or underlying partisanship of voters; this is reinforced by contextual factors like the social bases of the party system, class, religion, and so on. Once a voter has acquired an allegiance to a party he is usually never again so open to the possibility of change. Factors which make for change are the issues and personalities associated with each election, and are essentially short-term. These last factors explain why voters deviate from their normal party allegiance, into either supporting another party or simply not voting. Another source of change in the relative strength of the parties is to do with the effects of physical replacements in the electorate. From one election to another, some voters have died and left the register, while others have come of age and are able to cast a vote for the first time.

We now turn to an examination of these factors.

## Party Identification

Party identification refers to a person's psychological attachment to a party. If he thinks of himself as Conservative or Labour, or feels close to one of the parties, then he is called an identifier with that party. Many people learn a party loyalty early on, often from parents and over time the attachment tends to strengthen as it becomes rooted in community, social class, personal and other ties.[2] Young or first-time voters provide fewer and weaker identifiers with the parties and they are more volatile in their voting behaviour because they are less 'immune' to the pressure of events. Older voters, hardened in their loyalties, are more immune to the forces of change than young voters;

they are more likely to interpret issues and events in a partisan perspective and so maintain their party loyalty. In Britain, where a person's partisanship is typically shared by his or her spouse, neighbours and workmates, defections from the preferred party have been rare. But where the identifier's partisan environment is less homogeneous, then leakages are more frequent (Butler and Stokes, 1975, p. 65).

Party identification has been compared fairly to allegiance to a church. Graham Wallas long ago suggested that voters required 'something simpler and more permanent, something that can be loved and trusted, and which can be recognised at successive elections as being the same thing that was loved and trusted before; and party is such a thing' (1921, p. 83). The usefulness of the concept in research depends on identification being distinct from actual behaviour. In the United States, where there is such a distinction, a number of claims have been made for the concept:

(1) It provides a 'base-line' for a party's 'normal' vote. A party's 'normal' vote is based on its share of identifiers in the electorate or its basic underlying support (Converse, 1966), if we discount the influence of short-term factors.
(2) It helps the analysis and classification of election outcomes, particularly where the result differs from that predicted by the 'normal' vote.
(3) It relates to many other political attitudes. Party identifiers, particularly strong identifiers, compared to non-identifiers, are more likely to be politically interested, informed and active, agree with their parties' stands on issues, and vote on election day. Strong identifiers with a party are also more likely to believe in the efficacy of the electoral process.
(4) It reduces information costs for many voters (cf. Wallas, 1921, and Downs, 1957).

Knowledge of the partisan disposition of the electorate enables us to talk about the parties' probable electoral fortunes, *other things being equal*. In postwar American presidential elections only once (in 1964), has the Democratic candidate's support exceeded what would be expected on the basis of partisanship. Republicans have managed to exceed their anticipated share because they gained on the candidate and issue factors. Trend data on party identification enable us to trace the changing level of commitment to the parties, apart from election results. In the United States the proportion claiming to be Independents rose from 22 to 36 per cent between 1952 and 1976; in the same period the proportion claiming to be Democrats fell from 47 to 40 per cent, and to be Republicans from 27 to 23 per cent. The decline in attachment to the parties has been particularly marked among the young; by 1972 more than half of the 21–24 age-group were political Independents. Democrat identifiers still outnumber Republicans by a 2:1 margin and therefore have an inbuilt advantage. Yet the impact of other factors is seen in the fact that since 1944 the Democrats have only once gained a decisive majority of voters in a presidential election – in 1964. In Britain the trends have been similar. Between 1964 and 1974 the proportion of 'strong' identifiers with the two main parties fell from 40 to 24 per cent – though there was little change in the proportion of party identifiers, which remained around four-fifths (Crewe *et al.*, 1977).

These changes in level and intensity of partisanship become significant when we link them with the signs of the decline of the parties in Britain and the United States. In the United States (cf. Nie *et al.*, 1976, ch. 4, and Dennis, 1975) these signs include:

- – declining turnout in presidential elections;
- – growth of split-ticket voting (the proportion 'splitting' their votes between a presidential candidate for one party and a congressional candidate of another party rose from 20 to 42 per cent between 1952 and 1972);
- – volatility of voters (e.g. the landslides for the Democrats in 1964 and then Nixon in 1972);
- – support for third party candidates (e.g. Wallace in 1968);
- – growing electoral importance of candidate and issue factors compared with party identification;
- – distrust of parties.

In Britain, the symptoms are fewer but one may point to:

- – greater volatility;
- – the decline in the numbers perceiving a difference between parties or thinking that party competition makes politicians responsive;[3]
- – decline in the aggregate support from the two main parties (90 per cent in 1970 to 75 per cent in 1974 and 81 per cent in 1979).

The usefulness of the concept of party identification has been criticised on two grounds. The first questions the continuing validity of many of the former assumptions and findings. The growth of Independents among young well-educated and informed Americans has undermined the association of partisanship with the civic virtues, mentioned on page 89. If a steadily diminishing proportion of voters identifies with a party, then it limits the base for constructing a 'normal' vote and opens the possibility for more issue voting, greater electoral volatility and even a realignment of the party system. In both countries one can point to likely explanations for the weakening of partisanship: new issues, a new generation of voters, the spread of television as a less partisan form of communication compared with the press, disappointments with the performance of parties in office and general social change. Beck (1976) has suggested that there is a generational pattern in the strength of popular attachments to the parties. During the early years of a realignment or the emergence of a new party system, voters are strongly attached to the parties. The next generation of voters is also firmly attached because, during childhood, it is socialised into the system. By the third generation, however, the attachment wanes because young people are so physically and psychologically distant from the forces which brought the original alignment into existence. The passage of time weakens the underlying partisanship of the electorate. The weakness is reflected particularly in the youngest generation, who are most prone to vote in accord with the contemporary climate of opinion or for new parties.

We are presented with an apparent paradox. At the individual level we have been led to believe that partisanship, once acquired, hardens over time. But the passage of time from the original party alignment tends to make it more difficult to pass on intense partisanship to succeeding generations. Hence the number of partisans in the electorate weakens over time.

A second objection concerns the use of the concept in cross-national research. In each country the different party system has different meanings to the voters. Children, for example, conceive of voting and parties differently in France, England and the United States (Caldeira and Greenstein, 1978). In Britain, for example, voting is seen largely in terms of a choice of party, in America largely as a choice of person. In Britain the relation between vote and partisanship is more complex than that in the United States. In the 1960s, 85 per cent or more regularly admitted an identification with one of the two major British parties, though there was great fluctuation in support for the parties in the opinion polls (Butler and Stokes, 1975, p. 40). But in contrast to the United States, a change in vote at a British general election was very likely to be accompanied by the appropriate change in identification (ibid., p. 43).[4] One way of tapping the context of partisanship is to learn about the voter's sense of distance from the other parties. Butler and Stokes found that about a third of their respondents used a positive (to one party) – negative (to other party) criterion in evaluating the parties.

## Social Structure

A second source of stability is the social structure, or the social bases on which the party system rests. Some idea of the durability of party choices is seen from the fact that party systems in the United States and, till recently, Northern Ireland, have dated from cleavages associated with civil wars, one 120 years ago, the other 60 years ago. Neither the social structure nor the party system is immutable, although in the short-run they are relatively fixed for most voters.

One criterion for stating that a party is based on a social group is that at least two-thirds of its supporters share a characteristic. Thus, for a party to be middle class, at least two-thirds of its supporters should be white-collar workers. Rose and Urwin (1969) have analysed the social characteristics of the electoral followings of 76 Western parties that fought at least three postwar general elections. They found that 35 parties were based on a common religious or anti-religious outlook; these were divided almost equally into 18 pro-Christian and 17 anti-clerical or similar parties. Social class was a source of cohesion for 33 parties. The British Labour Party for example, is clearly a working-class party in that it draws some three-quarters of its support from manual workers and their families. But the Conservative Party is not a middle-class party, for it draws its support evenly from the two classes. National and language divisions are important bases for parties in Belgium, Canada and Northern Ireland, and in all three societies the separatist claims of groups threaten the stability of these regimes.

## The Weakening of Stabilising Forces

Before we turn to an examination of the short-run factors which make for change, it is worth noting how the stabilising factors may themselves be weakened. Consider first the case of partisanship, or the psychological ties between a voter and *his* party. We have already noted the decline in party identifiers in the United States and the decline of *strong* party identifiers in Britain. In America the decline of partisanship, has been a *generational* one, affecting the younger generation most. In Britain the decline has affected all age-groups, though it is more marked among the middle class and well educated, and seems to be a *period effect,* related to the issues and events of the time (Crewe *et al.,* 1977, p. 168).

A similar weakening is visible if we turn to the traditional social bases of the parties. In Britain there has occurred, during the 1970s, a marked depolarisation of the class base of the party system. An increasing proportion of voters are now voting with a 'class deviant' party, i.e. there are more Conservative workers and middle-class Labourites. In the 1974 and 1979 general elections these amounted to nearly 40 per cent of two-party voters. Labour's average share of approximately two-thirds of the working-class vote in general elections (1945–70) has now fallen to around a half. The Conservative average share of about four-fifths of the middle-class vote (1945–70) has now fallen to three-fifths. Some of this 'leakage' is accounted for by the rise of support for the Liberal and Nationalist parties as well as cross-party votes.

There are many factors contributing to the weakening of the class alignment; social class itself is not a salient concept to many people (only a half spontaneously accord themselves a class identity), economic and social change has diminished the proportion of manual workers and expanded the proportion of 'service' and white-collar workers, and weakened the cohesiveness of both. A 'looser' social structure has meant that the two main parties are more often perceived in less class-related terms. The class alignment, in terms of both voting behaviour and class-related attitudes to the parties, was at its strongest in the generation which came of age politically in 1945. Butler and Stokes (1975, pp. 201ff.) show how those attitudes have weakened in subsequent cohorts. The erosion of the class-party ties is in large part a function of the entry of new voters. Both parties are now less protected by ties of social class and party identification, particularly among the newer generation of voters.

In the United States the party coalitions dating from the New Deal era have also been undermined by the passage of time and new issues. The parties attracted groups of voters who divided clearly in the 1930s on the issues of welfare and a greater role for the government in intervening in the economy. Nie *et al.* (1976, ch. 14) chart some of the changes as follows. Jews and Blacks have become more liberal. The white South has become more conservative and Catholics have become less liberal. Outside the South, lower- and middle-class whites are more conservative while upper-status and better-educated whites are more divided (Axelrod, 1974). The Democratic electoral coalition in the 1970s has become more black and middle-class and suffered a sharp reduction in its Southern white component. The Republicans have become less Protestant, less middle-class and more a Southern white party. The inversion of the old New Deal relationship between social class and party means that more 'liberal' and 'egalitarian' sections of the middle class turn Democratic and 'conservative' workers turn Republican (Ladd and Hadley, 1976). The changing strength of groups in the party coalitions affects the salience of issues; the Democrats have been particularly divided over questions of race and economic and symbolic redistribution between blacks and whites.

## Issue Voting

Studies of the role of issues in voting behaviour usually become entangled with assessments of whether or not elections produce mandates and the rationality of the 'typical' voter. A traditional portrait of the ideal or 'rational' citizen is of one who is open-minded, well-informed and decides his vote on the basis of issues. The findings of voting studies have provided an empirical if controversial input to this aspect of democratic theory.

The early voting studies downgraded the role of issues in electoral behaviour. They suggested that most voters had already decided how to vote before the campaign began and sometimes either misperceived or were unaware of the stands of the candidates they professed to support (Lazarsfeld *et al.*, 1948; Berelson *et al.*, 1954). The conclusions of Campbell *et al.'s* (1960, pp. 169–71) study of the impact of issues on voting was even more negative. The study applied three tests to assess the force of issues on the voter:

(1) Public opinion is skewed in one direction on the issue.
(2) The voter not only perceives differences between the parties' positions on the issue but sees that one party represents his position better than another party.
(3) He must care about the issue.

When the study applied these criteria to sixteen issues in 1956 it found that few issues passed all three tests. Obviously excluded from the ranks of potential issue voters were the third of the voters who simply had no awareness of any of the issues. Other respondents were familiar with an issue but were not concerned about it. On all three criteria, only between 18 and 36 per cent could be classified as potential issue voters, that is, they might switch parties on the basis of an issue. Most of these voters, however, were already firmly committed to a party.

The conventional portrait of the American electorate accorded slight importance to issues and was part of a larger view of public opinion which was dominant in the 1950s and 1960s. Most voters, according to this view, had little understanding of political ideology in the sense of employing general concepts to explain political preferences, their views were often inconsistent and unstable, and they were partisan. Even in Britain, the alleged home of an issue-oriented and 'responsible' party system, the general direction of the findings was not much different. In the 1960s voters' views on the Common Market and public ownership were unstable and very few issues passed all three criteria (Butler and Stokes, 1969, chs. 8–9). On public ownership, for example, a clear majority of voters were opposed to further nationalisation, and clearly differentiated the parties' positions. But it was not an issue on which many people felt strongly enough for it to affect their votes.

This analysis does not exclude the possibility that some issues may be important, even decisive. In the early 1960s British public opinion favoured increased public spending on the social services and, by a good margin, regarded Labour as the best party for this. Some of these voters switched to Labour. In 1979 voters who favoured cuts in direct taxation and regarded the issue as important overwhelmingly saw the Conservatives as the best party to advance this goal. As a result many of them switched to the party. Another example of a decisive issue was immigration in the 1970 election. In the 1960s many voters had strong views on the issue and public opinion was unevenly divided on it (a large majority wanted a halt to immigration). But, because most voters were unable to differentiate the positions of the parties, the issue was not significant. In the 1970 general election the outspoken opposition to immigration of a dissident Conservative, Enoch Powell, identified the Conservatives (even though the party dissociated itself from him) with an anti-immigration line and swung many votes to the party (Butler and Stokes, 1975; Schoen, 1977).

The portrait of the low issue awareness of most voters, has, of course, changed in several respects in recent years. The Nie, Verba and Petrocik analysis of the American SSRC election data has measured a marked increase in the proportion of American voters who think of candidates and parties in ideological terms. The main shift in attitudes occurred in 1964 when Barry Goldwater stood as the Republican Presidential candidate and offered, in his own words, 'a choice, not an echo'. In that election more voters employed ideological terms in talking about the election, the comments were mainly directed at Goldwater, they were mostly negative and he suffered as a consequence (Nie *et al.,* 1976, p. 143). But in succeeding elections the policy differences between the parties' supporters have sharpened, with partisanship being more correlated with issue preferences, and with the Democrats becoming more liberal and Republicans more conservative (Pomper, 1972). Between 1956 and 1972 the proportion of voters who could be classified as left or right grew from 25 to 44 per cent; those in the centre fell from 41 to 27 per cent (Nie *et al.,* 1976, p. 148). Over the same time there has been a growth in the consistency and integration of the issue preferences of voters.

How might we explain the change? It is not, as might be expected, a function of more voters having more education, because gains in conceptualisation are no larger for the well-educated than for those who left school early. What seems to be more important in promoting a voter's issue consistency is his interest in politics. Political interest usually encourages a person to learn more about politics and then develop integrated views. And to understand why the level of interest in politics has increased in America from the 1950s to the 1970s, we have to take account of the emergence of issues like Vietnam, race and Watergate, which were of intense concern to many voters. Not surprisingly, surveys showed that the fears and hopes of a growing number of Americans related more to issues which appeared to fall within the area of government activity (ibid., p. 108).

A second explanation of the limited impact of issues must take account of the elites and parties who shape the political agenda. In both Britain and the United States rival politicians often seek to blur the differences on issues. In the most divisive postwar election in Britain, in February 1974, the two main party leaders presented themselves as models of 'fairness' and 'strength' on the one side, and supporters of 'unity' and 'the family' on the other. In America, Ben Page's (1978) study of the politically ambiguous stands adopted by presidential candidates shows how difficult it can be for voters to discern the issue positions of candidates who are determined to occupy the political centre. In 1968 Vietnam was regarded as an important issue by some two-thirds of American voters, but only a small fraction thought the election result would make a difference to the issue! The statements of Humphrey and Nixon were too ambiguous and the positions too qualified for voters to see a difference between them. American public opinion was 'dovish', in so far as most people wanted peace and the return of American troops. It was also 'hawkish' in so far as most people wanted victory or an honourable conclusion to the war. Where parties differ and are seen to differ on issues, we may speak of *position* issues. Many issues, however, are *valence* issues, that is, they concern policy goals or methods on which the parties and most voters are largely agreed – for instance, reducing inflation, or unemployment. In these cases, the voter is likely to be swayed by his perception of which party or candidate is more competent. To a larger extent the voters' responses echo the choices they are offered; a perception of little difference between the parties may reflect the fact that there is little difference. Where clear choices are offered, then voters are more issue-oriented in voting.

Where issues are single-peaked, that is, the preferences of the majority of voters bunch at or near one point in a continuum, then candidates obviously have an incentive to assume a position near the point. If, however, preferences bunch at different points or are evenly spread along the continuum, then the candidates have an incentive to be ambiguous as in 1968 on Vietnam. By contrast, the views of George Wallace – on segregation, law and order and Vietnam – were clear to most voters and his support was highly issue-based (Converse *et al.*, 1969).

Where new issues run athwart traditional party lines, the potential volatility of the electorate is enhanced. The partisans have traditionally been less informed about and interested in politics than the stable partisan; the latter has been more likely to approximate the ideal (Campbell, *et al.*, 1960, p. 143). But the new 'negative' type of voting – usually issue-based – requires information on the parties' stands. As with the converts to Wallace in 1968, so converts to the British Liberals in the 1960s and supporters of Powell scored highly on political information.

There remains, however, a substantial problem in recognising an issue vote or issue voter. It is difficult to disentangle the issue motive from other motives behind the vote. A voter's issue preferences may reflect his evaluation of a candidate and/or his party preferences (they may also coincide, or be mutually influential). Alternatively he may attribute, mistakenly, his own issue preferences to the candidate or party. These processes of rationalisation and projection may easily be taken for issue voting. The problem lies in our inability to study the precise linkages between issue, party and candidate preferences and the vote decision from a cross-section survey. In the best discussion of these problems, Brody and Page comment (1972, p. 452):

> In fact, if causality runs from opinion to behaviour for some citizens (the 'policy voters') and from behaviour to opinion for other citizens (the 'rationalizers') tables such as this will still look the same. If, however, voters are simply rationalizing a defection which is otherwise caused, and if we cannot distinguish them from those who switch their vote on the basis of policy considerations, we are in danger of overestimating the extent of policy voting by the number of such voters.

They continue (p. 458):

> The discovery of these independent causal factors is no easy matter. There is no statistical procedure which will uncover them. They must come from our theories of behaviour and our knowledge about the act of voting. However difficult it is to specify such causal factors that is exactly where the problem is.

The 1972 presidential election provides a good example of the difficulties in distinguishing the candidate and issue bases of a person's vote. Democrats regarded Nixon as closer than McGovern to their positions on eleven of fourteen issues, and he captured 42 per cent of the votes of the Democratic identifiers. Senator McGovern, by contrast, failed to carry many of the Democrats who agreed with his position on issues, largely because they doubted his competence on the issues. Questions of issue agreement were caught up with questions of the candidate's perceived political competence. The question of issue confidence (who will deal better with the problem of inflation, for example?) became at least as important as issue proximity (Miller *et al.*, 1976; cf. Popkin *et al.*, 1976).

It may well be that the textbook requirements for issue voting, inherited from the Michigan approach, are too stringent. There is ample evidence that awareness and issue constraint among voters increase where an issue is salient. When interviewers give voters the opportunity to choose issues which concern them, then surveys find higher levels of issue voting. One critic, RePass (1971), has shown that combining a voter's choice of the most salient issue with his perception of the best party to handle it greatly improves one's ability to predict the vote. On these personally salient issues, voters do see differences between parties and vote accordingly. The problem with this approach for explaining electoral behaviour in general is that it covers a tiny proportion of such voters. Moreover, party programmes are presented to voters as 'blocks' and voters do not simply pick and choose among issues. Again, it can be argued that to demonstrate a disagreement between a voter's partisanship and issue preference is not the most decisive criterion. In Britain it is among the strong party identifiers that partisanship determines perception of a party's position and among these that attitudes, perceptions and preferences are brought into line. Among the weaker partisans, perception of the party's position is more likely to precede preference for the party. We need also to study whether the voter is aware of the disagreement and thinks it important. For example, many people, regardless of partisanship, see the Conservative and Labour parties as being more competent on different issues, but the preference for one's own party is more marked on issues which the voter regards as important (Alt *et al.*, 1976, p. 278). Strong party identification does influence issue preferences but among weak party identifiers there is a greater tendency to vote in accord with their own issue preferences and perceptions of the parties' stand, rather than with partisanship. And because the proportion of strong party identifiers is declining in Britain and America, the potential is present for issues to have a greater impact in the future.

## Economic Circumstances

One of the most powerful short-term influences on the vote is the state of the economy and how it is perceived by the voter. The economy has both an objective and a subjective dimension in relation to electoral behaviour. In the postwar era most Western governments have accepted the goal of full employment as a priority of public policy and have regulated the level of aggregate demand accordingly. But an expansionist or full employment policy is also potentially inflationary. Because of an implicit trade-off between levels of unemployment and inflation, governments have had to choose a balance point in the continuum between the two goals which would preserve or boost their popularity at election time. According to a simple political economic model of voting behaviour, voters have come to see the government as playing an important role in affecting how well off they are and judge the government accordingly, punishing it for bad times and rewarding it for good. The voters' attentions and evaluations are not concentrated equally on the main political parties but on the government.

The study of the impact of the economy on voting behaviour is part of a larger sub-field on political economy. Clearly, the political and economic sectors interact more frequently today. The state is a major economic actor, as employer and financier of a large public sector, as investor, and as general regulator of economic activity. According to a systems view of politics and the environment, the parties compete for public support and, in response to the promises and policies of the parties, support – negative or positive – is generated through a feedback loop. If the feedback is negative, then the parties or government try to change their promises or performance. Political support is determined by many other factors, of course, but voters' perceptions of the economic outputs are important in colouring the electorate's satisfaction with a government.

There is good evidence that in America and Britain in the 1950s and 1960s a government's level of support in the opinion polls was affected by changes in economic conditions, particularly the rates of inflation, unemployment and real disposable income, with voters rewarding the government for improvement and punishing it for a worsening in conditions. The finding applied both at the aggregate level (Goodhart and Bhansali, 1970; Kramer, 1971; Tufte, 1978) and the individual level (Alt, 1978; Kernell, 1977). In Britain until 1968 the important indicator was unemployment and, thereafter, inflation. In the United States there has historically been a close relationship between electoral success and improvements in voters' real disposable incomes, closer than that with unemployment and inflation (Kramer, 1971). In the 1960s there was also an impressive correlation between British voters' satisfaction with the government's handling of the economy and the voters' personal sense of economic improvement, and between both and changes in support for the government (Butler and Stokes, 1975, ch. 18). Voters who felt that their personal economic circumstances had declined in 1963–4 were likely to defect to the opposition Labour Party in the 1964 election. The same pattern was repeated among those who felt their economic position had declined in 1969–70; they shifted from Labour to the Conservatives in 1970. Economic changes include not only 'real' improvements or declines in individuals' living standards, but their perceptions of these changes as well.

Yet the model of economic improvement ⟶ reward, economic decline ⟶ punishment has its limitations for understanding voting behaviour. Carried to extremes, it would predict that continued economic decline (as reflected in the deteriorating economic indices of the 1970s) or dissatisfaction would lead to the eventual demise of established parties. Yet in the 1970s opposition parties in most Western states have failed to profit electorally from 'bad' economic times (Rose and Mackie, 1980). At some point, other factors disturb a pure one-to-one relationship between changes in economic conditions and changes in levels of party support. Voters' expectations of economic benefits may be scaled down, a foreign crisis or another issue may be dominant, or the major alternative party may, after consideration, be found less appealing. There is also evidence that a government's popularity is related to the stage of electoral cycle, with a government's popularity dipping in mid-term, regardless of how the economy performs or is seen to perform (Miller and Mackie, 1973), and recovering somewhat as the election approaches. Surveys show that there are high levels of life satisfaction, regardless of an economic recession, particularly in those areas which are not the responsibility of government.

The criteria of sound economic performance may change over time. In the late 1960s many British voters switched from regarding the rate of unemployment as the key indicator of economic performance to the balance of payments. For most of the 1970s the key indicator became the rate of inflation. Because the general economic goals are widely agreed, they are valence not position issues. All parties favour prosperity, stable prices, a surplus on balance of payments and full employment. Voters, therefore, decide more on the expected competence and *performance* of the parties. But over time the trend is for the government to lose support as it offends or disappoints a growing coalition of minorities. And it appears that more voters are likely to punish governments for disappointments incurred than reward them for good deeds performed (Bloom and Price, 1975).

James Alt's study of voting behaviour in Britain contains ample evidence on the complex, adaptive and context-bound ways in which voters relate the economy to politics. He shows that between 1964 and 1974 the voters' satisfaction with their real incomes bore little relation to actual rises in incomes; that voters' expectations regarding the country's future economic performance were more influenced by the content of the mass media than their recent experience; and that in three general elections, 1964, 1970 and February 1974, the government party, although regarded as best on maintaining prosperity, lost the election, and the opposition party, which was regarded as best on prices, won.

Politics and economics interact in another way. Government ministers time their economic measure to have maximum electoral impact and, where they are able, choose the date of the election to coincide with 'good times'. Voters and politicians have the same political-economic outlook. The effects of the electoral-economic cycle are seen in the general tendency for levels of unemployment and inflation to fall in election years and for real wages to increase sharply in years of, or immediately following, general elections (Miller and Mackie, 1973; Tufte, 1978).[5] In Britain, there have been sharp increases in real disposable incomes in most election years, followed usually by a sharp slowdown or even decline in mid-Parliament. Only in February 1974, an unexpected election, was there a fall in real disposable incomes (Alt, 1978, p. 136). Richard Crossman, a minister in the 1964–70 Labour governments, confessed in 1971: 'The main fact is that we won the 1966 election by choosing the moment of wage inflation before the prices had really been felt to rise and obviously we were seeking to do it again in 1970.' The Watergate tapes show that President Nixon and his advisers also calculated explicitly along these lines.

The general picture is clear enough. There is a political economic cycle – 'as goes politics, so goes the economy'; Tufte shows that the economic growth rates are twice as high in the year when the incumbent seeks re-election as in other election years (1978, p. 24). But we need to move cautiously in our selection of the economic indicators. Nordhaus (1975) shows that while changes in real disposable incomes operate in line with the theory of the economic cycle in Japan, Britain, Australia and Canada, they do not in other countries. In Britain, Frey and Schneider (1978) find that the government's popularity in Gallup polls has been most sensitive to rises in unemployment: each increase of 1 per cent in this figure led to an average fall in popularity of 6 per cent. Each increase in inflation of 1 per cent, or reduction of 1 per cent in living standards, produced a fall in popularity of less than 1 per cent on average. Other studies have shown that left or right parties in government are more sensitive to economic indicators, according to the perceived interests of the bulk of their social class support (Hibbs, 1977; Cameron, 1978; Cowart, 1978). Thus, left parties tend to increase the size of the public sector, equalise post-tax incomes and respond more to unemployment than to inflation.

Free elections and the vote-seeking roles of politicians and benefit-seeking voters have led some commentators to fear for the stability of liberal democracy. Indeed, Goodhart and Bhansali (1970) suggest that the logical outcome of parties competing to maximise public support would be intolerable inflation and then political collapse (see also

Brittan, 1975). The cycles of the economy are 'distorted', it is claimed, as they are manipulated to produce short-term pre-election 'booms', to be followed by bouts of inflation and deflation. To balance this pessimism, one should note the survey evidence which suggests that most voters are generally sceptical of politicians' claims about 'good times' and have realistic expectations about the economy. In recent years expectations have been scaled down in line with the slowdown of economic growth. People are more willing to look elsewhere than to the government when allocating blame for inflation and unemployment – to the trade unions, world conditions, the Common Market, and so on. This change in perceptions of the relations between the economy and government has lessened the instrumental value of voting. As Alt comments (1978, p. 270):

> In large measure, then, the story of the mid 1970s is the story of a politics of declining expectations. People attached a great deal of importance to economic problems. People saw clearly the developments that were taking place, and people expected developments in advance and thus were able to discount the impact of the worst of them.

## Physical Replacement

In exploring the different pathways of change between two successive elections, we should not overlook the impact of the physical replacement of the electorate. Demographic changes alter the strength of the parties over time. Longitudinal analyses (Butler and Stokes, 1969; Nie *et al.*, 1976) acknowledge that changes in party alignments stem more from changes in composition of the electorate than from changes in the attitudes of those already in it. In a typical five-year Parliament in Britain the changes in the composition of the electorate due to immigration, emigration, deaths and coming of age produce a turnover of about 10 per cent in the electorate. The rise of Labour support in 1945 was explained less by conversions from other parties than by the combined effects of the greater death toll among elderly Conservatives and Labour's strength among a new generation of voters. The generation which came of age in 1945 contains the largest proportion of those who see sharp differences between the parties and see politics as representing conflicting class interests (Butler and Stokes, 1975, p. 201). Labour also gained advantages by the dying-out of those who had first entered the electorate before 1918 and been socialised into partisanship before the party's rise, and the higher birth-rate of families in the manual working class compared with those in the middle class.

The massive gains by the American Democrats in the 1930s, similarly, were largely due to the entry to the electorate of immigrants and their offspring once they had both come of age politically and been naturalised. More often than not they inherited an allegiance to the Democrats. The new voters are less set in their political allegiance and more receptive to the prevailing climate of political opinion when they first vote. Hence the effects of the Labour victory in 1945 and the Democrats' victories in the 1930s were still reflected in later years in voting behaviour.

There is ample evidence that the particular set of circumstances and be associated with each election produces large-scale departures from basic voting loyalties, either in the form of differential abstention rates among each party's supporters or as a net gain for one party from conversions between the parties. In most American presidential elections since 1948 these short-term factors have usually been a net advantage to the Republicans. In 1968 voters' positions on Vietnam, civil rights and law and order were important. In 1972 ideology and issues were more decisive than the personality of the candidates or partisan identification in explaining President Nixon's landslide. When Carter won in 1976, party identification was restored as a factor of importance. In Britain we have noted how the balance of long-term change, in the form of deaths and comings of age, has been working in favour of the Labour Party. But this demographic advantage has recently been offset by the party's choice of issue positions and its record in office. In 1970 in Britain the Conservatives managed to win, notwithstanding their having a lower level of base-line support than Labour. In 1979 the party had a fractional lead on party identification but managed a landslide victory *vis-à-vis* Labour.

## To What Effect?

What are the consequences of elections? Do elections matter? It is a fair comment that the studies of what elections decide are remarkably few when set against the shelves of studies of what decides voting. In large measure this disparity is because the question 'What do elections decide?' is particularly difficult to come to grips with.

At a general level, one can speculate that competitive elections in Western states have a number of functions for individuals and the political system. For the individual, elections provide an opportunity for political participation; for designating the government (or the party or parties which form the government); and for an exchange of influence between voters and candidates. For the political system, elections help to choose the government, provide an opportunity for the peaceful replacement of teams of leaders and the promotion and demonstration of legitimacy, and may act as a safety-valve. The dismissal from office in Britain of the Conservatives in February 1974, and Labour in 1979, of the long-established Social Democrats in Norway in 1973 and Sweden in 1976 or Mrs Gandhi in India in 1977, were seen as major events in those states. Similarly, the shifts in strength of parties, particularly those in government, are important. Elections organise conflict and are institutionalised means for making decisions. Most conceptions of democracy emphasise that government should be derived from public opinion and be accountable to it. Hence the role of elections as a means by which opinion may express itself, government may represent it, and at a later date the government may test its representativeness. Authoritarian and one-party states appreciate the benefits of elections, even when there is no effective choice (Hermet *et al.*, 1978).

But once we move to a more specific question – do elections decide policy? – then we encounter more severe problems. It may immediately be objected that the question is unfairly phrased because it lends itself to a simple and misleading yes-or-no reply. Elections *alone* do not decide policies and their influence may be greater on some issues and in some circumstances than others. General elections are not referenda; they are devices for choosing candidates or parties for the legislature or, in presidential systems, the head of the executive. Finally, elections do not immediately affect the composition and policy preferences of other elites – business, finance, trade unions, bureaucracy, and so on. Therefore, we may expect that the policy impact of an election may be *indirect*: it affects the choice of political incumbents and the climate of opinion, and it gives a general policy direction. But the conventional defence for elections as a democratic instrument is that the vote should make a difference, that the choice of parties and men is at the same time a choice of policies.[6] And the rhetoric and promises contained in politicians' election speeches and party programmes explicitly state that the results of general elections do make a difference.

At the risk of overlapping with the criteria of issue voting presented earlier, one might suggest the following conditions for a programmatic election:

(1) Parties present a choice of programme, or they make different promises.[7]
(2) Voters cast a vote on the basis of these programmes or promises.
(3) The winning party or set of parties is able to form a government and carry its programme through the legislature.

A more stringent condition might be:

(4) The winning party or set of parties is able to carry out its programme, i.e. it enforces its will over other groups.

In both Britain and the United States the two main parties at general elections or presidential elections do present a choice on most issues, though until 1983 the extent of difference between parties has actually narrowed in Britain (Robertson, 1976) and candidates tend to de-emphasise divisive policy positions and emphasise the consensual goals (Page, 1978). It is a matter of dispute as to whether the differences between the party are trivial or important. A large body of scholarly opinion has advocated a sharper and more coherent differentiation of the American parties, while in Britain more recently critics have complained that the differences have produced an 'adversary politics' (Brittan, 1975; Finer, 1975).[8]

We have seen that it is not possible to give a general answer to whether most voters decide on policies or not. The impact of specific issues and general programmes on the electorate varies with the circumstances of each election. Issues are only one component of the electoral decision, to be set alongside the party and candidate factors (Pomper and Lederman, 1980). Most voters decide on the basis of their perceptions of a government's record, its general image of competence, fairness, strength, and so forth, and their appraisal of how the opposition will perform. Specific issues play a part in the formation of this image. Yet many Labour supporters have disagreed with key planks in the party's manifestos in the last four general elections (1970–9) while still voting for the party, and the same has been true of many American Democrats. To some degree, also, the ambiguity of parties and candidates weakens the potential for issue voting.

On the third count, the record shows that governments in Britain and the United States are faithful in carrying through those promises which may be translated into actual legislation (Pomper, 1968; Rose, 1980). There are reversals or U-turns – Mr Heath's enactment of a prices and incomes policy and government intervention in industry, President Nixon's price and wage controls, or President Carter's federal budget deficit – yet the overall correlation between promise and performance remains impressive. But, crucially, a party's manifesto or platform covers only a small part of what a party in government does. Often a government has to deal with the unanticipated – a damaging strike, a foreign crisis, an abrupt change in the balance of payments or the value of the currency – or cope with circumstances not envisaged when the programme was originally drawn up. Moreover, there are many factors making for continuity between governments over many areas of policy (see below). According to one authoritative study of the British record, 'Nine-tenths of government legislation is stimulated by the ongoing policy process in Whitehall or by the force of events' (Rose, 1980, p. 72).

It is when we turn to the fourth condition, however – namely, the outcomes of policies – that doubts are most forcefully expressed about the directive role of elections. In the United States research into patterns of local state spending shows that what may be termed environmental factors (e.g. levels of urbanisation, per capita income, population density, etc.) are a better predictor of expenditure than political variables, such as extent of party competitiveness or type of party control. It may be objected that American political parties are less policy-oriented and there are greater limits on the influence of party government than in other countries. But in Britain, where the Conservative and Labour parties have concentrated many of their promises on macro-economic conditions – unemployment, inflation, economic growth and real disposable incomes – a rather similar picture emerges. A painstaking review of trends in these indicators since 1957 shows that party control of government is almost irrelevant: rates of change are both secular and negative over time. For each period of government between 1957 and 1979 the rates of unemployment, inflation, economic growth and rise in real disposable incomes have all moved in the same direction (Rose, 1980).

Reaction to these findings depends in some measure on one's expectations of elections and party government. In liberal democratic societies, with groups and individuals granted a fair amount of freedom and with both formal and informal restraints on government, there are limits on what governments can do. Some decisions about policy outputs are made largely through the political system, some largely through the market place, and some through a more balanced mix of the two decision systems. Voting is only a form of participation and elections only one means of representation. As Rokkan (1966, pp. 106–7) has observed of the corporatism in Norway, 'votes decide, resources count'. The choice of governors is not the same as deciding policies. Governments may attend merely to 'general arrangements' or take greater control over the society and the economy (Oakeshott, 1951). Indeed, some critics of vote-seeking politicians (Schumpeter, 1942; Brittan, 1975) wish to depoliticise policy areas, allowing a greater role to such non-elected 'experts' as bankers, bureaucrats, or industrialists, or to have more bargaining between the main interests. A limitation on the range of political decision-making is, of course, a devaluation of the electoral process itself, and a shift to more apparently depoliticised forms of decision-making poses problems of the accountability of the decision-makers to the public. The survey evidence on the declining levels of political trust and efficacy in Britain and America, or reduced confidence in the ability of government to solve problems, may reflect this sense of disappointment. A large majority in Britain and the United States still regard elections as a useful device for making politicians responsive to voters. But in both countries the proportions believing in the efficacy of parties and elections in making the government pay attention to what people think has declined (Asher, 1976, p. 10).

## Party Activists

The Downsian assumption is that parties are vote-maximisers, just as voters are utility-maximisers. Therefore, where two parties are evenly matched, one expects that the leaders will adopt 'moderate' policy positions if most floating voters are in the 'centre'. Such a two-party system makes, therefore, for 'moderate' politics. The fact that the Goldwater and McGovern candidacies defied the analysis in 1964 and 1972 respectively may weaken the theory's descriptive accuracy but heighten its prescriptive strength. Parties and candidates are impelled by other forces to take positions which will gain votes.

Explanations of why parties assume particular positions and an understanding of the electoral connections between candidates and voters have to take account of the role of party activists. In the age of the mass media and the development of new campaign techniques, the activists may have lost part of their role in carrying the party's message to the electorate. But they may still have an important place in influencing the party's policy position and its general image among voters. A major theme of both the academic literature and political folklore is that activists are 'extreme', or more strongly committed on issues, than voters. By contrast, the politicians, more interested in attracting voters who are not ideological and have various policy preferences, are more 'representative' of the electorate. The activists, it is suggested, are often activated by issue concerns to become active in the first place – particularly where politics does not offer material gains, mix in a more partisan environment, and are impatient with administrative and political complexities raised by the politicians.

McClosky *et al.*'s (1960) survey of delegates to the Republican and Democratic conventions in 1956 found that this type of activist was indeed more 'extreme' than voters, in the sense that the Republicans were markedly more 'conservative' and the Democrats slightly more 'liberal' than their parties' respective electoral followings. Twenty years later the 'gap' between activists and voters remains, except that the 'gap' has grown larger between Democratic voters and activists (Nie *et al.*, 1976, pp. 200–9). Democratic activists have moved more to the liberal end while the party's supporters are more divided between liberals and conservatives. In 1964, backers of the right-wing Barry Goldwater pointed to his strong support among right-wing letter-writers to newspapers. These, it was claimed, were symptomatic of 'a silent majority' which Goldwater's candidacy would mobilise. In fact, both the Republican party activists and the letter-writers were unrepresentative of the electorate (Converse *et al.*, 1965). We have no directly equivalent evidence for the British political parties. But a number of the policy positions favoured by Labour MPs and of the resolutions favoured by Labour conferences have not reflected the views of most Labour voters (Crewe *et al.*, 1977; Rose, 1974b; Crewe, 1982).

Issue disagreements between activists and voters are likely to have important consequences if the former are accorded a significant role in the party's decision-making structure. This is so with the British Labour Party which historically has been attached to the ideal of intra-party democracy, or the accountability of leaders to members, and has recently given even more influence over the formation of policy and selection of leaders to the activists. And in the United States reforms in the two major parties have given a greater say to the activists, particularly in the election of delegates to the party conventions. Most of the delegates are now elected through the primaries; but with primary turnouts of less than 30 per cent of the registered electors, these voters are unrepresentative of the parties' supporters, in socio-economic terms but also in opinions (Ranney, 1972). The reforms have, on balance, appealed more to 'purist' rather than 'professional' types of activist. The former are activists who are more committed to issues and candidates than concerned with the party's electoral appeal. By contrast, the 'professional' is prepared to accommodate and adjust to different interests, and even dilute ideology in the search for votes (Polsby and Wildavsky, 1976).

Hence greater participation by activists may produce less representative outcomes. The new participatory politics is likely to reward the activist who, by definition, has the necessary time, energy, ability and concern about issues. Party leaders may be forced by internal party pressures to adopt issue positions which go against their better electoral judgements, and voters may be provided with policy choices they do not welcome.

## Conclusion

Elections are only one source of feedback to the politician. There are also pressure groups, the mass media, opinion polls and the private behaviour of citizens (e.g. buying foreign goods, turning aside from public transport, refusing to pay taxes, and so on), all of which compete with a politician's own reading of public opinion. The different sources of public opinion on particular issues may or may not reinforce the results of a general election. In fact, it has often been noted that general elections are not useful instruments for conveying voter preferences to politicians or allowing voters to rate their preferences. The mandates of most election outcomes are susceptible to a variety of interpretations. It is not too difficult to set up two competing straw men – the representative as an *instructed delegate*, reflecting the views of the majority of voters in a constituency or the nation, and the representative as an *independent* where there is little direct relationship between most voters' preferences and the opinions and actions of the representative. We can find many exceptions to these 'pure' models and therefore dismiss them. There is a substantial literature which deals with conceptual and normative aspects of representation, the meanings of the term and the relationships between representatives and constituents which ought to prevail. But it is only recently that political scientists have begun to study the relationships between, on the one hand, elections and public opinion and, on the other, the role perceptions and behaviour of legislators and legislative outputs.

Theories of responsiveness and responsibility to the voters turn in some measure on the representative's desire for re-election. Where there is less competitiveness or the incumbent is indifferent to re-election, then he does tend to be less sensitive to the voters' views (Prewitt, 1970). Competition and the fear of losing office or the incentive of gaining office influence politicians. We have noted the evidence of changes in economic conditions in tandem with dates of elections. And incumbents may take policy positions and generally conduct themselves with an eye to the next election (cf. Mayhew, 1974). Moreover, even if elections are less important in binding future policy commitments, they still have a role in allowing the electorate to deliver a retrospective verdict on the performance of incumbents. And it is that sanctions element which is important.

The precise role of elections in this relationship varies according to such variables as time, type of party and electoral system, political culture, nature of the issues, and so on. The political culture and weak party discipline made localism and local mandates important in French politics during the Third and Fourth Republics. A multi-party system allows voters to cast more issue- and group-specific votes than may be possible in the more aggregative two-party systems. Yet if the government is a coalition between parties, then the voters' preferences may be heavily diluted in the coalition government's programme which emerges from the bargaining. The model of the responsible party system sees voters choosing on the basis of party programmes and the representatives of the governing party carrying out the programme.

Examples of different methods of establishing an 'electoral connection' are available in British and American politics. In the United States the 'incentive' system encourages the congressman to make his own reputation: variations in swings in constituencies show the importance of local issues and personality factors, and the relative weakness of national party ties. The congressman ambitious for re-election has to build his own power base and, given the advantages of incumbency, he has many resources and opportunities to do this (ibid.). In Britain, by contrast, voters respond more to national party loyalties: withdrawal of the party label is tantamount to electoral oblivion for most candidates. As a result, candidates and MPs have an incentive to toe the party line. The point is that there are different models of representation in different conditions.

One portrait in the literature is of the voter who lacks opinions on many issues, who has little awareness of the parties' stands on issues and whose vote is often shaped more by social background, tradition, or habit, and enduring party loyalty. A study by Miller and Stokes (1963) tried to examine which model – that of the instructed delegate, the Burkeian independent, or the party representative – best described a congressman's legislative behaviour. They found that the congressman's vote was a function (*a*) of his preferences on issues and (*b*) of his perceptions of constituency (or the majority of his constituents') opinion. There was little association between a congressman's opinions on the issues of social and foreign policy and the majority opinion of his constituents. Many constituents were poorly informed about the stands taken by their representatives; in typical constituencies about half of the voters knew very little or nothing about their congressmen. On some issues, therefore, congressmen are able to go their own way with little fear of electoral disadvantage. But on a highly salient issue, like civil rights at the time, on which many voters had strong views and congressmen were aware of their constituents' mood, they did represent them. In Britain the policy stands of MPs are perceived in very faint terms. Low awareness of the MP's position on issues weakens the possibility of voting on this basis. But the MP's party tie is well known and, for many voters, the candidate is absorbed within the outlook on his party. In asking if the legislature is representative, one always has to add: representative in relation to which issue? The relationships vary because public opinion varies in the extent both to which it is formed as an issue and to which it impresses itself on representatives.

How might we assess the role of elections in influencing governments? In the first place, elections are likely to matter more where an issue looms so large in the campaign that the result is widely thought to give a mandate to the government to move in a particular direction. The presidential elections of 1936 (support for the New Deal) and 1964 (support for the 'Great Society' programme) in America were important in this regard. In Britain 1906 (free trade) or 1945 were examples. Where the electorate's views are firmly held, then that pressure gets through, notwithstanding the shortcomings of elections as instruments of mass-elite communication. The losing party may also alter its policies in the wake of damaging or successive election defeats; in the 1950s and 1960s the British Labour Party and German Social Democrats both toned down their radical socialist policies of public ownership. The rise of Scottish nationalism in Britain in 1974 was important in bringing devolution on to the political agenda. By 1940 most American Republicans came to terms with many achievements of the New Deal and Conservatives in Britain accepted the mixed economy and welfare state which the 1945 Labour government had consolidated. Secondly, elections are more likely to have an impact where the winning party's intentions can be fulfilled through legislation, for example, allocating funds, raising the school-leaving age, or creating entitlements. But many of the targeted outcomes or conditions (e.g. prosperity, health, or peace) are more dependent on the actions of other domestic and international factors. Thirdly, the conditions of specific groups may be improved in the wake of enfranchisement; the expansion of black voting in the American South coincided with improvements in opportunities in education and other areas (Pomper, 1968). Fourthly, we have also seen that voters do influence the mix of government policies when an election is imminent; desire for re-election is important in heightening a politician's sensitivity to perceptions of voters' views. Theories of political ambitions and legislative behaviour emphasise how politicians play roles and adopt policies which promote their political advancement (Schlessinger, 1966). Those who argue that competitive elections 'make no difference' might wonder why so many governments in the world refuse to hold them. Finally, elections have a symbolic role, providing a symbolic reassurance and promoting political consent because the established procedures have been observed (Edelman, 1964, p. 17).

## Notes: Chapter 5

1 Important changes on all three dimensions occurred between the Fourth and Fifth Republics in France. A number of other influences were at work to produce the change, but changes in the constitutional and electoral 'rules of the game' were of major importance.
2 In Britain in 1970 it was found that in over 90 per cent of cases where both parents voted the same way, the offspring's first vote was similar to his parents' (Butler and Stokes, 1975, p. 51).
3 Between 1963 and 1970 the proportion who felt that the British parties had 'some'

or 'a good deal of' effect in 'making the government pay attention to what people think' was a half; 72 per cent claimed that elections had such an effect (Butler and Stokes, 1975, p. 467).

4 More recently there is evidence of some 'Americanisation' of British voters. In the February 1974 general election only half of the vote-switchers made the appropriate change in partisanship and between 1964 and 1974 the proportion voting in accord with partisanship fell from 86 to 79 per cent (Crewe *et al.*, 1977, pp. 141–4).

5 There is 'a bias towards policies with immediate, highly visible benefits and depressed hidden costs' (Tufte, 1978, p. 139).

6 Recent definitions of political democracy and free elections by Dahl, Lipset and Schumpeter certainly stress the role of choice between competing teams of candidates. They are silent about (or take for granted), however, the role of the parties in providing a choice between competing policies.

7 Such a set of conditions rules out elections in which (1) there are no significant policy differences between the parties, (2) differences may exist but are not perceived by the voters, (3) governments subsequently adopt policies contrary to those promises to the voters. In each case, there is a lack of popular control.

8 Compare the claim of Samuel Brittan (1968) that, because of policy differences within parties and among their supporters, the British parties present 'A bogus dilemma'.

Chapter 6

# Politics and the Socio-Economic Environment

Political behaviour is frequently seen as part of a wider pattern of social behaviour. Many of the topics covered so far have dealt with the relationships between the political behaviour of individuals and groups and various social or psychological factors. At a more general level, the relations between politics and society, culture, economy, or religion have also been of long-standing interest. For example, Aristotle's famous typology of regimes rested in part on their social structures. The instability of a regime, he argued, would be favoured by a 'balanced' society, one in which a large middle class would be able to mediate between the claims of the very rich and very poor. Montesquieu emphasised the influence of physical and climatic factors on the functioning of political institutions. Marx and Engels claimed that political structures were ultimately derived from social and economic forces. According to their theory of historical materialism, the laws, religion, culture and political institutions of a society are part of the superstructure, being shaped by a 'material' base, the economic structure. Man may make his own history, but only under certain conditions. In the twentieth century such different writers as Weber, Schumpeter, Galbraith and Bell have perceived tendencies in the process of industrialisation which act to produce a 'convergence' between societies, regardless of their different political and ideological outlooks.

One could continue in this vein. There is no shortage of informal or formal statements, for example, about the improbability of stable democracy in a country which has a dominant Catholic church, or the association between a free enterprise economy and liberal democracy, or between a collectivist economy and a centrally controlled political system. Relations between the political and other phenomena have for long been a major part of 'grand' social theory.

I have already referred to the concept of the political system (see above, p. 8) and the context or environment within which it operates. The political system is the set of institutions which makes authoritative decisions for society, and is analytically distinct from its environment.

The environment consists of various sub-systems such as the economy, culture, social structure and geographical position. It includes both the international and domestic social environment, for instance, the international economy or an outbreak of war in the former, and factors such as industrialisation, urbanisation, food supply and social structure in the latter. The system both influences and is influenced by the environment; political behaviour is 'set in an environment and open to the influences stemming from that environment, as well as from internal sources' (Easton, 1957, p. 479). Critics have pointed to the problems involved in establishing the exact boundary between the two, and deciding exactly what is in the environment. Yet we are aware of how the differing contexts, across time and space, have given rise to distinctive patterns of political development: the military security historically afforded by Britain's island position, the material abundance in the United States, or the racial and tribal divisions in so many African states.

But the relationship between politics and the environment does not operate in one direction only, from the latter to the former; political decisions and events also have an impact on the society or economy. Indeed, the so-called 'revolution of rising expectations' in the twentieth century is primarily a reflection of the growth of citizens' demands and beliefs that governments can improve social and economic conditions. Stalin's successful drive to industrialisation in the USSR illustrates how political decisions can transform one part of the environment. By shifting millions of peasants from the land to work in factories, the Communist Party was reshaping society. The growing interest in the politics of non-Western states, the process of modernisation and the shift from agricultural to industrial societies have heightened awareness of the part played by environmental factors in shaping politics and of the role of the political system in supporting them.

Studies of the relationships between politics and the environment have concentrated on a few broad areas. They include:

- Which types of political system are found with which types of society, religion, or economy?
- What is the direction of influence between politics and these various sub-systems?
- Are different political systems or structures associated with different policy outputs? (See Chapter 8.)

Of the two major domestic environmental factors, the socio-economic and the cultural, the role of political culture has been considered in Chapter 4. We now turn our attention to the socio-economic part of the environment. Karl Marx's theories about the relationship of politics and the mode of production in a society have obviously had a major impact on our thinking in this area. For purposes of empirical research, the availability of quantitative data on socio-economic indicators has also encouraged research which establishes the relationships between these indicators and other political factors. By contrast, institutional, cultural and group approaches lack such comparable 'hard' data, and the general flabbiness of such concepts as 'political development' or 'political performance' has long plagued the discipline. It will soon become evident that far more ingenuity and work has been applied to fashioning indicators for the former variables of socio-economic development (hereafter termed SED) than for the political variables of political development, democracy, stable democracy, and so on. A possible consequence has been the relegation of the less precisely defined and measurable political factors to the status of dependent variables (see Chapter 10).

## Politics and Socio-Economic Development

This section examines a number of propositions on the relations between SED and politics. They include relationships between:

(1) SED, or social mobilisation, and political participation;
(2) democracy and the level of SED;
(3) democracy and a high level of SED;
(4) SED and political instability;
(5) SED and political instability in post-industrial societies;
(6) SED and politics in hegemonic or one-party regimes.

### (1) SED, or Social Mobilisation and Political Participation

The process of social mobilisation refers to a complex of interrelated factors. These include such features as industrialism, urbanism, education and communication, and they tend to change together. As Karl Deutsch (1961, p. 494) observes:

> Social mobilisation is the process in which major clusters of old social, economic and psychological commitments are eroded or broken and people become available for new patterns of socialisation and behaviour.

A particular consequence of this process is the diffusion of a participatory outlook among people and an increase in rates of social and political participation. Lerner (1958), in *The Passing of Traditional Society*, has suggested a sequence in which this broad social change occurs. Urbanisation and industrialisation precede the growth of literacy and education; the latter encourage exposure to the newly created mass media and, with this, the development of a sense of empathy, or the enlargement of a formerly parochial outlook. This change in orientation is the last crucial link in the chain of factors promoting participation. Inkeles's (1969) study of participation in new states emphasises the role of socio-economic modernisation,[1] particularly factory employment and education, and Almond and Verba (1963) regard education as the key variable which has promoted this outlook.

If we shift our attention to already industrialised societies, then a similar logic of explanation seems to apply. It is well established that higher socio-economic status increases the likelihood of political participation, at both individual and aggregate levels (cf. Crewe, 1981). The crucial links between the macro-social processes and the behaviour of citizens are the attitudes which are developed. In the *Civic Culture* study it was Britain and America, the countries with the highest levels of SED at the time, which had more participatory cultures. The study showed that across the five nations, people with higher socio-economic status attributes, such as further education, white-collar jobs and group memberships, were more likely to be participants. The crucial links in this chain are that SED produces changes in the class structure. In particular, it produces more people with high socio-economic status who have more participatory attitudes, and therefore these societies include more participants. It is this change in the overall distribution of political attitudes in the population that is important. Re-analysis of the *Civic Culture* survey (Nie *et al.*, 1969) shows that organisational involvement and social status, both key components of the SED process, are two independent factors making for a more participatory outlook. Socio-economic status has to be coupled with such attitudes as sense of political efficacy and a sense of duty and civic interest, and it is these intervening variables which explain how a citizen's social status facilitates his political activity. But membership of organisations and activity in them are an independent influence.

## (2) Democracy and the Level of SED

The claim is an example of what May (1973, p. 1) has called the Linearity Thesis, that is, that political democracy is more likely to be found in societies with high levels of economic development. Perhaps the earliest, and certainly the most often cited, empirical study in this field is Lipset's 'Some social requisites of democracy'. The hypothesis he tested was that 'the more well-to-do a nation, the greater the chances that it will sustain democracy' (1959, p. 75). Lipset classified over fifty states into four political categories, on the basis of their political histories between 1918 and 1958. They were English-speaking Stable

Democracies (13), European and English-Speaking Unstable Democracies (17), Latin-American Democracies and Unstable Dictatorships (7) and Latin-American Stable Dictatorships (13). Democracy was defined in terms of open electoral competition between contenders for government. The main criteria for the European democracies were the uninterrupted continuity of political democracy since the First World War and the absence during the previous twenty-five years of a major political movement opposed to the democratic rules of the game. Rather less stringent criteria were applied to the Latin-American countries. SED was conceptualised in terms of four broad components: wealth, industrialism, education and urbanisation, with more specific indicators for each component (e.g. persons per doctor, persons per telephone, literacy, and so on). Mean scores on each of the components and indicators were computed for each group of countries. For each component he found that the average score was much higher for the more democratic countries. Their average per capita income, for example, was twice as high as that of the Unstable Democracies.

Lipset's assumption is that SED leads to democracy or sustains an existing democracy because it is associated with certain features and processes like a moderate working class, the reduction of sharp economic inequalities, a larger number of voluntary organisations, more communications, and so on. It is, therefore, possible to envisage countries of high SED which are not stable democracies, because those crucial intervening conditions do not occur (e.g. Germany in the 1930s, or Ulster). To deal with the exceptions Lipset resorted to other explanatory factors, such as history, or legitimacy, or effectiveness of the democratic regime which qualified the relationship.

The main criticisms of Lipset's pioneering analysis have focused on his methods. He frequently slides between the language of correlation and causation; ideally one needs to study the two broad variables over time to explain causal relationships, or to employ more refined statistical analyses to establish the relative weight of particular factors. There is also a problem with the classification of the regimes. Why, for example, are the European Unstable Democracies and Dictatorships regarded as more democratic respectively than the Latin-American Democracies and Unstable Dictatorships? Computing mean scores for the socio-economic factors in the groups disguises the ranges on some of the variables on which highly developed European dictatorships score higher than the less developed European democracies. The extent of overlap on some of the items between particular countries in different groups is disguised by the differences in group averages.

Philip Cutright (1963) made an advance on Lipset in several respects. He measured National Political Development (conceptualised in terms of specialisation and complexity of political institutions) and SED. His range of seventy-six countries includes African states, which had been excluded by Lipset. He provides for a scaling of the political and SED factors by awarding points, for example, for each year a system has had a government chosen in competitive general elections and a party opposition in the legislature between 1940 and 1961. This approach enables him to plot expected levels of political performance for a country, given its level of economic development. Among the 'deviant' cases, Ireland scores higher on democracy than one would expect from its economic development, while Germany, Spain and East European countries score lower. To explain the deviation from the expected ranking, Cutright suggests that we bring in other factors like leadership, culture, defeat in war, and so forth. What is odd is that some of the countries like Italy, West Germany, France, Japan and the Netherlands, which were under military occupation for some of the period, score higher than states which preserved their independence intact for the entire period.

### (3) Democracy and a High Level of SED

Neither the Lipset nor the Cutright study effectively tackled the question of linearity: do higher levels of SED bring further increments of political development (in Cutright's sense) or stable democracy (in Lipset's)? Alternatively, is there a threshold effect, with SED exercising an influence up to a certain level but not beyond? An attempt to confront this problem was made in Neubauer's (1967) study of twenty-three democratic states. The question he posed was: are the more economically developed societies more democratic? Alternatively, is it the case that above a certain threshold, further SED is not important for democracy? Democracy was conceptualised in terms of electoral competition and equality. Scores for democraticness were based on five indicators:

(1) equality of representation, or the relation of a party's popular votes to its allocation of seats in the legislature;
(2) scope of the suffrage or the percentage of the adult population eligible to vote;
(3) equality of information, or ownership of newspapers in capital cities;
(4) turnover of parties in government;
(5) selection of the executive.[2]

The 'scores' give some interesting results, with the United States being placed sixteenth out of twenty-three, behind Italy and India. Neubauer concludes that it is only where SED is low that the probability of a country being a democracy is effectively excluded and that above a certain level of SED other social, historical and cultural factors are more important in affecting democracy. Once democracy has been established, further gains in SED do little to improve the degree of democracy. Moreover, he suggests that the political importance of SED derives from its creation of supporting features like pluralism, tolerance, and so on. Many other quantitative studies (e.g. Russett, 1964; Dahl, 1971) have demonstrated a positive relationship between SED and political competition or polyarchy. The most persuasive explanation of the relationship is the likelihood that SED leads to a pluralistic social order, and demands for more participation.

### (4) Social Mobilisation and Political Instability

In contrast to the proposition that SED helps to stabilise a democratic regime (proposition 1), or that beyond a certain stage it makes little difference (proposition 3), this proposition suggests that the relation between the two may be curvilinear. SED, instead of bringing in its train conditions and circumstances favourable to democracy, may at a certain stage lead to its breakdown or to further strains on government. The actual timing and rate of industrialisation (perhaps the key component of SED) do seem to be important; many states which score high on Lipset's list of stable democracies, for example, started their industrialisation relatively early and achieved it gradually. Many states which start to industrialise late and proceed at a rapid pace tend, in the process, to exacerbate social divisions and cultural differences, and thereby increase their own 'load' of problems. Rapid economic growth, with its new methods of production, loosens class, caste and family ties, promotes social and geographical mobility, and creates more people who are *déclassés*. (The same argument, about social dislocation, relative deprivation and groups of relative gainers and losers, applies to rapid economic decline.) Huntington (1968) claims that it is social modernisation which causes the problems. Many Third World states are achieving social modernisation but not political modernisation in the sense of greater democracy, stability, structural differentiation, and so on. Instead, their lot seems to be one of *coups*, riots and revolutions, a process in which 'modernity breeds stability, but modernisation breeds instability' (p. 41). The crucial point is whether the society has developed the political institutions (e.g. political parties) and governmental skills to accommodate the extra demands and expectations associated with modernisation.

What is interesting is the claim that states can decay as well as develop politically in response to SED. Huntington wanted to separate the concept of political development from modernisation: the equation of the two made it difficult to conceive of political decay in a modern society. If social mobilisation and modernisation outrun the capabilities of the political institutions, there may be political decay and the established institutions may be found wanting. Rapid social mobilisation and, in the short run, rapid economic growth increase popular awareness of, and resentment at, inequalities, and promote social frustration. There are various pathways along which 'modernisation breeds instability', according to Huntington. In large part, the problem is the shortage of opportunities for social and economic mobility and adaptable political institutions. Inadequate opportunities promote social frustrations; where opportunities are sufficient, then modernisation leads to political participation. But where the participation is not channelled through established institutions then this gives rise to political instability (p. 55).

An alternative perspective on the importance of SED is that its consequences depend primarily on their impact on the political culture or authority relations in society. According to Eckstein, 'the level of economic development . . . matters only because the speed of economic development matters' (1966, p. 279). Eckstein embraces aspects of other explanations of stable democracy only where they may be subordinated to his congruence theory (see Chapter 4 above). He continues: 'the theories hold to the extent that they are special cases of the present theory and fail to hold to the extent that they are not (p. 270). A gradual rate of SED allows time for authority relations and the political institutions to adjust and adapt to changing circumstances. Later industrialism is usually more rapid and therefore generates the strains. Hence, according to Eckstein 'the modification is, in effect, the really crucial theory' (p. 279). A more precise formulation may be that the nature of the transition only matters where it actually produces these consequences.

## (5) SED and Political Instability in Post-Industrial Societies

So far we have examined claims that there is a relationship between stable and unstable democracies and 'high' and 'low' SED. A related question is whether there is a qualitative difference in a society as it moves through the first stages of industrialism to a highly advanced level of industrialism (sometimes termed post-industrialism)? Several countries, including Anglo-American and Western and North European societies, together with some East European countries and Japan, have already attained this status. Its characteristics include almost total literacy, relatively high per capita GNP, a shift from a manufacturing to a service-based economy, and the growth of a professional and technical class. Might it be the case that the social and economic trends in these societies actually make government more difficult?

Huntington (1974) argues that the combination of a more educated and participatory population, a more critical and inquisitive mass media, and an increase in demands in these societies threatens the insulating space which a government requires. While popular aspirations and expectations about the 'performance' of society, economy and government increase, the capabilities of government do not necessarily keep pace. With advanced SED there may be 'increasing socio-economic dislocation, frustrated expections, intensifying conflicts, disorder and violence' (p. 189). The values of post-industrial society, he suggests, challenge many of the political institutions and are at odds with the needs of efficient government.

This perspective is, of course, derived from Huntington's early work, suggesting that political order 'depends upon the ratio of institutionalisation to participation' (1968, p. 79). An increase in popular participation can only be contained if the participatory institutions become more complex, autonomous and coherent; otherwise they will be swamped.

In many respects Huntington's approach relates to the social psychological studies of political revolution and violence. The theory of relative deprivation (Davies, 1970; Gurr, 1970) suggests that as aspirations and expectations outrun gratifications, so dissatisfaction triggers off a cycle of emotions, with frustration leading to anger and then to aggression and political violence. Expectations rise faster than the satisfactions, or the latter slow down or even go into reverse, after rising over a period. The process is like a J-curve in which there is a deterioration following a period in which satisfactions have kept pace with aspirations. When the resulting frustration leads to aggression which is general, intense and directed at the government, then we have the conditions for a revolution. Gurr adds that the aggrieved also have to feel justified in resorting to violence and confident that they can succeed.

The social psychological approach concentrates on changes in a person's perceptions, satisfactions, levels of tolerance and expectations. Sharp rises in unemployment or inflation, or other social changes (cf. Huntington, 1968), because they suggest new possibilities to people, may increase the sense of relative deprivation. The J-curve explanation suggests a way in which one may reconcile the divergent claims of de Tocqueville that revolution follows a period of economic improvement (or any increase in expectations which are not fulfilled) and of Marx that it follows a period of worsening economic conditions. Relative deprivation is a reaction to the decline which follows a long period of improvement, which in turn increases the level of expectation.[3]

The social psychological approach reminds us that we have to connect the environmental changes with their consequences in the perceptions of individual political actors. A problem with the above studies, however, is that they infer individual perceptions of relative deprivation from objective aggregate data. Research based on the former suggests that it is such features as uncertainty, ambiguity and change – both positive and negative – in levels of satisfaction that prompt aggression (Grofman and Muller, 1973; Miller *et al.*, 1977). Dissatisfaction may lead to political protest but relative deprivation is not a satisfactory tool for analysing it.

What seems to emerge from these theories is a modification of Lipset's linear view, and the suggestion of a curvilinear relationship between SED and political stability. Depending on the stage attained, political and socio-economic change may have negative as well as positive consequences for political stability. SED in societies which are not well-developed in terms of political institutionalisation tends to produce political disorder; among the politically developed it is stabilising (e.g. as in Lipset's sample of stable democracies in the 1950s); but among the post-industrial societies, it may be destabilising again.

### (6) SED and Politics in Hegemonic or One-Party Regimes

The more 'benign' propositions have essentially suggested that it is the creation of a more pluralistic society and the development of a participant outlook, both of which emerge in the train of SED, that promotes stable democracy/political development. Obvious exceptions to this relationship are found in the USSR and other industrialised East European countries in the Soviet bloc. In these countries SED is combined with central control by one party. It seems clear that the liberal democratising consequences of SED depend on the emergence of pluralism. The interesting question is whether SED is generating demands for a relaxation of central control and more political competition, and will ultimately undermine these political systems (cf. Dahl, 1971, pp. 78–9).

## Conclusion

The literature on the relationships between the socio-economic conditions and stable democracy has clearly invested substantial effort in collecting aggregate data on the two sets of phenomena, transforming them into variables, and examining the relationships between them. But before assessing the findings, it may be useful to scrutinise the actual concepts and indicators employed in these studies. It is clear that in spite of a common view of SED as a concept and process, the authors employ different indicators for their concepts. May's (1973) review of the literature shows that out of a total of 37 SED indicators used in ten studies, Lipset, for example, uses 15, Cutright 11 and Neubauer only 7. The authors also sample different universes of states over different periods of time.

When we turn to the dependent variables, usually dealing with political characteristics, there is even more variance. They range from concepts of participation and participatory outlook to more complex ones, such as Dahl's polyarchy (a system scoring high on both popular participation and opportunities for political opposition), Lipset's stable democracy, Neubauer's democracy (political competition, equality, participation and information) and Cutright's political development (elections which affect the composition of the government and political competition). Both Cutright and Neubauer scale their political variables, whereas Lipset has a categorisation between stable democracy and other regimes. In the former, societies may be more or less democratic, but for Lipset the society is or is not a stable democracy. Finally, statistical approaches range from employing simple correlations (e.g. Lipset) to multiple correlation analysis (e.g. Cutright).

Yet in spite of the different definitions and choice of different indicators, the literature does cumulate in many respects. The main conclusion is also clear enough: there is a positive relationship between high SED and the chance of a state's being a stable liberal democracy in the West; below a certain level of SED, it is highly improbable that there can be a democracy;[4] above a certain level of SED further development does not make much difference to the chances of a state being a more stable and democratic society. Those studies which contain more elaborate statistical analyses suggest the particular stages by which social mobilisation shapes the political process. Lerner's (1958) correlation of each factor with political participation suggests that the pattern of causation is:

urbanisation ⟶ education ⟶ communication ⟶ political participation.

In general, it has been the quality of the causal analysis in this literature that prompts the greatest doubts. On the face of it, to look at change in one set of variables *vis-à-vis* change in another set seems reasonable enough. In the study of democracy the search has been for the socio-economic correlates of existing democracies rather than a longitudinal study, or an examination of how these regimes came into existence. Conditions which are necessary to bring about liberal democracy, however, may be rather different from those required to maintain it. Historians have filled this gap by suggesting that a particular rate of change and/or a particular sequence in resolving aspects of state and nation-building, and establishing political competition and government institutions, are more conducive to liberal democracy

(Nordlinger, 1968). Rustow, for example, argues that the achievement of national unity should precede the establishment of governmental authority, and that both should precede the movement towards political equality and the conscious creation of democratic institutions. He dismisses the idea of social and economic factors as being 'preconditions': 'These social and economic factors enter the model only indirectly as one of several alternative bases for national unity or for entrenched conflict' (1970, p. 352). What is more important is conflict and disagreement between groups; for liberal democracy, in the shape of a wider suffrage, equal rights of citizenship, rights of political opposition and so on, usually emerges as a by-product of political struggles. Democratic institutions, once adopted, develop their own momentum as people gradually become habituated to them. Barrington Moore's historical study (1966) stresses the importance of achieving a balance between the monarchy and the landed aristocracy, and between the latter and the urban bourgeois, on the route to liberal democracy. On the whole, the detailed case studies provided by students of comparative history are more satisfactory as explanations of how particular liberal democratic regimes came into existence.

The problem is that cross-sectional analysis gives us correlations at one point in time, and may lead us, mistakenly, to ask functional rather than genetic questions (Rustow, 1970, p. 339). It is a *level of development* approach to the relations between SED and politics. If level of SED is decisive, then there should be a convergence in the politics of societies of similar SED levels. In fact there is not a convergence in political regimes. It differs from the *nature of the transition* approach which deals with the timing, pace and sequence of SED, and the *starting point* approach which concentrates on the type of political system which prevailed when the society started to industrialise (cf. Huntington, 1974). The last approach accepts the importance of precursive influences; a traditional pluralist society becomes a liberal democracy, and a traditional centralised autocratic regime evolves into an authoritarian one under the impact of SED. In this analysis, a given level of SED is compatible with different types of regime.

The studies examined above, as we have seen, tend to ignore these more historical factors. Yet it is worth reminding ourselves that an assumption or a claim that environmental change shapes the political system requires at least a demonstration that the former precedes the latter. Establishing a temporal sequence between the two sets of phenomena is essential if one is to demonstrate the direction of causality. Unfortunately, the above studies collect the political and socio-economic data over similar periods and fall at this first hurdle. Some of the most abrupt changes in regimes in the past forty years, for example, in Japan,

Germany and France, have had more to do with military defeat, the overthrow of dictatorships and institutional engineering. Studies of individual cases (e.g. Germany in the 1930s or India today) contradict any assumptions that there is a clear relationship between the two factors.

Having established a correlation between SED and democracy, one has to entertain the possibility that both may be determined by some other factor (e.g. culture, or historical patterns), or that the influence between them is reciprocal. It is here that Rustow's reference to genetic circumstances is so important. Once established, a democracy may create some of the supportive features mentioned by Lipset, even though its emergence originally depended, in part, on SED. In a related field, the study of revolution, Charles Tilly (1973, 1975) comments on the limited explanatory power of sociological and psychological approaches. Such factors do have an indirect influence in altering actual issues and their salience, the political resources and perceived policy options of elites, and techniques of control. But the major direct causes of revolution and the form it takes are usually found in the political process itself. These include such issues as taxation policies, centre versus periphery struggles, and conflicts over control of the central authority. Again, one is reminded that the political structure, broadly defined, is a set of opportunities and constraints, and is something more than just the outcome of social economic and cultural patterns. The political emphasis has the merit of tackling how the environmental factors, and changes to them, penetrate and affect the political arena.

It is a useful exercise to connect environmental factors to political behaviour. But studies to date may have been too ambitious in concentrating on the macro-political phenomena reviewed above. Democracy, stable democracy, political development, party systems, and so on, may (indeed will) also be *partly* explained by other factors and approaches. It may be more worthwhile to connect particular environmental factors to more limited phenomena, to particular events, or changes of government, of policy, or of parties' electoral strength, for example. A number of such studies (Almond *et al.*, 1973; Tilly, 1975) show the importance of such 'mundane' factors as availability of food supplies and crop failure, military defeat or expansion, changes in the terms of trade, or economic depression in generating demands and expectations and altering the responsive capacity of the system. They are particularly important in shaping the resources of political contenders, and the type of issues and elite perceptions of issues. Ultimately, the impact of the socio-economic environment is translated into the decision-making arena in the shape of the issue preferences and resources of political actors. As one proceeds to study a particular episode or the evolution of a country's political system, one finds that the dependent variables (e.g. rules of the game, policy outcomes, party in government, composition of elites) are transformed into independent variables over time (cf. Almond *et al.*, 1973).

In the next two chapters I turn to a study of the role of individual actors in politics and then to a study of what difference they make to the pattern of policy outputs.

## Notes: Chapter 6

1 The scale of participant citizenship included items on: interest in public affairs, information, activity, identification with supra-local public authorities.

2 May (1973) makes some fair criticisms of these indicators. The *information* indicator ignores the fact that many people in the highly industrialised societies gain their information from television and radio, and that plural ownership of newspapers is not the same as a plurality of political views. On the *opposition* indicator one may observe that it is the existence of political opposition as a legitimate institution, rather than its strength, that is crucial. *Turnover* may be irrelevant to democraticness; neither France post–1958 nor Sweden would score well on this test. High turnover may reflect voters' dissatisfaction with the performance of a series of governments.

3 Davies's (1970) study of black urban riots in the 1960s used aggregate changes in income and years of education as indicators of satisfaction and expectation, respectively, among whites and blacks. The average family incomes were divided by the average years of schooling to provide a quotient of relative deprivation for each group. An additional measure was the ratio of the non-white to the white quotient. The two scores were then plotted over time to show changes in the levels of satisfaction.

4 The United States in the early nineteenth century is a difficult case. In view of the provision of free land to many farmers, the widespread suffrage among white males, the high level of literacy and the pluralistic political system, the United States was hardly a 'traditional' society. In the United States a pluralistic social order existed before SED.

Chapter 7

# Political Leaders

Specialisation of labour is a fact of life in politics as in most other activities. Differences in political influence and participation seem to be an inevitable feature of all societies, regardless of their political ideology and levels of economic and social development. This inequality, in turn, has given rise to the phenomenon of political elites. Mosca spoke for many when he claimed that in society there is 'a class that rules and a class that is ruled' (1939, p. 50) and that definitive studies of politics and power should focus on the elites. It is undeniable that there is a stratification of political influence, that some people have more influence than others. More questionable, however, is the thesis that the influentials constitute a cohesive elite.

In this chapter I am concerned with 'the political stratum' (Dahl, 1961a, p. 60) – that small proportion of the population which is heavily involved in political activity. I begin by discussing some of the conceptual and empirical problems involved in studying political leadership. I then examine a number of the different approaches to the identification of leaders, and, finally, discuss the characteristics of leaders. Throughout, political leadership is equated with formal office-holding.

## Political Recruits

For several reasons we might expect full-time or career politicians to be rather atypical of their fellow citizens. It is useful, in constructing a theory of political recruitment, to think of a hierarchy of participatory acts. More 'difficult' acts demand more of the participant in terms of time, psychological involvement, and so on. Being an elected politician demands more of a person than being an activist, which in turn requires more than just being a member of a political party. In Britain about 75 per cent of the electorate vote at general elections, some 40 per cent at local elections; about 20 per cent claim to be very interested in politics and appear to be attentive and well-informed; about 8 per cent are individual party members, and about 2 per cent are party activists. In 1979 there were 2,576 candidates standing for Parliament and 635 were elected as MPs. At each stage we move nearer to those most 'eligible' for political recruitment and those who actually achieve office; at each stage also we deal with a smaller number. A first rule of thumb in narrowing the number of 'eligibles' is that a large proportion of the electorate is not effectively available, simply because it is not very interested in political activity. Most people lack the motivation to become active in politics.

But what are the characteristics of those who are left? To some extent, inequalities in motivation parallel inequalities in the distribution of social and economic resources. Those who are motivated are usually also politically informed, politically ambitious and possess a strong sense of political efficacy; they are also disproportionately drawn from upper socio-economic groups. In particular, they tend to be male, middle-class, middle-aged and well-educated. A number of voters, and selectors of candidates, seem to regard such background factors as education, a professional career, or possession of a prestigious family name as surrogate indicators of political talent. Certain occupations such as law, teaching, business and journalism are more easily combined with a political career than others. Possessors of these social and economic characteristics already markedly reduce the pool of 'eligibles', and if we couple them with the participatory orientations mentioned in the previous paragraph, we are reducing it further still. But social background alone is not enough to spot the potential politicans, for the great majority of well-educated middle-class males do not go into politics. Political interest, ambition, and self-confidence are developed by political socialisation, and are particularly likely to be encouraged by a home background in which politics is discussed. The pool of potential recruits to politics is limited and selective, in large part because of the screening-out of so many people and the self-presenting features of the few (Prewitt, 1970).

When we turn to actual recruitment, there are further barriers. In the Soviet Union one has to be a member of the only permitted party, the CPSU; in the United States one has to be resident in the state one wishes to represent; and in Ulster and most Southern states of the USA, till recently, not to run for the locally dominant party made it well-nigh impossible to get elected. Once one has a nomination for a party, then one has to win the election and that, in turn, largely depends on how 'winnable' the seat is. All these factors – socialisation, socio-economic features, recruitment and then election – have a winnowing effect on the process of the emergence of the politicians.

## The Study of Political Leadership

The study of political office-holders and decision-makers may prove fruitful on a number of grounds. The influences on political outcomes of such macro-phenomena as public opinion, culture, or social and economic trends have to be mediated through the actions of individual and group political actors. A focus on the behaviour and attitudes of leaders may also have more 'pay-off', because these people are more likely to affect the policies of governments and other political institutions. Where leaders are in or near the Cabinet, White House, or Politbureau, they have more opportunity to impress themselves on the policy process. Our understanding of the political relevance of the studies of the inputs to the political process (public opinion, voting, pressure groups, etc.) will be enhanced if we also study the predispositions and responses of elites. Finally, the political leaders play an important role in the elitist model of democracy. This model starts from the assumption that public opinion is as a rule so lacking in focus and direction that the elites themselves often have ample room for manoeuvre and discretion and therefore play a major role in shaping the way the system operates. It is in this sense that the elitist model claims to provide a realistic description of how politics is conducted. A separate claim made by some writers is that the elites are, by and large, more familiar with the content and implications of the ideals of representative democracy, more committed to them, and therefore safeguard the democraticness of the system (see Chapter 9).

One problem is that too few studies of political leadership actually make clear what leadership is. We may be able to recognise leaders easily enough as office-holders but discerning the exercise of leadership is another matter. Do leaders actually 'lead'? The old 'trait' approach by which the 'natural' leader was recognised as one who possessed certain skills (dominance, eloquence, or charisma), or a particular family and educational background – is now discredited, largely because we now know how variable 'power' is, and because we have to allow for situational factors. The elite or *positional* approach usually identifies leadership activity with what the office-holder does. In this sense, studies of presidents and prime ministers count as leadership studies. Holding office, however, is not the same as exercising power; in some political situations (e.g. Mr. Wilson and his plans to reform the trade unions in 1969, or the role of French premiers in the Fourth Republic) decisive action may actually endanger the leader's position. Alternatively, some leadership may be exercised by individuals who do not hold formal political office at all.

According to McFarland (1969), the leader has *influence* ('a capacity to make people behave differently than they would have otherwise') and *power* ('a capacity to make others do something that they would not do otherwise and that the person specifically wants or intends'). J. M. Burns (1975, p. 266) calls for 'a general theory of social and historical causation and for leadership to be embedded in it'. The difficulty, however, with such a recommendation is that power is an elusive concept when it comes to empirical research. A rigorous test of whether leadership was exercised in a situation would call for an analysis of the leader's original goals and the follower's original preferences and freedom of action, and an assessment of what would have happened in other circumstances. In real life we are not able to meet these exacting standards. Theorists of leadership, therefore, find that 'it is usually necessary to relax the methodological requirements of a causal model' (Edinger, 1976, p. 259). Leadership has to be viewed as a *relationship*: for the leader to exercise influence or power he has to have followers. The emphasis here may be on the leader's *power* to persuade others to follow, regardless of their wishes, or on his influence in directing people to action to which they are already inclined. But the ability to mobilise followers is a major test of his leadership.

The study of political leadership is separate from the study of elites or from elite theory which looks at leaders across a wide range of institutions. Pareto, for example, regarded elites as those who possessed most of the desired values in society, be they prestige, wealth, or power. He was careful to distinguish 'the governing elites' (in politics and government) from the non-governing elites in other sectors. For Mosca, the elite was simply a class that rules.

Our primary interest is in *political* leaders and leadership, and in questions of public policy rather than in any elites and influentials. As Parry notes (1969, p. 14), the object of *political elite* studies is

> to examine the structure of power in communities, to see whether it is in the hands of a cohesive, self-conscious minority, to test whether this is an inevitable or a merely *contingent* development, and in doing so to illuminate the question of the nature of 'power'.

The study of political leadership has been characterised as an orphan of political science. If this is so, the cause of the bereavement is hardly neglect or lack of acknowledged importance.[1] Analytic and prescriptive writing about statecraft has been an abiding interest of political theorists. Traditionally, types of government were equated with forms and character of political leadership, particularly with the leaders' mode of selection and style of rule, such as dictatorship, monarchy, or representative and responsible government. Aristotle, for example, evaluated different forms of government according to the qualities, motives and number of the rulers. Whether the rulers governed in the common interest or in their self-interest determined whether they were monarchies or tyrannies, aristocracies or oligarchies, polities or democracies.

In fact, the study of leadership has not been so much neglected as side-tracked by much postwar political science. The moves to a more hard-nosed, quantitative study of politics, the adoption of the language of variables and relationships, and the search for regularities and testable generalisations have left little scope for (*a*) the scientific study of leaders and the contexts in which they operate or, paradoxically, (*b*) the employment of 'subjective' skills such as empathy and intuition. Such approaches as systems analysis, structural functionalism and social mobilisation take a rather determinist stance in explaining political and social change, thereby narrowing the scope for individual and collective choice. They also preclude examination of the particular contexts within which individual leaders operate. Many political scientists are uneasy with some of the techniques employed in leadership studies. From psychology, for instance, the emphasis has been on the dynamics of the individual's personality. Too few political scientists, however, are competent to go beyond amateur psychoanalysis. From economics the emphasis has been on game theory and rational decision-making perspectives. But for all their mathematical rigour, too few exponents of coalition theory have actually applied their methods to concrete political events.

Above all, perhaps, the subject has been bogged down in the mutually exclusive claims advanced on behalf of the 'great man' or, alternatively, social forces, in explaining social causation. This competition between approaches which emphasise choice or determinism is part of a more general methodological debate in the social sciences. Most writings on leadership belong broadly to one of two schools, depending on their assumptions or images of man and society (Searing, 1972). A *mechanistic* image of leadership sees society as atomistic, conflictual, and emphasises the importance of the sub-systems of individuals and groups. An alternative *organismic* image sees society as interdependent, change as revolutionary and the sub-systems as playing a subordinate role within an interdependent society. If we relate these images to the explanation of social change, then we find that the mechanistic invariably attributes an important place to individual actors, whereas the organismic emphasises the importance of institutional norms, political culture, social structure, and so on, in explanation.

Of course, we may reconcile these differences by saying that the disagreement is about the margin allowed to the choices of actors. In effect, the problem becomes one of deciding how malleable the situation is, and specifying the conditions under which the preferences of the political actor(s) can alter the outcome from what it would have been without the actor's intervention. Behaviour emerges from the interplay of both the predispositions of individuals and the logic of the situation. Unfortunately, as Searing observes, however, the images are often converted into 'monolithic images of man and society [which are] presented in the form of universal generalisations' (1972, p. 21).

There is no simple answer to the question 'Do political leaders shape events?'. The Great Man perspective erred in explaining too much in terms of human choice and underplaying the structural limitations. Determinists, whether Marxists emphasising economic causation (though even Lenin admitted the need for a correct reading of historical circumstances), or theorists of post-industrial society, with their emphasis on the inherent logic and 'imperatives' of the new scientific technical order (e.g. St Simon's *industriels*, or Galbraith's educational and scientific estate), have neglected the importance of personal choice by political actors. The significance of the leader varies with the malleability of the situation, the relevance of his skills and his location in the environment. Appreciation of an actor's indispensability does not involve an assumption of the 'great man' perspective but an acknowledgement that in any analysis, abstract socio-economic changes have to be mediated through changes in individuals' attitudes and behaviour. Ultimately grand theories or macro-level explanations have to come to terms with the actions of political leaders.

The task, then, is to focus on the interaction between the individual and the context, and to investigate the margin of choice or range of possibilities open to a leader; these expand and contract over time and, to some extent, are subject to alteration by him. The actor's capacity to shape the 'givens' of history and political culture are severely constrained. However, he has more scope in his own spheres of law-making, political appointments and designing institutions, and these, in turn, may affect the larger environment.

There are a number of research strategies for diagnosing the amount of voluntarism in a situation. By concentrating, for example, on a key event one may identify an event-making person. A bold attempt to tackle the question of whether or not an individual has decisively affected an outcome is Sidney Hook's *The Hero in History* (1943). This argues that whereas *a* Russian revolution in October 1917 was inevitable, the revolution's final character was determined by a number of Lenin's personal interventions. Hook makes a strong case that without Lenin there would not have been *the* October Revolution, and that many other consequences would not have followed. Lenin was significant because the situation was malleable, his skills were relevant in restructuring it and he was strategically placed. After the collapse of the Russian autocracy, and the failure of Kerensky, the situation was extremely fluid. Lenin was a key figure in urging the Bolsheviks to seize the initiative and take advantage of the political vacuum. Other Bolsheviks looked to him and he had the drive and confidence to urge action. Lenin combined a belief in historical determinism with a view that it was also possible for individuals to give history a push in the right direction. The scope for the actor's impact may also be enlarged in unfamiliar or new situations, that is, where there are not familiar cues or where they are ambiguous or contradictory. As Weber appreciated in his discussion of political charisma, wars, revolutions and crises usually belong to a class of events in which the established routines break down and people are prepared to turn to personal leadership.

Another way to interrelate institutional and behavioural aspects is suggested in de Jouvenal's distinction between the *auctoritas* or power inherent in a position or role, and the *authority,* the element contributed by the holder of the office. We may think of the former as being relatively fixed (e.g. the formal powers of a President) but of the latter as varying with the skills of the incumbent. The appropriateness of the skills depends on the office and the situation, and a skilful entrepreneur may augment or exploit the power resources. Neustadt's (1960) study of the American presidency is sensitive to the variability in a President's performance, to factors which determine his power and the way different incumbents have used circumstances and their own personal skills, role definitions and goals to reshape expectations of the office.

In the Fourth French Republic, to take another example, a premier possessed little formal power. The fragmented party system, short-lived ministries, severe limits on the premier's rights to dissolve the Assembly and other formal and informal rules of Assembly politics, all combined to weaken the executive and make the premier something of a figurehead. A would-be activist leader, therefore, required both great skill and exceptional circumstances if he was to assert himself. For a short time (1953–4) Mendes-France was able to use the crisis of the Indo-China War to play an active role which went against the institutional and cultural matrix until his affronted Assembly colleagues overthrew him. By contrast, after 1958 the political institutions of the Fifth Republic were redrawn to facilitate the exercise of personal leadership by the President and strengthen the executive against the legislature. In a study of leadership and policy-making in the Fourth Republic an emphasis on the external and institutional forces, which narrowed the formal power of the premier, is necessary. In the early years of the Fifth Republic, however, the emphasis shifts to the personality, political goals and values of de Gaulle. These features were important in creating both the new institutions and the 'rules of the game', and in providing more leeway for the leaders.

## Locating the Leaders

One way of identifying leaders is by a *reputational* approach, in which the researcher relies on a panel of knowledgeable observers to select leaders or influentials. The method provides knowledge about the *reputation,* or insiders' perceptions of holders of power, and may help identify influentials who wield indirect power or do not occupy formal political positions. Floyd Hunter employed this method to identify the top 100 decision-makers in Atlanta (1953). It goes without saying, however, that the reputation for power is not the same as its exercise.

With a *positional* approach, as noted, the researcher equates power with the incumbents of formal office. Mills in *The Power Elite* (1956) identified the leaders in the military, corporate and governmental sectors as the power elite. Thomas Dye defined the elite as occupants 'of the top positions in the institutional structure of American society' (1976, pp. 11–12), and proceeded to identify some 5,000 office-holders in the corporate, governmental and public interest sectors.[2]

Office is certainly a source of influence. A Churchill, a de Gaulle, or a Khrushchev ceases to command once he surrenders the seals of office. But again, office is no guarantee of influence; if it were, then simple retention of office would be the test of leadership. Yet a common theme of students of premiers and presidents and other executives is about the variability of performance with each incumbent. Some incumbents prove to be strong and some weak – a case of 'the office is what you make it'. Neustadt saw the office of the American President as 'the power to persuade', and the effective President as one who, by skill and personality, is able to expand the power of the office. The effective incumbent was likely to be a skilled political entrepreneur, someone who is sensitive to the power possibilities in a situation and in the office. The positional approach may also miss the wielders of indirect or informal influence. Both the positional and reputational approaches, however useful, are flawed in that they provide us only with the criteria for locating *potential* power-holders.

A more explicitly behavioural approach is to study concrete *decisions.* By identifying the major actors in political processes and examining the extent to which they achieve their objectives, in terms of initiating or resisting policies, one is also able to check the claims for the positional and reputational leaders. But because leaders may vary according to issues, we face the problems of deciding 'How many issues?', 'Which issues?, before we can generalise about leadership in a community, political party, or country. The approach, as critics have noted, is not useful for identifying a 'second face of power', that is, how the political agenda is shaped and the context within which policy alternatives are presented and decisions taken or not taken.

There has been a heated debate between the advocates of the different approaches. We shall see in Chapter 8 that in studies of American communities the decision-making approach has usually found a pluralist system, or a dispersion of power, while the reputational one has found a concentrated power elite. On account of the awareness of the shortcomings of any one approach applied on its own, there is now some general agreement that one should employ a mix of the methods (Parry, 1969; Putnam, 1976).

## Personal Characteristics of Leaders

In this section we turn to an examination of the studies of the characteristics of political leaders – their social backgrounds, personalities and political styles. Interestingly, these studies invariably define the politician as one who holds an elected office.

### Personality

Few would now doubt the importance of personality in affecting a person's behaviour in politics, or other forms of behaviour. The main problem is whether one can grapple satisfactorily with the problems of evidence and inference and assess the importance of personality relative to other factors (Greenstein, 1969). From the time of Plato and Aristotle, political theorists have commented, often intuitively and impressionistically, on the personal bases of politics. In the twentieth century Freud developed psychoanalysis into a systematic field of study and political scientists gradually borrowed the tools and insights of this new approach. The pioneer in the application of psychology to politics was Harold Lasswell. His original formulation of the *political type* emphasised a search for power as the distinctive feature of the politician. He claimed that the private power drives of the political leader were displaced on to the public stage and then rationalised in terms of the public good (1948, p. 38). Politics was an activity which invited irrational behaviour. Lasswell also emphasised the one-sided nature of this striving: it was for power or dominance over others, and was sought as a *compensation* for damaged self-esteem – 'power is expected to overcome low estimates of the self' (p. 39). According to this formulation, the situation is less important in affecting a person's political behaviour than are his unconscious drives.

A rather similar effort to relate the politician's personality needs and their displacement to a political situation is found in the psycho-historical school best exemplified in Erik Erikson's studies of Luther (1958) and Gandhi (1969). These studies examine the conjunction of the individual's personality needs with a social and historical context. The great reformer, like Luther and Gandhi, settles 'a personal account' or personality problem on a large scale, being 'called upon . . . to lift his individual patienthood to the level of a universal one' (1958, 67). Individuals who are concerned to transform private ambitions on to a political stage are particularly drawn to charismatic or crisis roles. A more singular illustration of the approach is Wolfenstein's study of revolutionary leaders (1967), where the revolutionary behaviour of Trotsky, Lenin and Gandhi was related to their repressed aggressive feelings towards their fathers.

The intense ambition, aggressiveness and search for action of Winston Churchill also invite such an analysis (Kavanagh, 1974). Anthony Storr has suggested that Churchill's desire for 'personal distinction' was so abnormal and his aggressiveness in politics so marked that they should be traced to early deprivation of parental recognition and consequent lack of self-esteem. There is ample evidence of both (Storr, 1969).

The personality factor is of some significance for an understanding of Churchill's inspirational qualities. Storr also notes how closely Churchill (with his proneness to deep depressions and consequent search for excitement and drama) resembles Jung's intuitive-extrovert personality type (pp. 212–15). Such a person tends to be highly egocentric yet also to have an unrivalled ability to inspire his fellow men with courage. He further hypothesises that Churchill's own depressive temperament and his personal struggles to combat despair helped his inspirational role in 1940. Churchill, in other words, was able to meet his own personal need to find a suitable adversary on whom his aggression might be displaced by linking it to the defence of his country. Churchill offers a compelling illustration of the adaptive and constructive political consequences of the emotional and unconscious layers of the personality. The qualities of obstinacy, aggressiveness, neurotic sense of mission and lack of 'balance' which had hindered him in the past, were successfully exploited for political purpose. Like other crisis leaders in history he may have been enabled, because of the Nazi menace, to settle a personal account in a grand historical and political context.

Because Hitler and Stalin shared a number of paranoid personality features, Tucker (1972) has suggested that they illustrate a dictatorial personality. The paranoid person sees himself as surrounded by conspiratorial enemies, a factor present in Hitler's anti-Jewish campaign and military expansionism and in Stalin's purges. Tucker suggests that in certain 'fighting' or revolutionary organisations this personality is functional in energising the organisation and giving it a sense of purpose. In the hands of such leaders 'structured situations can be restructured, role expectations confounded and roles themselves decisively remoulded to fit the needs of the dictatorial personality' (p. 44).

The psycho-biographies inevitably focus more on the subject's inner drives and subconscious strivings and less on the situation. According to the Georges' (1956) analysis, President Woodrow Wilson gained his strength from his relationship with his autocratic father. He resented the intense pressures imposed by his father though he was always submissive. Wilson was compulsive in seeking achievements and justified himself, in his own eyes, by presenting them as moral ideas. He had great confidence whenever this drive for power was presented as service for some noble cause. Yet the perpetual struggle with his father made Wilson unwilling to compromise with rivals. His refusal to meet Senator Lodge's demands for changes in the Versailles Treaty in 1919 and 1920 concerning the United States' membership of the League of Nations eventually proved his undoing.[3] A particular strength of the studies of Woodrow Wilson and the German Socialist leader Schumacher (Edinger, 1965) is that they are set in an explicit conceptual framework, albeit one drawn from psychology. The authors see their subjects as a compulsive type of personality, seeking power as a compensation for feelings of inadequacy. By relating the personality to the nuances of political role, situation and task, they show how Wilson and Schumacher were markedly successful in some situations, and quite hopeless in other recurring situations. The politician's personal conditions were important in promoting success in one context and producing the maladaptive pattern of behaviour in another.

On balance, however, the evidence does not support the claim that the political type is paranoid, a person activated by damaged self-esteem. A study of South Carolina legislators found them to have a strong sense of self-esteem (McConnaughy, 1950). Barber's (1965) study of the Connecticut state legislators included some members with above-average and some with below-average self-esteem. His interpretation (p. 224) of his findings is that politics is an activity that appeals to those with both high and low levels of self-esteem but not to those on the middle level. The former are able to handle the strains and demands involved in public controversies and taking decisions. Their self-confidence helps to make them the most effective members of the legislature. On the other hand, a political career also appeals to those who are low in self-esteem. Politics provides a 'second chance' to gain attention and prestige for those who are dissatisfied with their occupations or disappointed on other grounds. One has to admit, however, that we lack a satisfactory study of self-esteem among politicians. Those who have high self-esteem, like Barber's *Lawmakers,* may have compensated for damaged self-esteem at an earlier stage. We can only tackle this problem by developmental analysis which looks at changes in self-esteem over time (George, 1968, pp. 47–8).

Many of the objections made against the personality in politics approach are simply misconceived. One may study the subject without reducing it exclusively to the pathological or irrational, rejecting traditional approaches, and dealing only with idiosyncratic traits or individuals. Personality characteristics are not randomly distributed in institutions; there is some evidence of a selectivity of personality types in different political roles. The more important task is to consider how and under what circumstances personality may be important for political behaviour. Greenstein (1969) refutes the claim that, because of the constraints of a situation the personality of an actor has little impact on the outcome by noting that the scope for personality depends on how indispensable the person is (what Greenstein calls Action Dispensability). Is the actor in a strategic position where his decisions affect what others do, like the position of Stalin or Hitler – or even someone lower – in a centralised totalitarian system? Is the situation malleable, as in a power vacuum following defeat in a war, a crisis, or while drawing up a new constitution? How relevant are the personal strengths or weaknesses of the individual in the situation? The importance of personality also depends on such factors as how fixed the expectations of the behaviour are, how intense the actor's emotional involvement is and how new the situation is. In a nutshell, we might say that at higher levels, where politics 'matters more' to the personality, so there is more capacity for personality needs to be expressed in behaviour. Greenstein's apt formulation of the problem (p. 29) is that we should see the environment and the personal predispositions being involved in a push-pull relationship. The stronger the situational constraints, the less scope for personality to be expressed in behaviour, and vice versa.

## Social Origins

The high socio-economic status of the politician and bureaucrat is a fairly universal feature across most societies, regardless of their level of economic development or dominant ideology. In many new states and less developed societies the social 'gap' between the middle-class, university-educated politicians and the rest of the electorate is even more marked than in industrialised societies (Putnam, 1976). I noted earlier that the social structure combines with other features to shape a person's opportunity for recruitment into politics. Gender, age, occupation and education combine to reduce, severely, the pool of those who are effectively 'eligible' for political recruitment. This pool may be further reduced to those who have the interest, motivation and skills to encourage them to undertake a political career. And these last qualities are more likely to be found in people from higher status groups.

The compilation of objective biographical data on politicians or other elites is now a large field. Such data on politicians may be used as a basis for studying the distribution of values in society (particularly among the selectors of elites), the social representatives of the elite and, by inference, its likely responsiveness to groups in the electorate, the cohesiveness of different elites, and the kind of interests they are likely to favour. The approach has been particularly crucial to the study of social stratification, or social differences in a society. Such data may also be employed as an indicator of qualitative change in the elite within a country or of differences across countries. In Britain in the twentieth century, for example, one may demonstrate the gradual erosion of MPs from working-class backgrounds in the Labour Party and a similar decline of the aristocracy on the Conservative benches. Yet, notwithstanding the growth of university-educated middle-class politicians in both parties, there are still differences between MPs of the two parties. The middle-class Labour politician tends to be drawn from the teaching, lecturing and social welfare professions, employed mostly in the state sector, and is often first-generation middle-class. The Conservative MPs are in law and business, usually in the private sector, and come from secure middle-class backgrounds (Kavanagh, 1980). Two factors are at work to explain a decline in the working class in the ranks of Labour and Socialist parties in Western societies. One is the general shift to white-collar or service employment at the expense of the manual and manufacturing sector of the workforce. This has been accompanied by a major growth in employment in the public sector, covering welfare services and state corporations. A second factor has been the expansion of educational opportunity, which has permitted a larger number (though not a larger proportion) of children from working-class homes to compete for elite positions. The emphasis on an MP serving a lengthy period of apprenticeship in the House of Commons before becoming a minister also explains why so few of the working-class Labour members become ministers. Most of them are sponsored by trade unions and are usually middle-aged before they enter the House of Commons.

One may also use this data to test the hypothesis that the greater the revolutionary upheaval in a society, the more dramatic the change in the social composition of the political elite. Nagle's *System and Succession* (1977) presents time-series data for political recruitment to measure the nature and extent of the change (or elite displacement) in the United States and Mexico, Russia and Germany. The last three countries, in contrast to the United States, have gone through cycles of revolution, economic crisis and peace in the twentieth century. Nagle's conclusion is that there have been only minor social changes in Germany and the United States; in Mexico the change has been one of generations, in Russia it has been of both generation and social class. The shift after 1917 was from the landowners and aristocrats to the middle-class intellectuals and then (as a result of Stalin's purge of the old Bolsheviks in the 1930s) to those from a peasant and proletarian background.

Data on the professional training and higher education qualifications may indicate changing skills in the bureaucracy and among politicians. In industrial societies, for example, there has been a shift to the recruitment of more managerial and technical qualities among administrative elites (Putnam, 1976, ch. 7). On the other hand, the administrative class of the British civil service presents a good example of how the self-presenting (and self-preserving) feature of elite recruitment frustrates attempts to change. In spite of efforts to break away from the recruitment of Oxbridge educated arts graduates, applicants (and, even more so, recruits) still come disproportionately from these groups. Other types of student appear to lack interest in such a career or the confidence that they will be selected if they apply. The sample of 'eligibles' is already biased by university, sex and subject (Halsey and Crewe, 1968).

Finally, social background data may provide a surrogate measure of the political influence of different groups in the policy process. The marked under-representation of blacks among politicians and the electorate in American Southern states for much of the post-Civil War period, or of Catholics in Ulster (under-represented among voters and politicians), are clear examples of groups which suffered systematic exclusion from power by white and Protestant elites respectively. This discrimination was only part of a wider pattern of bias in the allocation of goods in society. One analysis of the unrepresentativeness of Western elites, compared with the public in terms of education, social background and occupation, argues for 'the strong presumption which this creates as to [the elite's] general outlook, ideological disposition and political bias' (Miliband, 1969, p. 68). In particular, it is sometimes argued that the middle-class social background goes with a belief in the validity and virtues of the capitalist system. Some studies assume that there is something obviously 'wrong' with a socially unrepresentative political elite, on the grounds that it leads to a biased distribution of social goods.

But one has to tread cautiously in linking changes in the social composition of an elite to changes in its political style or changes in policy outcomes. There are several steps in establishing such relationships and they have to be demonstrated and not, as is often the case, taken for granted. A familiar argument that different social backgrounds produce different policy outcomes proceeds along either of the following lines. One line is that elites from a particular class background will produce policies which favour members of their own social class. Testing this particular proposition is not a simple matter. The history of Socialist parties, for example, is as littered with examples of middle-class MPs who are socialist and egalitarian as it is with working-class MPs who are very conservative. Where society is clearly divided, for instance, on class lines, and the party in government is predominantly drawn from one social class or group, then one might look for legislation of a class or sectional character. One would expect the British Labour Party, for example, to pass legislation favouring council tenants over home-owners, or trade unions over business, or press for more social and economic equality. But 'class interest' is not a self-evident term. Many working-class Labour voters are not council tenants or are hostile to many aspects of trade unions.

A second line is that differences in social background create different predispositions and policy preferences. On this we do have some evidence (see Kavanagh, 1982, for summary). Within Socialist parties, educated middle-class professionals have contributed an important expressive style of politics – interest in quality-of-life issues, humanitarian, pacifist and Third World problems, for example. In the United States Democratic Party in the1970s a middle-class intelligentsia or 'symbol specialists' (lawyers, journalists, teachers) have come to the fore. Such people appear less interested in bread-and-butter issues than in more abstract questions of ideology, social justice and 'quality of life' (Kirkpatrick, 1976). The evidence suggests that social background may have an influence here. What is not clear, however, is how significant or consistent the differences are, or how they compare with differences which correlate with other demographic factors.

Painstaking effort is required for the collection of biographical data. There is a problem of 'missing' data, or the suspicion that politicians misrepresent their backgrounds; Communist leaders in Eastern Europe overstate their proletarian or peasant origins, German Bundestag deputies tend to report their occupations 'in terms that do not provoke class-conflict images of interest representation' (Nagle, 1977, p. 15). The better research breaks up such gross independent variables as social class, occupation and education, on the one hand, and types of leadership orientation and behaviour, which they are supposed to explain. Edinger and Searing (1967) have shown that some background factors are better than others for predicting political attitudes among elites, and that the relationships differ across societies and types of elites. They found that the best prediction variables for politicians, for example, were adult or role socialisation experiences, particularly those involving political party and occupation. Many studies, however, lack sufficient specificity and precision in this area. The more useful work also spells out the theoretical linkages between the social background factors and orientations and behaviour; too often, however, description is equated with explanation, the data being regarded as self-explanatory. Some variables, particularly social class or higher education, are too 'lumpy' or indiscriminate; the danger is to assume that people from one class have undergone a common set of socialisation experiences.

Explanation is best achieved by integrating the social origins data with the political culture, political socialisation, legislative norms, recruitment procedures, and so on. W. L. Guttsman's (1963) historical study of the British political elite is a model of how these diverse threads may be woven together. One comes away from his book not merely with a perception of upper-class dominance of political life – which one gathers from most such studies – but also with an awareness of the relevance of particular occupational and social skills to politics, the criteria of prestige applied by the politicians' selectors and sponsors and by voters, and how these have changed over time.

## Typologies

Typological studies classify leaders on the basis of their having some characteristics or syndrome of characteristics in common. Much writing on leadership styles has taken Weber's ideal types of charismatic, traditional and legal-rational forms of rule as a starting point. At an elementary level, students distinguish between 'strong' and 'weak' leaders, 'conservative' or 'change-oriented' leaders. Machiavelli and Pareto made similar distinctions, taking account of a leader's skills and motives. Machiavelli distinguished between the *foxes*, leaders of intelligence and cunning, who rejected the use of force and relied on manipulation and bargaining to promote their ends, and the *lions*, men of strength and integrity, who by contrast were prepared to use force. More recent examples of the genre include Hoffmann's (1967) study of heroic leaders in France, Tucker's (1972) work on the totalitarian type of leader and James Barber's research into types of presidential character (1972).

Barber's analysis is complex and subtle and not easy to summarise. By political character he means his subject's orientation to life; this orientation encompasses a person's world view or basic beliefs and political style, and interacts with a 'power situation' and a climate of expectations. Working with two dimensions – of *active-passivity*, or how active and energetic the President is in the office, and *positive-negative affect* in his attitude to the job – Barber classifies his cases into four types: passive-positive, passive-negative, active-positive and active-negative. The *passive-positive* type is non-aggressive and co-operative; an example is President Warren Harding. The *active-negative* is ambitious, not easily satisfied and concerned with his self-image; for example, President Nixon. The *passive-negative* does not enjoy politics or the conflictual aspects of the job; for instance, Calvin

Coolidge. The *active-positive* both enjoys politics and is extremely active; Kennedy and F. D. Roosevelt were of this type.

This work grows out of Barber's earlier study, *The Lawmakers*, (1965) carried out in Connecticut. There he developed a four fold typology of legislative styles, on the basis of (*a*) the legislator's attitude to membership of the legislature, as reflected in his willingness to return for another session, and (*b*) his activity in the legislature. One type, the Lawmaker, felt positively about his membership and was very active in the legislature. The Reluctants were not emotionally attracted to the legislature and rather inactive. Another type, the Advertisers, were active but not committed, appearing to view membership primarily as a means of career advancement or self-advertisement. Finally, there were the Spectators, who were relatively inactive in the legislature but enjoyed membership. Barber persuasively explains these styles in terms of particular personality characteristics and links them with various social background factors.

There comes a stage in any field of study when a mapping and then a typology are desirable and even necessary for imposing some order on variegated data. But one needs to be reminded of the shortcomings of ideal types. Weber's analytical types of charismatic, traditional and legal-rational leadership, for instance, seem to break up when applied to the real world. Few leaders fall exclusively into one of his three categories and most possess some qualities of two or even all three of the types. The danger with typological analyses, including Barber's, is of squeezing the characters and straining for commonalities in the types and neglecting important differences between individuals in any one group.

## Belief Systems

There are three strong arguments for studying the political or politics-related beliefs of politicians. The first is that politicians are more likely than members of the public to have a coherent or integrated set of attitudes. Politics matters more to them than to the ordinary citizen; they are more likely to think about political principles and values, and how these relate to political practice; and they spend some time interpreting politics and explaining policies and events to the public. A second argument is that their strategic position provides them with an opportunity to act out their beliefs in the political arena. Finally, there are good reasons for thinking that how politicians think about politics sometimes affects their behaviour, and this in turn may influence the course of politics. We know that political actors apply certain rules of thumb to help them make sense of complexity. They have their own 'cognitive maps' of politics. Do they believe in the inevitability of conflict or that there is a natural harmony of interests in society? What is the role of chance in politics? What are their criteria for 'correct' political action? Such analyses have been applied to, among others, British and Italian MPs (Putnam, 1973), French MPs (Melnik and Leites, 1958) and Malaysian elites (Scott, 1968).

Putnam's study of ideology drew on depth interviews to delineate the *political styles* (how politicians think), and *cognitive predispositions* and *operative ideals* (what politicians believe). He was able to show that an ideological outlook was separate from intense partisanship. An ideological outlook in the sense of thinking in comprehensive, general, deductive and abstract terms was declining in his two elites. The ideologues were more politically extreme and alienated than other politicians, but they were not more authoritarian, intolerant, opposed to compromise, or paranoid. Putnam's findings, incidentally, are a warning against using 'ideology' as a portmanteau term into which too many ideas are poured. Students of comparative politics will not be surprised by Putnam's finding that Italian politicians are more ideological than their British counterparts and more frequently see politics as the expression of social conflict. No doubt the differences in the two countries' elite political cultures are a product of their difference histories, political cleavages, party systems, and so on. Yet the culture (see above, Chapter 4) also influences these factors. The British elite political culture has been characterised by a high level of interpersonal trust, general agreement on the essentials of the political system and the value of working within them, and a willingness to compromise. Such features have been, and still are, rejected by many Italian politicians. These qualities in turn have been reflected in the past performances of the two political systems.

Yet knowledge of this background information invites a legitimate 'so what?' question. What is the 'pay-off' in terms of understanding a politician's behaviour from knowing about his beliefs and preferences? Obviously much depends on how central the particular belief is to a person and the precise nature of the situation. Beliefs and opinions stated in a general context are less valuable as predictors of behaviour than those expressed in relation to a specific situation. In addition, knowledge of personal preferences and values may not matter in a highly structured situation; for example, the incidence of party voting of British MPs in the House of Commons. But on free votes[4] the MP's personal values may be important.

A political situation is not an objective datum which is perceived in similar terms by all actors. Situations have to be interpreted and assessed by political actors. Hence our interest in their values and orientations. Such knowledge of how the politician is likely to diagnose a situation will be enhanced given any of the following conditions:

> where the beliefs are well-integrated; where they are held in a manner suggestive of an underlying pattern, i.e. where there is a belief *system*;
>
> where situations are relatively open or unstructured and where the element of choice is such that personality factors are likely to be free to express themselves.

Also,

> study of the belief system is likely to be rewarding where the actor engages in controversial, important, or unexpected behaviour.

Another approach in studying a politician's belief system is to 'code' his instrumental and philosophical beliefs (George, 1969). The approach was pioneered by Nathan Leites in his *The Operational Code of the Politburo* (1951) and applied to the Communist leaders. The 'operational code' is a checklist for examining an actor's assumptions about the nature of politics and how he goes about relating political ends and means. Such a code, when developed, is useful for diagnosis and explanation, particularly to

(*a*) appreciate how an actor perceives and diagnoses a situation,
(*b*) narrow the courses of action likely to be considered by him and understand how he is likely to structure and identify the choices available to him.

It is helpful in enabling us to go beyond the conventionally impressionistic and *ad hoc* treatments of this sub-system of the personality: it signals some progress in making an actor's belief system a more explicit variable and thus a more useful tool for analysis. It does not, however, mean that the need for situational analysis or for linking beliefs with other components of the personality system can be eliminated. It helps us to limit the number of alternative ways an actor approaches a situation.

## Biography

Students of political leadership continue to look to biographies for much of their raw material. The biographer, however, is at the mercy of the passage of time. Time has to elapse for a substantial number of relevant private papers to become available and also for him to take advantage of a more considered perspective on his subject. *Ergo*, substantial biographies of prominent politicians are left to the historians, whose concerns are usually different from those of the political scientist. The historian, as biographer, is usually more concerned with description and with the idiosyncratic and personal aspects of his subject; the political scientist, however, looks for a framework, and a set of broadly comparable questions which allow the biographies to 'add up', or produce a body of generalisations. Unfortunately, questions about a leader's political style, his perceptions of his role, what he gets out of political activity, how he handles others and how he calculates political risks are often dealt with unsystematically, if at all. Descriptive biographies may, of course, lead to fruitful generalisations where they are subjected to theory-oriented secondary analysis. Most typological analyses (e.g. Wolfenstein, 1967; Barber, 1972), personality studies and social background work (e.g. Guttsman, 1963), draw heavily on biographical sources. But, overall, the contribution of political biography to political science has been limited.

## Conclusion

It is difficult to make useful cross-national generalisations about political leaders. We have good evidence that they are usually drawn from upper-status social backgrounds and are well-educated. But they tend to emerge in response to distinctive institutional-cultural milieux, across countries and political parties. Italian *deputati,* for example, have very different outlooks and political styles from British MPs. Particular systems of recruitment reward different styles of behaviour and different roles impose different patterns on political incentives. Yet politicians of similar social and economic backgrounds may behave very differently and, for all the personality studies, 'homo politicus' is capable of displaying various personalities. Even within a country, political emergencies or national crises open the way for different types of politician who would be spurned in 'routine' politics.

The different perspectives on leadership reviewed above are not mutually exclusive but need to be integrated. Greenstein has noted that social origins are part of the environment in which personality is developed. The two approaches are complementary, but not interchangeable, the former preceding and shaping the latter. Barber's study of legislative styles found that the particular types were associated with patterns of personality and social background. Law-makers, for example, tend to be high in self-esteem, well-educated, and represent a politically competitive urban area. These are examples of some integration of the different approaches.

The study of political leadership is beginning to look like a sub-discipline, one that has a shared vocabulary and interests and in which research can begin to cumulate. But we should stress the 'beginning' element. There is little prospect for a scientific study of leadership if this is to mean that we will be able to predict how individuals will behave in given roles and situations (Paige, 1977). The difficulties in establishing controls, replicability and making 'if this . . . then that' types of statement mean that we operate at modest levels of scientific rigour in studying leadership. But some steps could be taken.

First, leadership studies need to be clear about the *explanandum* – what it is they are explaining. Is it an event, an outcome, in which the choices and non-decisions of individuals may play a role, or is it the leader's actions and attitudes? These are two different questions. In the former, study of the political actor is tackled as part of an inquiry into a larger topic; in the latter, the task is to explain the actor's behaviour. Secondly, macro-approaches, drawing on history, culture, political institutions, the economy and social structure, are important in describing the context in which leaders operate. Although the leader may still have some room for choice, it depends on his particular skills whether he is able to exploit it. Identifying the margin for choice remains a suitable subject for study. Many of the leader-related features we have discussed are more likely to be important in non-routine situations. In crises, or new or ambiguous situations, the force of established procedures, group norms and traditional expectations is likely to be relaxed. Then the beliefs, role perceptions and personality of the individual actor have more scope for expression. A rich description of the situation, allied to an appreciation of the author's definition of the situation, and how he calculates and perceives situations, improves our ability to narrow the range of possible outcomes and to explain intelligibly what happens.

Leaders operate within and are influenced by a context. In Chapter 8 I examine the influence of broader environmental forces within which political actors take decisions. Debate about the relative influence of environmental and political factors affecting the character of political systems and policies leads to examination of the question 'Does Politics Matter?'.

## Notes: Chapter 7

1 A bibliography in Paige (1977) runs to 166 pages.
2 This included the mass media, major private foundations, universities and law firms.
3 Opponents proposed modest changes in the Treaty. But Wilson was not prepared to compromise, even though the changes would not have affected the substance of the treaty, and the Senate failed to ratify it.
4 Votes on which the party leaders do not impose a three-line whip.

Chapter 8

# What Governments Do

## I Governments and Policies

The term 'government' has various usages and refers to a disparate set of activities, persons and institutions. It may refer to office-holders (e.g. civil servants or elected politicians), the institutions of the executive, the type of regime or system (e.g. parliamentary or presidential, authoritarian or democratic), the activities carried out by the government, or simply the process of ruling. Much effort by pressure groups and political parties is directed to influencing or controlling government in the first three senses of the term, because the decisions and policies of government affect society. This influence is obvious in state-dominated societies in Eastern Europe. But it also applies to a greater degree today than before in the mixed economies and welfare states in the West.

Government and politics involve, among other things, the exercise of power. Many familiar definitions of politics, such as 'the authoritative allocation of values', 'who gets what, how and when', or the Marxist perception of governments in capitalist societies serving the interests of the dominant social class,[1] emphasise this allocative role of government. What governments do, encompassing their policies, outputs and how these are decided, has been closely related to two important themes in political studies. One, reflected in the local community studies, concerns the distribution of influence and power in society. The other is concerned to assess the relative influence of political and environmental factors in determining the pattern of policies.

Governments carry out several tasks: they make rules for society, in the form of laws and regulations; they extract resources, particularly revenues in the form of direct and indirect taxes; they distribute benefits and goods in the form of payments, services and capital; they also provide symbolic gratifications for many citizens (Almond and Powell, 1966). Governments, in contrast to most private organisations, are interested in collective problems and take decisions for society as a whole. Inflation, safety standards at work, entitlement to vote and defence are examples of collective problems and are concerns of governments. In the past three decades there has been an almost universal tendency for the scope of government in Western states to increase, whether measured in number of central and local government employees, public expenditure as a share of the gross domestic product, money raised by taxation, or number of laws and regulations. Governments are also widely expected to try and affect the aggregate levels of economic activity, through their fiscal and monetary policies. In short, as extractor and distributor of revenues, and as manager of society, the government's role has increased greatly over recent years.

There has also been a historical pattern in the state's assumptions of activities. The 'defining' or 'federative' tasks of government like diplomacy, military defence, law and policing and taxation have been assumed first. The mobilisation of physical resources through programmes of public works, communications and industrial and agricultural development has followed. The final stage has seen the involvement of the state in providing social and welfare services such as housing, education and welfare (Rose, 1976a). The greater part of public expenditure in recent years has shifted into this last category. Increasingly, the substance of election campaigns and the promises of parties' election manifestos reflect this change in the concerns of voters and politicians.

The policies, decisions, laws, and so on, of government are often called *outputs*. They are to be distinguished from the *outcomes* or *impacts* of the policies on the society, economy, educational system, or whatever. Many policies, such as fixing a pension level or a maximum size for a school class, expanding the provision of higher education, or setting up a commission to combat racial discrimination, are inputs to a social process or the environment. The actual effects or impacts of such policies in improving standards of education or race relations depend on the influence of other factors as well.

In recent years the development of quantitative techniques has encouraged students to develop answers to such questions as:

- Is there a pattern in the policy outputs of different regimes or of societies with different levels of social and economic development?
- Where there are differences in outcomes, are political or environmental forces more important as determinants?
- Which models of the policy process – elitist or pluralist – best describe the pattern of outputs?[2]
- Finally, depending on the answers to the above, the more specific question may be posed: how important are democratic procedures (elections and party competition) in determining variations in outputs?
- In other words, does politics matter?

Some students have also relied on findings of how decisions are made and/or the types of policies and outputs achieved to arrive at conclusions about the distribution of power in society. This kind of research asks such questions as who participates in decisions, which interests favour and which interests oppose certain policies, and which groups gain and which groups lose from policy outcomes?[3] In other words, 'who governs?'. Some critics object that the distribution of power may not be fully revealed in issues and policies and that the agenda of politics, the issues and policy alternatives which are actually considered, are also a form of power. We are less concerned here with the methodological debate about the study of power (which has been covered extensively elsewhere) than with the use of the studies to appraise particular political systems and institutions. The question considered here is: do community power studies confirm or disconfirm claims that all interests are taken into account?

In the next two sections, I examine the findings of, first, community power and, secondly, aggregate statistical studies.

## Community Power Studies

One popular model of the distribution of power in society is the Ruling Elite Hypothesis. This derives from the elitist analyses of Mosca, Michels and Pareto, and claims that in every system there is a unified minority (the elite) whose preferences on policies regularly prevail over the choices of other groups. Pioneering studies of small towns in the United States by the Lynds (1937) and Warner and Lund (1941), and of Atlanta by Hunter (1953), appear to confirm this pattern. All claim to have found that a socio-economic elite (drawn from business, finance and the law) dominates politics in the communities, that the interests of workers and blacks are neglected, and that there is little in the way of political pluralism. At the level of national politics, C. Wright Mills claims that the United States is ruled by a 'power elite' (1956), or 'an interlocking set of overlapping elites' in the military, business corporations and politics. Such features as common social and educational backgrounds, the frequent transfer of members from one elite to another, and the system of co-opting new members by the established elites led Mills to claim that the elite was cohesive (also, Miliband, 1969). Marxist analyses of Western states also suggest the existence of an elite that is agreed on 'fundamental' questions, particularly those concerning the viability of capitalism, and that politicians of the left and right are protective of these socio-economic interests. Democratic political procedures, such as free elections and party competition, and pressure group activity, all operate within and are subordinate to this dominant consensus.

A decision-making approach to the study of power has challenged both the methods and conclusions of the ruling elite school. Robert Dahl (1958) claims that the detailed study of concrete political issues is the best way of testing whether or not there is a concentration of political power. Status, political office, reputation and wealth – all measures utilised by the Ruling Elite School – are types of *potential power*, resources which may or may not be exploited for *actual* power. This is a crucial distinction, for its advocates claim that the study of political decisions makes no initial presumptions that power-holders actually exercise power. It looks at who initiates, opposes and vetoes politics, and at who prevails in outcomes.

Dahl (1961a) studied three issues in New Haven – reorganisation of the city's school system, redevelopment of the city centre and nomination by the parties for elective offices. He found that the above types of resource were unevenly distributed among activists: they were 'non-cumulative', in his own words. No one resource dominated the others and the political weight of types of resources varied across issue areas. What Dahl found was a pluralist type of system, one in which there were different groups of decision-makers in different issue areas – a pattern of petty sovereignties. A decisional study of power in Chicago by Banfield (1961) similarly concluded that there was no power elite. Instead, the studies suggest, there are many leaders all of whom have some influence, though each is limited in scope; this pluralism gives rise to bargaining and compromises as well as competition between rival leaders to appeal for popular support. Only a few people have direct influence, but the mass has an indirect influence, through competitive elections and the democratic creed (Dahl, 1961a, p. 311). This, in turn, creates the opportunity for popular preferences to make themselves felt, as it includes the rights to dissent, compete and bargain and laws governing electoral competitors. A variety of groups participate, different interests prevail on different issues, and the existence of elections makes elites attentive to public opinion. But even if one accepts Dahl's contention that there is no ruling elite, it remains a matter of judgement whether the pattern of power he describes is pluralist or oligopolistic.

A not dissimilar pattern is found in Hewitt's study of policies in postwar Britain. He found that many groups had an intermittent and limited involvement in a number of issues. Moreover, according to the relevant public opinion data, the outcomes were, more often than not, in conformity with the majority opinion. Different models of the policy process fitted different issues. For example, the ruling elite model described foreign policy, but pluralism was more appropriate for domestic economic issues (1974).

Objections have been raised against Dahl's selection of issues, some of which were of minor interest to the economic influentials, and against the suitability of the New Haven case for generalising about power in other communities of the United States. But the major criticism of the approach has been of its behavioural bias; that is, it studies visible actors, groups, issues and outcomes. In addition, it is suggested, we have to turn our attention to the political culture, political routines and 'rules of the game'. These constitute a 'second face of power' and they determine which issues are brought on to the political agenda and which are excluded (Bachrach and Baratz, 1962). This 'second face' is reflected in two types of phenomenon. First, there is the 'mobilisation of bias', or the set of values, procedures and beliefs that work consistently and systematically to benefit some groups at the expense of others. Secondly, there are 'non-decisions', or proposals for change in the allocations of benefits and power which do not reach the political agenda. 'Non-decisions' involve both actual decisions (i.e. proposals that the elite manages to defeat) and potential issues (i.e. proposals that are not voiced, by the opposition, because of fear, false consciousness, or a belief that they would be defeated anyway). 'Non-decisions' cover 'deciding not to act or deciding not to decide' (Bachrach and Baratz, 1963).

The major objection to this approach is, by which criteria do we decide which of the several potential policies or other issues we should select for study? How do we, for example, distinguish between concerns which are suppressed as a result of deliberate manipulation by the 'system', and those which naturally do not exist? How do we distinguish between a person's conscious abstention from political activity, and apathy? How far back in time or abroad do we go to determine which groups are responsible for the particular pattern of procedures, values and institutions? One school of thought (Merelman, 1968; Wolfinger, 1971) flatly asserts that the research requirements are so formidable or impractical that we should dismiss the concept of non-decisions as a suitable subject for empirical study. There is simply no way to disprove claims that there is always a hidden elite behind the observed elites, manipulating things.

Yet the consequences of political procedures, political culture and the socio-economic structure are important in setting the agenda of politics and do deserve analysis. Control of the agenda is a form of power. Lukes (1974) has suggested that we study both issues and potential issues and both observable and latent conflict. In answer to the question 'How do we study the covert and latent?', Lukes suggests that one makes a subjective judgement about policies which clearly and consistently work to the disadvantage of a group and cases in which groups fail to recognise their real interests. In finding 'a contradiction between the interests of those exercising power and the *real* interests of those they exclude' (pp. 24–5), one is able to arrive at a judgement, though clearly a value judgement, about what their 'real' interests are.

Crenson's (1971) study of the different reactions to air pollution in two cities is useful in this regard. The failure of politicians in one American city to take measures to combat air pollution, while politicians in another city do take such measures, does require explanation. Similarly, the failure, until the 1960s, of civil rights legislation for blacks to make progress in the United States, or the disadvantages and discriminations historically suffered by Catholics in Northern Ireland, are phenomena which clearly can be explained in terms of this approach. But many other 'routines' or patterns of bias are not so clear-cut as to lend themselves to this line of analysis (Parry and Morris, 1973). For example, capital punishment is not an 'issue' in British politics in so far as no major political party has a policy on it, beyond leaving it to a free vote in the House of Commons. It is difficult, however, to see that this particular routine favours a particular elite or discriminates against a group. The difficulty here, however, is that some allocations of values are achieved without explicit decisions being made, or as a side-effect of decisions, or as a result of events and forces outside the society. The approach comes close to asserting that who governs is who gains (Polsby, 1980).

The rival schools in the community power debate differ about many methods, assumptions, findings and conclusions. Most studies of decisions conclude that power is contingent, diffused among different groups, and each group's power is limited in scope. So-called elitists and neo-elitists, who use various methods, find that power is centralised. Both sides can agree on identifying *some* of the participants, but they do not agree on what this tells us about power. One side claims that we should study only decisions as an objective empirical datum, while the other claims that we also have to make normative judgements about people's interests. My own view is that the neo-elitists have effectively made their point that decisions alone are not sufficient for the complete study of power. They have not, however, proved their own claim about the existence of a ruling elite. (The important consequences of this particular debate for pluralist statements of democratic theory are considered later in Chapter 9.) Neither side has yet shown that it is possible to provide a complete answer to the search for power. Hence Wolfinger's (1971) 'plea for modesty', or Mackenzie's sceptical aside: 'it is by no means certain that [the enterprise] can pin down the sources and operation of political power' (1970, p. 61).

In the next section I shift my focus from studies of *who* determines policies to *what* determines policies. Whereas both sides in the community power debate agree that the activities of individuals and groups count, while disagreeing about who these actors are, the output studies disagree about the relative importance of individuals and groups.

## Aggregate Studies

A broad range of studies, covering local, national and comparative governments, has produced various answers to the questions raised on page 149. Most studies have conceptualised the policy process in terms of a system, and measured the correlation between particular outcomes (usually policy expenditures) and inputs of the socio-economic environment or party political variables. The size of the coefficients between the selected policy variables and the selected environmental and political variables is then taken as a measure of the comparative influence of the last two factors.

A view of the policy process is sketched in the flow chart in Figure 8.1. On the left we start with the system, or environmental resources; this covers such 'givens' as the society's level of industrialisation, wealth and urbanism, and so on. These are relatively fixed in the short term, though they may change over time and in response to political initiatives. Next there are factors which express or influence the demands, such as interest groups, political parties and political leaders. Finally, there is the decision-making arena, sometimes called the black box of government. This includes the modes and institutions of decision-taking, as well as the rules of the game or the elite culture. Environmental explanations emphasise the importance of the first group of factors, the system's level of resources. Political explanations accord more influence to the factors treated under Demand Patterns and the Decision System, namely, the more explicitly political procedures and actors.

Aggregate statistical approaches to the study of policy outputs have a number of advantages; they readily lend themselves to quantification and measurability and one can examine a large number of cases over time and space. On the other hand, the studies have operated with a rather narrow range both of dependent policy variables (e.g. levels of public expenditure, redistributive effects of programmes, or levels of programme expenditure), and of independent political variables (e.g. party competitiveness and left versus right party control of government) or environmental variables (e.g. urbanism, per capita income, industrialism).

The approach is associated with three further important problems. The first is obtaining cross-national data of adequate quality. Much of the information collected by international agencies such as UNESCO and the OECD is initially supplied by national governments. Aside from their accuracy (and one has to allow a margin for error, particularly in less industrialised societies), the data on, say, welfare provision are often submitted in a non-comparable form. In such cases the researcher

| SYSTEM RESOURCES → | DEMAND PATTERNS → | DECISION SYSTEM → | POLICY OUTPUT |
|---|---|---|---|
| e.g. | e.g. | e.g. | |
| Wealth<br>Industrialism<br>Population density | Parties<br>Groups<br>Leaders | Rules of game<br>Structure of authority | |

Figure 8.1 *Policy-making.*

*Source:* Salisbury, 1968, p. 165.

has to fall back on a 'second-best' strategy (Castles, 1978, pp. 57–8) and rely either on incomplete information or on surrogate indicators and make inferences from them.

A second problem is the interpretation of the data, particularly on expenditure. The global level of public expenditure (expressed in constant prices) across different governments is a crude measure of policy. The total level may remain constant, though spending is reduced on some services and increased on others. Expenditure on a programme may increase, largely through growth in the number of clients (e.g. old age pensions), or fall, largely because of reduced demand (e.g. declining school rolls). Alterations in total levels of expenditure may disguise a constant level of service provided per capita: in such cases a decision to maintain the existing policy alters the total level of expenditure. There are also shortcomings in looking at public expenditure as an indicator of the values of countries or parties in government. Governments find levels of public expenditure difficult to control, often using public expenditure as instruments for other policy goals. Again, one has to guard against the assumption that amount of expenditure is equivalent to the quality of service – what Sharkansky calls 'the spending-service cliche' (1970, ch. 7). Money is a visible, measurable input, but there are many other determinants of the quality of a service and of its outputs. Sharkansky points to cases of negative service–spending relationships, such as American states which are low spenders on law and order but have low crime rates, and states which are low spenders on highways but achieve a higher mileage per capita and greater road safety. Many other factors are at work in these cases; the point I want to make is that money is not all that matters.

Finally, some important factors will not show up in statistical exercises. Governments, for example, are also concerned to influence the climate of opinion or popular expectations, or to shift the content or form of a service – say, comprehensive schooling, or economic planning – while leaving expenditure levels constant. Indeed, many national governments have allowed for greater absolute public expenditure on the assumption of economic growth.

A frequent test of whether politics matters (or its impact compared with that of the environment) has been to examine the effects on policy of control of the government by parties of the political left and right. The left/right distinction of political ideology has some disadvantages; if applied cross-nationally it regards the American Democrats as being politically left like the British Labour Party or Swedish Social Democrats. We are inevitably pooling together disparate 'left' parties. What matters in such an exercise is not the 'left' parties' precise location on a continuum of ideology, but their placement in the context of the national party system. Political 'leftism' is invariably conceptualised in terms of a party being *more* sympathetic (compared with the national party of the political right) to an interventionist role for the government towards society and the economy, and more sympathetic to egalitarian policies.

The party political explanation sees contrasting policy preferences between left and right emerging from the different ideological preferences of partisans and/or the different demands of each party's electoral followings. The left parties, supported by the organised labour movement and the bulk of the working class, are expected to favour more government direction of the economy and egalitarianism; the right, backed by business and the middle class, to favour a market economy and place a lower value on equality. Interestingly, the development of Keynesian techniques has provided postwar governments with the policy instruments to choose between levels of price inflation and unemployment. For most of the postwar era higher levels of unemployment could be traded off against lower rates of inflation and vice versa. Governments, of course, want to maximise all desirable economic goals but this is rarely possible in practice. According to the above theory, a government's definition and choice of the lesser evil is shaped by the above forces.

Against the 'political' explanation there is frequently pitted an 'environmental' one. According to this, the party political variables are either subordinate to or mediated by economic factors or various other 'givens'. An early study by Fabricant (1952), for example, found that the growth in state and local expenditure in the United States over time was best explained by the rise in per capita income and such factors as urbanisation and population density. The correlation was confirmed by later studies. In so far as economic indicators are surrogate measures of a society's economic resources, the relationship is plausible enough. We might expect economic growth and such demographic trends as a growth in the number of old age pensioners and schoolchildren to result in higher levels of public expenditure as the extra resources become available to meet the rising demand for services.

Students of budgeting have noted the tendency of programme budgets to grow incrementally. A useful rule-of-thumb guide to what a department will spend next year, *other things being equal*, is to start with this year's total and allow a margin for growth or 'improvement' (Wildavsky, 1964). Rarely is there zero-based budgeting in which a programme is reviewed from scratch. The same logic has been true of public expenditure programmes in many countries. The expansion of the welfare state and the government's role in economic management have given rise to so many statutory commitments by the government and entitlements to state benefits that it is extremely difficult to cut programmes or central budgets. A number of studies have shown that the length of time a programme has existed affects its size; again the explanation hinges on incremental growth.

In the next section I present a series of propositions, the main burden of which states, summarily, that (*a*) political factors are important in affecting policy outputs, and (*b*) environmental factors are more important than political factors in affecting policy outputs.

## II Politics Does Make a Difference

### II.1 Party Control and Local Policies in Great Britain

Provision of many basic local services and the bulk of local government expenditure in Great Britain is affected by central government laws and regulations. Central government lays down minimum and sometimes uniform standards for services. It has other pressures at hand in that it supplies some 50 per cent of the finance of local authorities, and has the power to audit local authority expenditure. Yet where there is room for local discretion there are variations in local services according to party control. Labour authorities, for example, spend more money on council housing than do Conservative authorities (Alt, 1971; Boaden, 1971). The picture is confirmed in Sharpe's (1981) examination of total expenditure and programme expenditure for English counties and county boroughs at three periods, 1960/1, 1968/9, 1972/3. For both types of authority he found that the two political variables, Labour party strength and Conservative party strength,[4] correlated with expected outcomes. Labour control was associated with higher total expenditure, higher expenditure on the politicised and redistributive services like education and housing and lower spending on highways. Sharpe's view is that for various structural and ideological reasons the effect of the Labour Party in Britain on local policy outputs is greater than that of left parties in Western Europe.

### II.2 Party Control and Local and State Policies in the USA

Many early studies of the policy outputs of state and local government in the United States downgraded the role of political factors (see below, and p. 164). Subsequent studies have qualified the claim. Political factors, for example, have been found to be influential in state expenditures on welfare and education policies, though not on highways (Sharkansky and Hofferbert, 1969). Fry and Winters (1970) showed that, even if party and electoral factors were not important in influencing the absolute level of state expenditures, they did influence the redistribution of revenue burdens and benefits across social classes. A crucial and neglected point, however, has been whether competing political parties actually favour significant policy differences or are supported by different social groups. It is in such circumstances that one might expect party to make a difference. Jennings's (1979) examination of changes in welfare policy in eight American states between 1938 and 1970 found that where the electorate was divided on class lines, control by the lower-class party, the Democrats, did produce a shift to the lower class in per capita state welfare expenditure. The conclusion is that one should only look for differences in outputs where one might expect the differences.

### II.3 Changes in Party Control of Government in Adversarial Party Systems and Policies

The normal procedure for assessing the policy consequences of a change in government is to look at the association between a party's period in office and such outputs as actual legislation, or patterns of government expenditure, or the policy outcomes during that period.

One has to admit at the outset that there are certain constraints on our ability to study satisfactorily the effects of party government. Where the main parties which alternate in government are broadly agreed on policy goals, then we have no reason to look for or find differences. Where there are limits on the party's power in government – in the shape of a constitutional separation of powers (as in the United States) or coalitions (as in many West European states), or where there are infrequent changes of party control (as in France post-1958, Sweden, Italy post-1948) – then it is difficult to separate the influence of party from that of other factors.

Britain, however, presents a good test. For the entire period since 1945, when either Labour or the Conservative Party has been in sole control of the government, except for three years the party in government has enjoyed a majority in the House of Commons, and the government has not been checked by a written constitution, Supreme Court, or federalism. The party in government has the opportunity to implement its programme and the parties do provide a choice at elections. According to the *adversarial* critique of British party politics, this system has produced abrupt reversals of policy when one party replaces another in government because of the growing disagreements between the parties (Finer, 1975). One can certainly point to a number of fields – secondary education, the Common Market, industrial relations, regional aids for industry and prices and incomes – where this has occurred in the 1970s. The adversarial critique is correct in one sense. The Conservative and Labour manifestos promise different policies and, when in office, parties do achieve a large number of their promises. This is particularly so when the promises can be cast in the form of parliamentary legislation and the government has the disciplined majority in Parliament to get the measure passed. British governments find it more difficult, however, to achieve promises of broader policy goals of 'prosperity', 'equality', or 'lower inflation'. And some alterations in major areas of policy – such as the shifts in levels of public expenditure or adoption or abandonment of a formal prices and incomes policy – are as likely to occur within the lifetime of a government as to follow changes of government.

## II.4 Different Political Systems and Different Policies

It is not surprising that countries with different levels of resources and different histories have different maps of policies. In this sense, perhaps a trivial one, each system possesses some characteristics which make it unique. This does not mean, however, that one cannot make some useful general statements about policies across industrialised states.

First, there are important differences in policies between East European Systems and the pluralist regimes in Western Europe. The former governments take a much higher share of GDP in public expenditure and are more active in the extraction and distribution of resources (Pryor, 1968). In the centralised East European system, per capita income is important in affecting spending for foreign aid and research development, but not for education, health and defence. Parkin (1971) similarly sees important differences between what he terms *command* (East Europe) and *market* societies. Governments in the *command* societies, because of the centralisation of power, are better able to impose their values on society. In market or *pluralist* societies, by contrast, governments are limited by having to share power with other groups, a factor which inhibits the radicalising policy effects of any change in government.

Secondly, there are also differences across industrialised societies in the West. One study which mapped the different role of the state in services across the United States and West European states explained the more limited role of government in the United States not in terms of different elites, demands, political institutions, or pressure groups, but in terms of ideas and political culture (King, 1973). In the United States there has been a suspicion of state power, and a respect for traditional liberal ideas of self-sufficiency and individualism. The country was slower to adopt nationwide programmes for social welfare and, except for education, still spends less on them as a share of GNP than other comparable Western states. The greater commitment to education could also be related to American values of equality of opportunity and individualism. Historical approaches have shown the national differences in handling problems of social welfare (Heclo, 1974), or different emphases on aspects of social policy, or differences in starting dates and components of programmes (Heidenheimer, 1973).

Thirdly, public opinion enters any analysis in establishing the broad lines of 'acceptable' policies. Almond and Verba (1963) touched on this subject in examining the role of culture as a 'background' factor to the way different political systems operated. But how do different national complexes of institutions, elites and experiences interact with public opinion to shape the political agenda? Both Marxist and liberal analysts of postwar Western capitalism have agreed that the achievement of welfare provision and full employment were important in gaining the consent of organised labour to established political and economic arrangements. In the United States, Wilson and Banfield (1964) have shown how a different 'ethos' or orientation to politics has shaped the political agenda in different communities. A *public-regarding ethos* supports programmes which benefit the whole community; a *private-regarding ethos* takes a more parochial view of desirable policies.

### II.5(*a*) Left Party Control of Government and Macro-Economic Outcomes

A large number of studies have found that left party control of government produces expected differences in patterns of policies compared to those of a right-controlled government. Hewitt (1977) found a consistently positive relationship between left-party dominance in twenty-five Western states and egalitarian policies (reflected in redistribution of incomes and access to higher education). Cameron (1978) reported that greater left strength in government in eighteen Western states was associated with a sharper growth of the public sector between 1960 and 1975. Hibbs (1977) found that across twelve West European and North American countries between 1960 and 1969 leftist governments were more sensitive to increases in unemployment, while rightist governments were more sensitive to increases in inflation. Socialist parties seemed to reflect the greater concern of their working-class supporters over unemployment while parties of the right reflected the middle-class concern over inflation. The different political values of the parties resulted in different perceptions of whether unemployment or inflation was the greater economic threat, and their selection of policy responses entailed different public expenditure and taxation policies. Left governments induced lower levels of unemployment than governments of the right, but at a cost of higher levels of inflation. Elsewhere Hibbs (1978) shows that the rate of strike activity has decreased in those states with governments which are wholly or partly leftist in composition.

There is, therefore, an impressive array of studies showing that the control of government by different parties, with different ideological and class-interest propensities, affect policies. A more specific statement of proposition II.5(*b*) follows.

### II.5(*b*) Left Dominance Accompanied by the Weakness of the Political Right and Macro-Economic Outcomes

The finding that Sweden, Norway, Denmark and the Netherlands devote more public resources to welfare expenditure than other Western states appears, at first sight, to suggest the importance of party political control of government (Castles, 1979; Castles and McKinlay, 1979). The composite index of welfare used by Castles is based on infant mortality, government share of GDP, spending on public expenditure as proportion of GDP, and GDP per capita. All four of these countries have a higher than expected welfare score, while Belgium, Switzerland, Luxembourg and Finland score lower than expected. What the three Scandinavian states have in common is long periods of Social Democratic dominance of the government. Although the Netherlands is also highly placed, the left has had a much weaker presence in Dutch governments than in governments of the other three states. What appears to be important in the Dutch case is the weakness of the political right, a factor shared with the other countries. Castles suggests that it is large parties of the political right that are major impediments to high levels of welfare provision; this, as much as the strength of the political left, is important. It is the feature which *all* four high-spending societies have in common.

### II.6 Political Systems and Economic Growth

There is some evidence that, under *ceteris paribus* conditions, authoritarian and one-party regimes do better in promoting economic growth than competitive regimes. Protected from the threat of electoral competition, significant political opposition, or a free press, the governments are more willing to sacrifice personal consumption to investment (Adelman and Morris, 1967). It is worth noting, however, that these claims have been confirmed only in the case of the less economically developed states.

The above propositions argue that politics is important in determining the form of policies and policy outputs. Political variables (e.g. party systems, party control of government, and institutions) are important in shaping policy demands (e.g. socialist parties press for greater welfare expenditure, redistribution, full employment) and the adoption of policies (e.g. parties choose policies on the basis of their ideologies or the perceived interests and demands of their supporters). In the next section I examine a series of propositions which suggests that the impact of political factors is weaker than that of environmental factors.

## III The Environment Makes More Difference than Politics

### III.1 There Is No Significant Difference in Economic Policy Outcomes with Changes of Government

For reasons already mentioned on page 159, Britain furnishes a useful case to test this proposition. Note that the test here is not of intention and legislation but of outcomes; the parties may differ in terms of their policies and legislation but be unable to produce different outcomes. British elections in recent years have increasingly dealt with economic matters – inflation, growth, unemployment and prosperity. Yet if we turn to the record of different party governments it is striking how little of a consistent partisan pattern there is in outcomes. Richard Rose's recent *Do Parties Make a Difference?* (1980) is perhaps the most systematic examination yet of the differences in macro-economic conditions which have been associated with the periods of Labour and Conservative government since 1957.

For example, increases in the growth of public expenditure correlate hardly at all with changes in party control of government. The sharpest discontinuities in the rate of its growth have often been within the lifetime of a government. For example, the Conservatives' record of containment in 1953–7 was followed by the expansionist period of 1957–64; and record of the Labour government 1974–6 (a sharp rise) contrasted with that of 1977–8 (a sharp fall). In constant price terms, public expenditure has increased in eighteen of the twenty-one years between 1957 and 1978. In the last two decades the proportion of public expenditure as a share of GNP has increased over the lifetime of all governments. The picture is broadly the same for other OECD countries. Klein (1976) finds no clear and consistent relationship between levels of spending on particular programmes and which party is in power. Both British parties have regarded public expenditure as a policy instrument, part of general strategy for depressing or stimulating aggregate demand, and have allowed for its expansion out of anticipated economic growth. The three years of decline in amounts of public expenditure were all achieved under Labour and were all undertaken as part of the government's general anti-inflation policies. If there were steep surges under Labour in 1964 and 1974–6, the major reduction was under Labour in 1977–8.

If we turn to the redistribution of wealth between 1960 and 1977, the share of the nation's wealth claimed by the top 10 per cent of people fell from 63 to 44 per cent, a trend that continued regardless of party. On other macro-economic indicators, such as the size of the public sector deficit, rates of inflation, and levels of unemployment, economic growth and minimum lending rate, there have been similar changes in direction – a secular rise in each over time, regardless of distinctive party programmes and policies. The trend in average rates of economic growth for each successive government has also been downward for all governments since 1959. The economy grew by 2·6 per cent per annum under the Macmillan government, 2·2 per cent under the first Wilson government, 1·4 per cent under Heath and 1·1 per cent under Wilson and Callaghan (Rose, 1980, p. 128). The record of economic decline does not constitute proof that the parties do not differ in their intentions. The lack of variation according to party does, however, argue more for the constraints of circumstances than the positive influence of party ideology.

### III.2 Party Makes Little Difference to the Rise in the Government Share of GDP

The evidence is fairly clear about the continuous rise in public expenditure as a share of GDP over the past twenty years; spending on social programmes has increased as a proportion of public expenditure and the proportion spent on defence has declined in the postwar period. Rose and Peters (1978, p. 55) studying West European states between 1951 and 1976, found no significant statistical relationship between the number of years a party of the left controlled a country's government and the growth of public expenditure. The biggest percentage increase was in Italy, which has had right-dominated governments for the entire period, and the lowest percentage increase was in Britain which over this period has had approximately equal Labour and Conservative periods of rule.

Cameron (1978), while allowing a role for left governments in expanding the size of the public sector, accords more importance to a country having an 'open economy' (p. 1255), that is, a relatively high exposure to, and dependence on, external producers and consumers. His explanation is that national decision-makers assume that the vulnerability which stems from this situation is best offset by the state assuming a more active role in promoting political and economic objectives. His leftist-governed countries scored high on government's intervention in the economy, but so did the Netherlands, Belgium, Ireland and Canada, countries that have not had frequent spells of leftist rule. What the two groups of political systems have in common is an 'open' economy and a high level of industrial concentration. This last feature in turn tends to be associated with a high degree of worker unionisation, a leftist outlook in government and a larger public sector.

There are several studies which argue that rises in public expenditure are due to general trends, and proceed regardless of politics. In the late nineteenth century the German economist Wagner suggested that the supply of government services expanded more than the growth of GNP. Other economists have noted a tendency for public expenditure to grow during wars and, because of a 'displacement effect', to be sustained at a high level in peacetime (Peacock and Wiseman, 1961).

## III.3 Political Variables Have Little Relation to Policy Outputs in American States

The famous early studies by Dawson and Robinson (1963), broadly confirmed later by Dye (1969) and Hofferbert (1966), suggested that socio-economic factors (per capita income, urbanisation and industrialisation) were more important than political variables (inter-party competition, turnout, party controls and malapportionment) in affecting expenditure on welfare policies. The studies regarded the policy variable as total level of expenditure, though Dye also included measures of expenditures on health and welfare programmes. Dawson later showed that high party competition and high amounts of expenditure were both independently related to socio-economic development. Controlling for the political factor showed that the economic factors were more important influences on the level of expenditure. Such a conclusion was chastening to proponents of the efficacy of the electoral and party process (cf. Key, 1949). It also challenged the tendency to assume that democratisation expressed in party competitiveness, equal representation of districts and high turnout at elections would continue to stimulate higher spending.

### III.4 Political Variables Have Little Relation to Policy Outputs in West European Local Governments

Replicative studies have broadly confirmed the earlier American findings on local state expenditure. Fried (1971) found that, contrary to his expectations, Communist-controlled cities in Italy pursued more conservative fiscal policies than cities controlled by Christian Democrats. More generally, he later commented (pp. 337–43):

> The socio-economic constraints are such, it would appear, that it makes little difference for urban policy who controls local urban government, what their values are, how many people turn out to vote, what policies the community-at-large or the activists prefer, or how the community is organised for governmental purposes.

### III.5 Politics Has Little Relation to Variations in Social Security Expenditure as a Proportion of GDP

Cutright (1965) found that the best predictor of levels of welfare expenditure was socio-economic development, though the representativeness of the political institutions was not far behind in importance. Similarly, Wilensky (1975), in a study of twenty-two industrialised societies, found that levels of social welfare expenditure varied more with three environmental factors:

- economic development, or per capita GNP,
- population structure,
- age of programme.

Such factors as gross categories of economic system (capitalist versus communist), or political system (liberal democratic or authoritarian), or elite ideology (e.g. beliefs in equality and planning on individualism) were, by comparison, unimportant. To quote Wilensky's assessment (p. xiii):

> economic growth and its demographic and bureaucratic outcomes are the root cause of the general emergence of the welfare state. As for the political system and ideological factors, these categories are almost useless in explaining the origins and general development of the welfare state.

There were general pressures in all industrial societies for a common set of income-maintenance programmes.

Parkin (1971, chs 4, 6), with a rather miscellaneous set of data, agrees that there have been limited moves to egalitarianism in Western capitalist societies. Yet he suggests that the role of left parties in promoting this redistribution has been limited, for the changes have proceeded under right-wing governments as well. His explanation (p. 183), like that of Miliband, is that socialist egalitarianism is incompatible with pluralist democracy in capitalist societies. The political procedures, dominant values and major economic interests continue to weaken the radical impact of socialist parties.

The burden of these findings is fairly clear. Politics, operationalised largely in terms of party political factors, is not so important in shaping policies, certainly when compared to environmental factors. Welfare and mixed economy policies appear, for the most part, to be part of a package that goes with being an industrialised, urbanised, affluent Western society. Implicit in this view is the presence of pressures or so-called 'imperatives', both on the demand side (consumers, pensioners, students, general awareness of problems) and the supply side (resources, competing politicians and bureaucrats), which operate to produce a convergence of policies. These pressures are largely determined by the environment, even though there is a recognition of their interaction with groups and electoral politics, and so on. The force of incrementalism, even of the disjointed kind, in which established policies gradually evolve over time, are supported by many powerful groups and are not thoroughly reviewed *de novo,* only emphasises the difficulty of change when one government replaces another.

## IV Conclusion

It is understandable if such a welter of contradictory findings from so many studies invites a reaction close to despair. The body of literature points to no clear-cut conclusion. Some studies show that some factors have an influence on policy outcomes, while other studies show the reverse. Although follow-up studies provide some elaboration and specification of earlier findings, what emerges is a set of almost idiosyncratic findings, confined to particular periods, places, policy output, political and/or environmental variable(s), and even research approaches and statistical methods. The last point is illustrated by Sullivan (1972) who, for example, by employing different statistical methods, reversed the findings of Fry and Winters (1970) about the relative importance of political factors and the redistributive effects of policies. The conclusion about the relative importance of political to other factors remains somewhat indeterminate. This is rather chastening, given the large number of studies, the elaborate collections of data and the statistical ingenuity employed.

One reason for this note of caution is simply that, contrary to the frequent claims that the studies are cumulative, so many are non-comparable. Precise testing of previous claims and the accumulation of a body of knowledge is not helped when studies choose different countries, different time-periods, different independent and dependent variables and different indicators for the same variables (e.g. for the provision of social welfare). Thus, 'the use of discrete indicators, methods, and hypotheses in each study results in a non-additive body of literature, unable to establish a major relation among the environmental political systems and policy' (Munns, 1975, p. 667). Parkin (1971), for example, talks about the ineffectiveness of Social Democratic parties in *changing the reward structure* of capitalist societies, whereas Castles (1978), using fairly similar indicators to Parkin's, talks about the success of these parties in *improving the socio-economic conditions of the working class,* in societies where parties of the political right are weak. Wilensky (1975) concludes that political factors are relatively unimportant in welfare expenditures. Yet he also acknowledges the influence of a well-organised working class in affecting the expenditure, which others might regard as a political factor.

The tendency to regard the political and environmental factors as competitive has hardly helped understanding of the policy process. Clearly, at extremes of high or low economic development, the environment and its repercussions on resources are important. Some environmental factors, like the age composition of the population, or level of industrialism and urbanism, affect the demand for services. Some factors, like per capita income (for taxable capacity) and population growth, affect both the demand and supply for services (Fried, 1975, p. 325). Walker (1969) found that the more economically developed, affluent American states were more innovative when it came to starting new programmes. The greater resource base appeared to provide an extra margin for creating new policies or adapting existing ones. This is a speculative linkage, yet most studies, with their correlational approaches, fail to establish the linkages between the environment and the outputs. We have to remind ourselves that not all environmental conditions are transformed into policy demands and responses; some problems become political issues and reach the political agenda, and some do not. And here the perceptions and activities of elites, parties, interest groups and the shape of public opinion are important in transforming the inputs from the environment.

Party politics is more likely to have an impact under certain conditions. Impact in this context means the production of an intended outcome which would be different from that if another party were in control of government: that is, party difference produces outcome difference. The first condition is that the parties should have distinctive policy attributes and/or distinctive electoral followings. If there is no disagreement between the parties, no contrasting policies and/or no distinctive clienteles, then there are a few *a priori* reasons to expect parties to have an impact. A second condition is that political office allows sufficient leverage *vis-à-vis* society for the ruling party to make changes. This is obviously more likely where the party rules alone or is the dominant partner in a coalition, and where political power is effectively centralised in the executive. Political systems with written constitutions, provision for judicial review and a separation of powers are effectively power-sharing systems which impose formal checks on the government (e.g. the United States, Canada, Australia and West Germany). Britain and France, which lack all or most of these features, provide examples of power centralisation. The same broad line of argument applies to local government as well. Local governments in Italy and Scandinavia usually have all-party or coalitional executives, and the power executive systems represented by the mayor (United States) or the *Burgomeister* (West Germany) give the local political leadership some independence from party pressures in formulating policy. Both systems tend to depress the possibility of party ideology producing distinctive policy outputs (Sharpe, 1981).

A third condition is that the party will be in office long enough to have an impact on policies. A long tenure in office also increases the ability of the party to modify the context of politics – the institutions, socio-economic structure and climate of opinion – to its liking. Castles comments (1978) that Sweden reflects a 'Social Democratic image of society', which is the product of the lengthy period of Social Democratic rule. Parties of the political right in Sweden have gradually had to compromise with a set of assumptions and expectations which have been largely shaped by the forty-year dominance of government by the Social Democrats. The period of Labour rule in Britain between 1945 and 1951 produced a convergence of policies as subsequent Conservative governments accepted the new policies. A similar process was achieved by Roosevelt's 'New Deal' policies. (Ironically, this line of analysis is usually appropriated by left-wing critics of the 'hegemony' of ruling-class ideas in other capitalist societies; they argue that the political left is neutralised by the dominant values which are hostile to the left.) The outcome is a paradox: changes in party control of government may not produce much difference in policy outputs, largely because one party or group of parties has dominated government for so long, and the policy agenda to such an extent, that new parties in government have to come to terms with a consensus shaped largely by their opponents. The limited policy impact of a new government is not a reflection of the limits of politics but of the influence at an earlier stage. Many policies or agendas emerge from the interplay of various factors at one point *in time in the past:* cross-sectional analysis tends to miss the importance of the originating conditions. In other words, in trying to measure the 'impact' or 'influence' of parties, we are likely to find influence of only one side at a formative period, and that in creating what then becomes the status quo.

The neglect of the distribution of public opinion is curious in the treatment of policy outputs. The responsible party model assumes, at the outset, that parties will differ on policies and that these differences will bear some relationship to the preferences of their electoral followings. But, on a number of issues, public opinion may be so consensual that a party provides a different and minority choice at its electoral risk. In Britain, for example, there are constraints on sharp class-related differences in policies between the two main parties. Both parties draw more of their support from the working class – even though there remain class differences in the profile of support for the parties – and a majority of voters agree on many of the policies raised at elections. The same observations are true of the United States. In such cases there is a push from public opinion for some similarity or overlap in many policies between the parties. A theme of the 'end of ideology' literature of the 1960s was that, as the traditional divide between parties of the left and right had been narrowed, so a new consensus – a 'conservative socialism' – on the mixed economy and welfare state had emerged.

We are surely interested in how the outputs are perceived by the public or by the clients or groups at which they are directed. Marxists (O'Connor, 1973; Gough, 1979) have been sensitive to the role of full employment and welfare policies in helping political stability in Western states in the postwar era. During the economic recession the welfare commitment and the squeeze on corporate profits may be producing a 'fiscal crisis of Western capitalism' (O'Connor). In Northern Ireland policies by the Unionist majority over the years have alienated the Catholic minority and further undermined the legitimacy of the regime. Consociational styles of decision-making in other divided societies (e.g. Switzerland, the Netherlands and Austria) have purchased higher levels of consent from the population. Students of political culture are aware of the non-instrumental basis of legitimacy to a regime. Outputs alone are not enough. In the 1970s levels of life satisfaction in West European states appear to have remained steady, notwithstanding a worsening political economy (Rose, 1980).

The findings of the aggregate statistical studies are the beginning rather than the end of an explanation of what determines the policies. They provide a wide range of relationships between factors across countries. But given the heterogeneity, even confusion, of the sum of the findings, and the gap between causation and correlation, there remains much room for argument. The detailed historical studies of the development of particular policies in a country or a sample of countries may provide a more promising approach for gaining an understanding of the precise linkages in the process and testing the general relationships suggested in the aggregate statistical approaches (Heclo, 1974; Heidenheimer *et al.*, 1975). Of course, the environmental factors are important and one is not suggesting that the political scientist should limit his consideration of possible causes of policy outputs. It would be premature, however, to suggest that politics does not matter.

At the same time, we do not have to oversell the case for the influence of politics. The policies of a government are but one factor affecting the policy process. They interact with the social and economic context, interest group pressures, the climate of opinion, the pre-existing situation, and international and other influences. There are claims anyway that parties – because they choose to be 'catch-all' bodies and de-emphasise ideology to win elections, or because they are relatively weak institutions in comparison with, say, the bureaucracy (King, 1969; Rose, 1974, 1980) – may count for less than we might have expected. Again, there are constraints on any government which is limited by its dependence on the co-operation of other actors, shortage of resources and the sheer intractability of problems. These pose obstacles to party government. In a sense, the environmental emphasis on social and economic factors, because it reminds us of the administrative and economic feasibility of policies, is a framework that represents a set of constraints and opportunities. On the other hand, the political, institutional and the culture factors touch on what is politically possible.

One wonders, therefore, how useful an exercise it is for students to regard these as mutually exclusive factors and then to proceed to weigh their relative influence. An appreciation of how they interact in different contexts and time-periods is apparent in recent work. For instance, when Klein examined the utility of different governmental political and socio-economic explanations of changes in the level of public expenditure in postwar Britain, he found that no one approach, taken alone, was a sufficient explanation. Each approach contributed an element to the general explanation. The explanatory power of the particular model in part depended on its focus – whether it was total expenditure on a programme or expenditure on a sub-programme. The problem was to fit the approaches together, given the reasonable assumption that the level of public spending was determined by the interaction of these factors. A further step in this direction was taken by Sharkansky and Hofferbert (1969), who showed that high levels of local state expenditure on education and welfare were related both to level of affluence in the state and levels of party competitiveness and high turnout, while the programmes on highways and natural resources were inversely related to industrialism and population density. There is, it appears, no simple answer to the question 'Is it politics or economics that has the greater impact on public policy?' (p. 878).

Simeon (1976, p. 556) has sensibly suggested the potential usefulness of the voting behaviour model, 'the funnel of causality'. With this approach, one starts with those factors which are distant from the actual policy decision – the environment, history, geography, culture, resources, and so on. As one moves closer to the actual decision, to the demands, the framing of policy alternatives, the preferences of elites and the decision-making institutions, so the political variables become more central to the analysis. One clearly requires the former perspective for a preliminary mapping of the available economic resources, the social structure and for an appreciation of what is probable or improbable (e.g. generous provision of welfare spending or higher education is unlikely in an economically backward country). One needs the political variables to understand the short-run changes in policy, differences in detail, and the timing and exact shape of policy. The field illustrates the unfortunate tendency

> for each discipline, or specialty within a discipline, to develop a proprietary interest in a variable, taking it as a matter of honour to prove that its variable is most important or at the very least is not cast into the outer darkness of statistical insignificance. (Heclo, 1974, p. 285)

In political science we seem to be stranded between the studies of inputs (Chapters 2, 3, 4, 5) and outputs (Chapters 6, 8), while neglecting what happens in between. As Simeon comments (1976, p. 556):

> Much of the literature has tended to focus on one end of the funnel without taking account of the other. Thus work on the environment has tended to ignore the 'black box' of the political process, while work on the process has tended to ignore the setting within which it operates.

Finally, it is worth considering the possibility that continuities over time, similarities across cases and incremental change may arise from 'routines' which are deeply embedded in the political process, and have little to do with socio-economic factors. Incrementalism is a form of policy routine or decision rule which helps to simplify the process of making budgets (Sharkansky, 1970). It is also a way of sheltering the policy-makers from critical scrutiny; concentrating on the increment narrows the policy area for examination and means that existing lines of policy are not examined from scratch. Incrementalism is a means by which past decisions determine most future expenditure (Wildavsky, 1964). Limits of time, intelligence and information encourage decision-makers to adopt incrementalism rather than the rational comprehensive method (Lindblom, 1959). In other words, the importance of politics is reflected as much in continuity of policy as in change.

But policy routines may be jolted by circumstances and by policy-makers who provide new ways of looking at problems, redefining options and recasting the costs and benefits of alternative policies. Examples of the former include wars, new legislation, rapid economic growth or decline, or a sharp increase in the number of clients for a programme (e.g. for unemployment, or higher education). Such factors weaken the routine of incremental budgeting (Sharkansky, 1970). A fair retort to proponents of socio-economic determinism is made by Hofferbert (1974, pp. 226–7):

> a full explication of environmental contexts is essential to aid illumination of the behaviour of policy-making elites. Interactional analysis (*à la* community studies) . . . is insufficient without a specification of the external boundaries that define, to a greater or lesser extent, the range of probable behaviours by those doing the interacting.

## Notes: Chapter 8

1 'The executive of the modern state is but a committee for managing the common affairs of the whole bourgeoisie' (The Communist Manifesto).
2 Most elite studies have been concerned more with demonstrating who participates in policy-making than with assessing who gains and loses from the pattern of allocations. The answer about who participates in policy-making may or may not be identical to the question of who gains from the outcomes.
3 It is difficult to assess the effects of a particular measure because so many outcomes have a number of causes. Not only does the measure interact with other inputs but immediate effects have to be separated from those stemming over the passage of time.
4 'Strength' was indicated by the party percentage of seats and the number of years it controlled the council.

Chapter 9

# Political Participation and Political Democracy

There are many definitions and many types of democracy. To offer the popular definition of 'the rule of the people' invites a series of further questions on what is meant by 'rule' and 'the people'. Democracy is a complex, ambiguous term and one which, of course, carries evaluative overtones. Most states claim to be 'democratic'. Revolutions are made in the name of democracy, and to be charged with being undemocratic is a mark of disfavour. In most formulations of democracy, widespread participation by the population in influencing important political decisions is a recurring feature: in definitions of liberal and representative democracy, for example, the designation and control of the leaders by the electorate is the key element. One writer, Robert Dahl (1971), has recently used the term 'polyarchy' to refer to regimes which provide for extensive participation and a choice or competition between teams of leaders. These are systems which provide for a continuing responsiveness of the government to the preferences of its citizens, considered as political equals; such institutions as political parties, pressure groups and competitive elections, and such procedures as limits on government, constitutionalism, and so on, are means to this end. For the moment let us accept a democratic system as one that permits participation, by the adult population, either directly or indirectly, in influencing political decisions and the selection of rulers.

This chapter looks at two important aspects of the question of political democracy. First, it looks at the normative implications or conclusions of empirical studies of political participation. Secondly, it examines some of the recent findings about participation – findings which I consider to be interesting and important in their own right.

## Political Theory and Democracy

Studies of political behaviour have certainly had an impact on political theory, both normative and empirical. Some students have, however, raised the question whether or not the methods of modern social science are suitable for grappling with traditional and/or normative political theory on such issues. In no area, perhaps, has the impact been more marked than in that of democratic theory. There is a continuing difference of view as to whether studies of public opinion and electoral behaviour, for example, should have such an effect on theories of democracy. Those who accept that theory is descriptive, in part at least, logically accept the relevance of empirical findings for testing appropriate parts of those theories. Others who regard theories as normative, as statements of ideals, may consider the findings interesting but ultimately irrelevant to the purpose of theorising. Clearly, these are two separate views of 'theories'. Only the former acknowledges that those parts of theories which do relate to empirical conditions may be set against or derived from such findings. Among those aspects of democratic theory and of democracy as a form of government which have been studied empirically (cf. Cnudde and Neubauer, 1969), we may refer to the following features which have been examined as 'conditions':

- the level of education of the population;
- consensus on democratic values;
- political structures and institutions;
- historical development of the society;
- social and economic conditions.

These studies usually proceed to a definition of democracy by seeking the common properties which are found across a range of democracies and/or seeking the properties of those states which distinguish them from non-democracies. The problem with this approach to defining democracy, however, is that by starting off with a view of which states are already democratic, and deriving a definition from this, we end up with a tautology. The United States and Britain are democracies; democracy is what we find in the United States and Britain. A radically different view of theory is to specify the concept in advance and then see to what extent real-life conditions approximate it. Such theories of democracy are essentially normative, arguing the case for a particular value or outcome, regardless of whether or not the condition is achieved.

One problem with current debate on this subject is that much of the analysis has been largely narrowed down to two rival schools. On one side are the so-called *traditional* or classical democratic theorists; these theorists are rarely specified but usually encompass Rousseau, the two Mills and de Tocqueville. The common link between them is thought to be their agreement on the worth of participation, at least for the individual. Ranged against them are the 'democratic elitists', such as Lipset, Almond, Dahl, Berelson and Eckstein. These scholars favour democracy but, in contrast to the classical theorists, grant a positive role to the autonomy of elites and to a degree of popular apathy. Yes, attempts to divide these scholars into two groups risk ignoring differences between them, the different occasions and purposes of their writings, the subtleties and ambiguities within each individual's work and the developments in it over time. There is a good dose of elitism in the work of de Tocqueville and J. S. Mill, for example, and Dahl has been sensitive to the shortcomings of contemporary political institutions and to the case for more participation. In the next section we examine the main planks of the two schools (Kavanagh, 1972a, 1972b).

## Traditional or Citizenship Theory

The belief that an intrinsic merit of extensive political participation is the possibility for the individual's self-realisation or self-development is appropriately associated with John Stuart Mill. This argument is separate from the instrumental claim that participation by a group or an individual is important for the protection of interests. In the early decades of this century Mill's argument was carried further by a group of 'citizenship theorists' (Thompson, 1970). At that time these writers had to confront claims (e.g. by Mosca or Pareto) that elite or minority rule was inevitable and also conservative criticism of popular participation. Citizenship theorists, who were optimistic about the prospects for and consequences of greater public involvement in politics, included Charles Merriam, T. V. Smith and John Dewey in the United States, and Graham Wallas and A. D. Lindsay in England. These writers differed from contemporary elitists over two presuppositions. As pro-participants they believed in the individual's *autonomy* (that the individual is the best judge of his own interests) as well as his *improvability* (that the individual's existing stock of political wisdom could be increased given greater education and certain social and political changes). What would emerge, given greater participation, would be better citizens, endowed with a 'largeness of spirit', and a more responsible and public-minded society. By and large, this school is normative – though empirical – in its approach to political participation. It regards participation as a worthwhile end in itself, and defects in public opinion are not regarded as inevitable (i.e. as part of human nature) or as a sufficient reason to restrict public participation in politics. And political participation is certainly regarded as something in addition to voting in elections.

## Democratic Elitism

A more empirical theory of democracy has moved the old debate between defenders and critics of democracy, which had been largely normative, on to a new plane. Many behavioural students of politics have taken issue, implicitly or explicitly, with the citizenship theorists on three main grounds. First, they have observed how widespread is political apathy, how great is the individual's shortfall from the ideal. Many voters are not well-informed about issues and have little sympathy with liberal and democratic principles. Almond and Verba (1963), for example, set out to test a model of the good citizen of democratic theory (a rational-activist model), in which the individual is informed, active and interested in politics. When they found that the ideal citizens were only a small minority, they proceeded to revise democratic theory along more 'realistic', 'elitist' lines to take account of the findings. Secondly, these writers have charged that the traditional concern to promote mass involvement in politics took inadequate account of a major requisite of the political system, namely, that of stability. They feared that this could be upset by high levels of participation. Thirdly, they have alleged that the pro-participants undervalued the importance of political elites. Because the qualities of civility, tolerance and support for liberal democratic principles were disproportionately found among people of higher social status and education, then apathy among other groups could be a useful safeguard for liberal values. Agreement on democratic values among the activists was important in stabilising the system. The desired political balance, according to these behaviouralists, involves a measure of apathy by citizens which will permit a wide degree of governmental initiative. Campbell *et al.* suggest that our traditional ideas need to be revised because the electorate 'is almost completely unable to judge the rationality of government actions; knowing little of the particular policies and what has led to them, the mass electorate is not able either to appraise its goals or the appropriateness of the means chosen to secure these goals' (1960, p. 543). This behaviourally oriented interpretation claims to be based on the observed attitudes and conduct of citizens and thus to be more in tune with the *real* political world. Previously, it is asserted, there was a marked discontinuity between democratic theory, as developed by J. S. Mill and his sympathisers, and democratic practice. The techniques of social science enable the behaviouralists to claim to distinguish themselves from the traditional elitist and democratic theorists on two methodological grounds: (1) that they are non-normative, or neutral with regard to values, for they are concerned with what is and not with what ought to be; (2) that they are concerned to develop hypotheses which can be given an empirical content, operationalised and thus tested.

These authors believe, however, that in spite of the shortcomings of individual citizens, the political system (usually Anglo-American) is working satisfactorily. According to Berelson *et al.* (1954) for example, 'where the rational citizen seems to abdicate, nevertheless angels seem to tread' (p. 311), and '*Individual voters* today seem unable to satisfy the requirements for a democratic system of government outlined by political theorists. But the *system of democracy* does meet certain requirements for a going political organisation. The individual members may not meet all the standards but the whole nevertheless survives and grows' (p. 312). Instead of clinging to atomistic concepts of political behaviour, as traditional theorists were inclined to do, the new theorists claim to be more sensitive to the likely consequences of the summation of individual acts and orientations for the political system. The needs of the political system for stability and effectiveness require that a wide measure of initiative be left to the elite. These requirements in turn, according to Almond and Verba, demand that 'the involvement, activity, and influence of the ordinary man be limited . . . the ordinary citizen [needs to be] relatively passive, uninvolved and deferential to elites' (1963, p. 478). In bringing about and sustaining a stable democracy and a civic culture, then, apathy on the part of a large section of the electorate is a positive good. Participation, according to this restatement, though clearly necessary if the government is to be sensitive to popular demands, needs to be curbed or traded off so that other desirable goals may be achieved. This concern about the 'excesses' of participation is not confined to behaviouralists. Students of public policy and political development have pointed to the politically destabilising consequences of rapid increases in participation or high levels of 'demand' participation (cf. Huntington, 1974; Brittan, 1975). It is possible to envisage 'trade-offs' between increases in participation above a certain (but which?) level, and negative consequences for other goals. It is extremely difficult, however, to state the relationships in terms which are susceptible to measurement (cf. Huntington and Nelson, 1976).

In this restatement, democracy is seen as a political method, rather than as a form of society, or political system, or as an end in itself. According to Schumpeter (1942, p. 269; emphasis added) it is '*that institutional arrangement* for arriving at political decisions in which individuals acquire the power to decide by means of a competitive struggle for the people's vote'. Lipset (1959, p. 27) describes democracy as the system 'which supplies regular constitutional opportunities for changing the governing officials and a social mechanism which permits the largest possible participation of the population to influence major decisions'. The behaviourally based thesis is highly sympathetic to the elitist restatement of democracy already alluded to. Both are hostile to the participatory ethic, as procedure and as goal, and doubtful about the practicality of achieving significant degrees of self-government and political equality. Bottomore (1965, p. 117) comments that in these revisions democracy has become a static term 'in which elite rule is sanctioned by periodic elections'. Both Lipset and Schumpeter attempt to fuse the once mutually opposed principles of democracy and aristocracy; both accord overriding priority to the stability and strength of representative government, the security of which is seen to be threatened by widespread participation. Leadership, competition between political parties and the provision of free elections to facilitate the expression of choice are the key concepts in both the elitist and empirical theories of democracy.

## Participatory Democrats

Separate and not always internally consistent criticisms are made of the above approach. Indeed, there has developed a distinctive school of critics of democratic elitism and what may be called the *participatory* theory of democracy. Before commenting on the criticism I should make clear, first, that elitism is not regarded here either as a pejorative term or as being necessarily hostile to democracy and, secondly, that I think it is reasonable to theorise about democracy on the basis of empirical findings about public opinion and electoral behaviour.

There are three main criticisms made of the so-called elitists. The first is that much of their work, indeed the new theory, is itself normative. This is ironic because a central thrust of the behavioural reaction against the traditional theorists was on account of the non-falsifiable nature of the latter's work. Much of the empirical research on the Anglo-American political system, however, has been highly satisfied with the status quo and has assumed that the conditions of democracy have already been achieved (and not, *à la* Mill, that the conditions, even if likely to remain unfulfilled, should still be striven for). Many of the writers adopt a pluralist perspective, one that assumes that different groups have adequate access to the authoritative decision-making structures, that all issues are properly processed by this machinery, and that the rulers are fairly responsive to a wide variety of demands, (cf. Chapter 8 above).

A second criticism is that the writers have invariably adopted a macro- not a micro-perspective, and looked at the question of the individual's participation primarily from the point of view of its consequences for the stability and effectiveness of the political system rather than from that of the individual. To assert or demonstrate that a political system is a stable democracy neither disproves nor renders irrelevant the contention of the citizenship theorists who were more concerned with the capacity of political institutions to promote the individual's moral, intellectual and social betterment. Indeed, a crucial part of the participatory case turns on the gains for the individual's personality and self-esteem which come from participation. There is, therefore, a clear difference between the contending schools on the vision of democracy and/or the relevance of empirical findings for democratic theory. For example, Almond and Verba, on the basis of the discrepancy between the ideals of the rational-active citizen and their findings for Britain and America, argue that the standards of the former may have been set unreasonably high. Any theory of democracy should be reformulated because 'theories of politics should be drawn from the realities of political life' (1963, p. 476). In contrast, Bachrach claims: 'I see no reason why a principle, serving both as an ideal to strive for and as a standard for judging the progress of a political system toward the achievement of that ideal, must be realizable in practice to perform its function' (1967, p. 86). In other words, unless one is able to show that the goals are inherently impossible, on account of human nature, the limited diffusion of the civic virtues in society is not reason enough for abandoning them as a target for society as a whole. If widespread political participation provides a schooling in democracy, then its achievement is the best means of buttressing a democratic order. The contrasting method of electing wise elites and, as it were, then insulating them from the demands of the masses is hardly calculated to produce a civic culture or a democratic society.

Finally, many of the empirical findings about political attitudes in the 1950s and 1960s, which buttressed the elitist case, have had to be revised recently. For example, we have seen that the findings about the low level of ideological thinking among the non-activists have been qualified in the light of later research (see Chapter 5 above). And the claim that the elites (be they defined as the activists, better-educated, politically interested, or local political office-holders) uphold the democratic principles also requires revision (Rackman, 1969, p. 21). Not only have some of the elites been inconspicuous defenders of the ideals (e.g. as in the American Watergate scandal or in Ulster), but a number of the original survey questions appear, in retrospect, to have been biased to the actual experience of the elites. In the 1970s in the United States political distrust was frequently found among the better-educated and other traditionally expected 'carriers of the [democratic] creed'. A good part of the cynicism among the political left and right in the United States is based on the perceived performance of the system. But critics of the pluralist interpretation of politics, even when they accept or do not dispute the validity of the original findings, question the conclusions. They complain about the failure to test alternative models of the policy process, the mobilisation of bias in a system, and how the political agenda and policy alternatives are structured by the 'routines' established by the institutions and values in society.

In one respect at least, there may be an important continuity between the 'traditional' and 'new' theories of democracy. Pateman (1980) usefully reminds us that there are different strands in traditional democratic theory. There is a participatory strand expressed, for example, in Rousseau, and found in the practices and values of direct democracy; the other strand is a liberal democratic one, which prefers mixed government, and places limits on the role of government and the range of decision-making by politics and popular participation. Liberal theory has regarded competitive elections as the cornerstone of democracy, allowing for majority rule, but providing guarantees for essential minority rights and liberties. Popular participation is regarded primarily as a means of checking and limiting the rulers, and 'not as something essential and valuable in its own right' (p. 63). In the West, much of our thinking and many of our procedures derive from the liberal or representative version of democracy rather than the participatory one. The arguments of the 'new' elitist theory are, therefore, not so new after all, but rather a re-working of an established strand in traditional democratic theory.

It is also possible to locate the 'new' theory within a conservative tradition in sociology (Bramson, 1960), particularly the fear of mass politics and the challenge to order, community and hierarchy posed by the rise of industrialism and democracy. Pluralist writers in this tradition have been critics of mass society/mass politics. According to Kornhauser, mass society is a social system in which elites are readily accessible to influence by non-elites and vice versa (1959, p. 39). Individuals who are socially isolated or not affiliated to groups which are intermediate between the family and the government are particularly likely to be susceptible to the appeal of mass movements. There is some evidence that such people are more likely to feel alienated from the political and social structure (Groth *et al.*, 1977). Pluralists have wanted people to belong to autonomous organisations and social groups. Groups such as trade unions, churches, business organisations and face-to-face groups have a claim to the individual's loyalty, 'mediate' direct contact between the state and citizens and act as a barrier against totalitarianism. The great fear of such writers is of a sudden increase in participation or of large-scale participation outside established procedures and institutions. Events in Weimar Germany and the breakdown of regimes elsewhere suggest that increased participation causes or reflects (an important difference) a heightening of social tension, political irrationality and political extremism. Hence the association of apathy with political moderation, and high activity with fanaticism and extremism.

## Political Participation

Until recently most discussion on popular participation in politics was confined to voting in elections and an examination of the various correlations of such activity. Historically, popular struggles for political 'rights' and entry to citizenship have concentrated on gaining the vote. For most people this is the most frequent form of political activity and much discussion interchanges political with electoral participation. Political participation has a variety of other meanings, however. For some writers it may refer to a set of attitudes, such as a person's sense of political competence, or high levels of interest in and information about politics. Others refer to a wide range of political activities, of which voting is only one. Perhaps non-electoral forms of participation have been neglected because they are less easy to analyse through sample surveys. If so, this is unfortunate, because if voting is a relatively low-salience activity for most people, then the forms which occur between elections may be more important for them.

There has been a remarkable stability in patterns of voting participation across many Western states. Many of the personal and social factors which correlated with turnout twenty years ago (Lipset, 1959, p. 184) have been confirmed by Crewe (1981) across various countries for the present. Personal characteristics making for high turnout include:

- high income,
- high education,
- middle age,
- married status,
- membership of organisation.

The social factors include:

- relevance of government policies to the individual,
- access to information,
- group pressure to vote,
- cross-pressures.

But we may also point to more strictly political factors which influence rates of electoral participation. One is partisanship or the cleavage structure. The intensity of partisan tensions between the political parties, the saliency of the election and the predicted closeness of the result are all factors which tend to stimulate a higher turnout. The socialist parties have been more successful in mobilising the working class to vote in class-based party systems than in societies which lack such a party. We have already noted the historical evidence that electoral rules governing ease of access to the voting booth and the nature of party competition affect the size of the political universe. In the United States race is now a factor that narrows the general participation between the social classes. What Verba and Nie (1972) term 'group consciousness' encourages blacks to participate at higher rates than would be predicted on the basis of SES factors alone.

But voting is only one among various forms of activity, and compared with most other forms of participation voting imposes fewer demands, at least in terms of time and opportunity costs. Verba and Nie show that, for the United States, election turnout has declined a little over the years, while more people have participated in other modes. These two authors have developed a rich typology of modes of political participation, one which appears to work well in some other countries (Verba *et al.*, 1978). They distinguish four main modes of political participation:

- voting,
- campaign activity,
- communal activity,
- particularised contacts.

These types of activity are fairly self-evident except perhaps for the last two. Communal activity includes contacting local officials about social issues, and particularised activity includes contacting local officials on highly specific problems. The modes differ along certain important dimensions (p. 73): (1) the amount of initiative each act requires, or how much time, effort and resources are involved; (2) the scope of the potential outcome; whether it affects all citizens (e.g. taxation) or only a few; (3) the amount of conflict entailed by the act; how much opposition is raised, whether policies involve a redistribution of benefits and costs; (4) the type of influence exerted by the act; whether the act conveys information to the leaders or pressures to conform to a policy. Voting, for example, requires little initiative, usually creates little conflict, but may have a widespread effect on the formation of the government and general policies. Communal activities require initiative, create little conflict and have collective outcomes (though they may be narrower than those of elections). Campaign activities are more obviously linked to conflictual activities.

Drawing on their surveys from a number of countries, Nie and Verba (1975, pp. 17–22) find that the different forms of participation appeal to persons of different types of orientations. The three basic orientations studied were:

(1) psychological involvement in politics, measured by interest in and attention to public affairs;
(2) partisanship, measured by strength of party identification;
(3) sense of contribution to the community welfare, based on the respondent's belief that he makes such a contribution.

*Voting,* for example, attracts partisans, those who strongly identify with a political party. It has little association with the individual's sense that he is contributing to community welfare, probably because the voting act does not require much psychological involvement. *Campaign activity* is associated with psychological involvement, partisanship and sense of contribution to the community. *Communal activity* correlates highly with psychological involvement again, but not with partisanship: participants in this area are less interested in conflictual aspects of activity. Finally, with *particularised activity*, there is, predictably, little association with partisanship or sense of community usefulness, and only a modest relationship with psychological involvement.

The authors suggest that the campaign and communal activities are the core of political participation. Across the five nations participants in these two modes also score high on psychological involvement.[1] The activity of voters and particularists is explained by more specific factors. What distinguishes the former activities is that they are concerned with more general political matters and a greater initiative is required by the individual engaging in them. We would, therefore, expect these types of participants to have a strong psychological involvement in politics.

Originally, political participation was viewed as being unidimensional; people who performed the more demanding acts (e.g. running for or holding office) also performed less demanding ones (e.g. being a member of a political party, discussing politics and voting). At the top of this national hierarchy were the 'gladiators' who were engaged in the more demanding activities; they were followed by more modest types of political activists, and at the bottom were the apathetics who did not participate. But the findings disconfirm the hypothesis of a hierarchy or ladder of forms of participation (cf. Milbrath, 1965). Verba and his colleagues found that in the United States political participation was multidimensional and that activity in the more demanding context did not entail a willingness to participate in the 'easier' context. What was more likely was that if one engaged in an act belonging to a particular participatory mode, then one was also likely to engage in other acts in that mode.

Table 9.1 *Modes of Political Participation in Britain and the USA*

| | *Britain* % | *USA* % |
|---|---|---|
| Inactive | 19·6 | 24·7 |
| Voting specialists | 62·6 | 23·6 |
| Group specialists | 8·1 | 22·5 |
| Party specialists | 6·7 | 16·9 |
| Complete actives | 3·0 | 12·4 |

*Sources:* Moyser, 1980, Verba and Nie, 1972.

In other countries political participation appears to be more cumulative. Barnes and Kaase (1979, p. 86) found that between 60 and 80 per cent of respondents in five West European states were identified by activity on the first three points of their scale.[2] In other words, political participation in Western Europe appeared to be unidimensional, in contrast with the United States where voters proved less likely to be generally active.

The different modes attract people with different political orientations, so that it is possible to build up psychological profiles of the participants. For example, the *general inactives* engage in hardly any participatory acts, and have little or no sense of involvement in politics or of political efficacy. By contrast, the *complete actives* participate in all modes, and are politically skilled and psychologically involved. The *voting specialists* include those who are regular voters but engage in no other form of activity. As seen in Table 9.1, most British adults fall into this mode. *Group specialists* participate in group activities and this mode accommodates most participants in the United States. Finally, the *party specialists* or campaigners specialise in activities related to political parties. It is interesting that the British score high on voting, the easiest form of activity, and must limit their activity to it; in the United States, by contrast, a smaller proportion vote but this participation more often carries over to other forms of activity.

In most societies there is a socio-economic pattern to political participation. Cross-national studies, such as those by Almond and Verba and Inkeles, have shown how this relationship stands up. Higher social class is associated with higher levels of political information, interest and commitment, resources which dispose people to be active in politics. Although high levels of political participation do not correlate with high levels of economic development (e.g. voting turnout in the United States compared with Turkey or Italy), there does appear to be a threshold level of economic development which is necessary for widespread participation. The reason is that at low levels of material possession a person's energies are taken up with other tasks. As Inkeles comments on the apathy which he found among the poor in developing societies: 'Good citizenship is, then, a kind of luxury which can be "afforded" only by those who have secured a standard of living above the minimum required for mere survival' (1969, p. 1134).

Other surveys (e.g. Inglehart, 1971, 1977) suggest that in the high consumption societies of the West, economically satisfied people may demand more far-reaching forms of political participation. Verba and Nie (1972, pp. 98–100) show how, for the United States, certain groups 'overparticipate' and some 'underparticipate', if we assume a uniform level of activity for all groups. The former category includes the middle-aged, males, above-average income earners, whites, Protestants and the well-educated. The socio-economic 'bias' in participation is not surprising and is a general phenomenon. The extent of the bias varies across countries, however. It is even stronger in India but far less marked in Japan and Austria compared with the United States (Nie and Verba, 1975, p. 44).

One factor which does weaken socio-economic influences on participation is the nature of partisanship among citizens. People of low socio-economic status but who are strong partisans are above-average participants in Austria, Japan and the Netherlands. In the United States and India, however, these people are below-average participants. What seems to differentiate these systems is that in the former the parties do help to structure the political divisions in the electorate; the main opposing parties are closely related to social groups on different sides of the political cleavage and stimulate the activity of farmers and industrial workers (Nie and Verba, 1975, pp. 52–4). In class-stratified societies a working-class party may substitute for education and status as a facilitator of political participation and sense of political competence among workers (Rokkan and Campbell, 1960).

But how do we test whether different levels of activity among groups actually affect the responsiveness of the elite? Verba and Nie questioned local political elites and the electorate about their perceptions of important issues. Their test of elite 'responsiveness' was agreement between the elites and groups on what were important policy questions. They found that there were higher levels of agreement between elites and those groups who 'overparticipated'. Local elites were more likely to agree with middle-class than working-class groups, for example, about the important issues. The inactives are mainly from the lower socio-economic groups, less educated and black (in the United States). Here is some confirmation of the charge that elitist democrats usually fail to note that political non-participation, like political participation, is both selective and cumulative: it tends to be concentrated among the already socially and economically disadvantaged and relatively unorganised, and elites may fail to recognise their policy preferences. [3] At the same time, high participation tends to produce more politically representative decision-makers.

## Political Protest

Political protest, so far as it is activity intended to influence the policies of the authorities, clearly is political participation. Till recently, however, most studies have excluded unconventional or protest activity, largely on the grounds that it was 'outside' the system (e.g. Verba and Nie, 1972). Yet demonstrations, sit-ins and strikes for political objects appear to have increased in recent years. Another implication, perhaps, is that orthodox and unorthodox forms of political activity attract different people. The import of most studies was that the more politically active and competent citizens were also usually the most supportive of the regime in Britain and the United States. More recently, however, the politically competent citizens have shown a willingness to resort to extra-legal or unorthodox methods beyond those associated with voting and working for a party. Alan Marsh's (1977) survey uncovered a widespread potential for protest in Britain (e.g. willingness to break a law the respondent considered unjust or harmful). Willingness to protest was highest among those who shared all three of the following characteristics: (1) a high sense of political efficacy; (2) cynicism towards the political system; (3) a developed sense of ideological and political conceptualisation. It was also related to dissatisfaction with perceived government performance.

This willingness to protest is not, therefore, a displacement from conventional forms of political participation; rather, it appears to be an additional means of redress. It is among the more politically competent that there appear to be higher levels of ideology and mistrust, and it is among people who possess these qualities that there is a greater potential for protest. The findings were broadly confirmed in a survey of West European countries (Barnes and Kaase, 1979). Here is an important qualification to the idea of a relationship between participation and a sense of political competence buttressing support for a political system. Where cynicism is allied to competence, we have the potential for protest; where it is allied to a sense of powerlessness, we have apathy (Gamson, 1968).

## Conclusion

That participation *per se* is a 'good', even 'rational', activity has long been assumed, even if only implicitly. Dahl (1970), however, has reminded us that increases in participation for more people may have 'costs' in terms of lower efficiency for the economy and society and of fewer opportunities for other activities for the individual. Downs and other exponents of economic models of political behaviour have suggested that in some circumstances it may be quite rational for a person, having calculated the costs and benefits of his electoral participation, to abstain from voting. He may calculate that his vote will make no difference to the outcome, that there is no important difference between the choices offered at the election (indifference), or he may feel negatively about the choices (alienation). The evidence for electoral turnout is that the more alienated or indifferent one feels about the choices, then the more likely one is not to participate (Brody and Page, 1973).

In the United States these features would seem to provide an explanation for the comparatively low and declining level of electoral turnout, with indifference being a more important factor than alienation. On the other hand, surveys show that levels of political interest, information and sense of duty to vote are as high as ever. In addition, more people now enjoy higher education and high socio-economic status, factors which should increase turnout. But, offsetting these trends, there has been a decline in sense of efficacy, trust in the government and parties, and perceived responsiveness of the political elites. These negative factors seem to be important in depressing the level of turnout. Similarly, in Britain the non-voters are poorly motivated (scoring low on party identification, political interest and information) and seem to be more politically apathetic than alienated (Crewe *et al.*, 1977). They tend to be young, single, not to own a home, and to have moved recently, all factors which weaken their links with the community.

We have already noted the evidence that higher socio-economic status, at both aggregate and individual levels, increases the likelihood of political participation. The importance of social status as a cross-national influence was seen in the Almond–Verba survey. Britain and the United States had more participants than Italy and Mexico, largely because they were more economically and socially developed and therefore contained more people with high social-economic backgrounds. People of equivalent social status in the countries participated at approximately the same levels. The precise relationship between these macro-economic processes and effects on political participation is mediated by changes in the attitudes of individuals

(Nie *et al.*, 1969). A simple statement of the relationship postulates that social and economic change produces changes in social structure which in turn correlate with increased rates of political participation. What seems to be more important is that changes in the social structure tend to go with higher levels of political efficacy, interest, information and sense of civic duty. It is these attitudinal variables which explain why higher levels of socio-economic development in a country and higher social status among individuals increase the level of political participation. The exception to this statement is the role played by voluntary organisations, which tend to proliferate with SED. Organisational involvement and higher social status raise levels of political participation through different routes, with higher status operating only where there are changes in attitudes, whereas organisational activity has a direct effect regardless of the attitudinal factors.

It is worth restating the cautions already given in the previous two chapters about explaining political behaviour through socio-economic or other environmental factors. Advances in socio-economic development usually accompany greater levels and more varied forms of political participation. With the growth of government functions, the diffusion of greater education, communications, and so on, people have more incentives and opportunities to participate. But SED itself is a complex and variegated process. For example, urbanisation, beyond a certain point, may have a negative effect on levels of political participation, as it weakens the sense of community. What determines the impact of urbanisation on levels and types of political participation is the socio-cultural characteristics of the residents and quality of community it creates (cf. Nie and Verba, 1975, p. 38).

In contrast to the social class and social psychological explanations of participation (in terms of information, efficacy and civic duty, for example), one may pose a 'rational' or instrumental explanation. Because high-status individuals frequently score highly on the above attitudes, have more political resources and are more likely to wield influence, they have more 'rational' reasons to participate (Goodin and Dryzek, 1980). Such an approach implies that widespread participation will be associated with a broad equality in the dispersion of political resources; in such circumstances more people have incentives to participate.

In recent years there have been impressive gains in our knowledge of the social, psychological and political correlates of political participation. And study of the participation process has not been confined to the electoral arena. A number of findings, about which people are more active than others, the reasons for this, or the consequences for public policy of different levels of activity between different groups, do have normative implications. To note this is to return to the argument raised at the beginning of this chapter: in an important sense the advocates of greater participation have been strengthened by the survey evidence that political elites are more responsive in areas of high political participation (see above, p. 179). In the final analysis, however, the differences between elitist and participation theorists of democracy boils down not only to differences of definition but also to their contrasting views of theory and its relation to empirical studies.

## Notes: Chapter 9

1 The other nations are India, Nigeria, Japan and Austria.
2 That is, talking about politics, reading about politics in the press and working on community problems.
3 The socio-economic bias in participation is found also in the Soviet Union (White, 1979, ch. 7) and Eastern Europe (Putnam, 1976).

Chapter 10

# Assessment

The previous chapters have demonstrated the impact of the 'behavioural revolution' on research methods and certain areas in political science and also looked at a number of findings in these areas. I have already considered a number of *ad hoc* criticisms directed at particular aspects. In this final chapter I turn to the doubts and questions which have been raised about behaviouralism. It is worth noting that a similar mood of questioning is found in the other social sciences as well. In political science the mood is termed a 'post-behavioural revolution'. This umbrella term embraces a wide range of critics, including humanists, proponents of traditional approaches and political radicals, all of whom attack in varying degree the methods, values and substance of the behavioural approach. David Easton (1969), in an effort to impose some order on a disparate set of complaints, has said that the critical reaction is characterised by a demand for *relevance* and *action*.

## Post-Behaviouralism

The efforts to fashion a more scientific study of politics, combined with the negative reaction to them, have certainly encouraged a greater sense of self-awareness among political scientists. Scholars are more technically proficient; more topics are covered and in greater depth; most subjects now have their own impressive shelves of studies to which a student may go; the discipline is less parochial, less Western-oriented; it draws on the insights and concepts of other social sciences. In sum, we have a number of generalisations and well-researched findings about many political phenomena. There is also, however, an awareness of the complexity of political phenomena and of the contingent nature of many of our statements. There is not a greater consensus about whether or not the study of politics is a science, and only an optimist would conclude that recent controversies represent yet a further stage in the development of the discipline. In this concluding chapter I would like to consider the validity of these criticisms and assess the extent to which the aims of the behaviouralists have been satisfied.

One may readily agree about a number of the shortcomings in specific aspects of the work. Opinion surveys, for example, are often a-historical, statistical correlation between variables is sometimes confused with causation, interpretations poorly fit the data presented or fit alternative but unexamined interpretations, there are macro/micro problems of analysis (e.g. see p. 71 on political culture) and much grand theory hardly connects with the real world of politics or the requirements of empirical research. But it is worth noting that such shortcomings are not peculiar to political behaviour or political science; they are also found across the social sciences, not least in traditional political science studies. (Indeed, reading some the post-behavioural criticisms, one has to remind oneself of the shortcomings which prompted the behaviouralist reaction in the first place.) In so far as they derive from the deficiencies of particular researchers they are no condemnation of the general approach.

It is useful to keep in mind the distinct types of criticism:

(*a*) fundamental or philosophical objections against the approach, its methods, assumptions and techniques; these question the possibility of distinguishing factual from value statements;
(*b*) objections against one aspect, e.g. use of quantification or surveys;
(*c*) sociological criticisms about the political – usually allegedly conservative – assumptions and values of the work;
(*d*) objections against the substance of the research or a particular piece of work rather than the approach itself.

Summarised, the most coherent attacks concentrate on the following major points.

### The Study of Political Behaviour Is Not and Cannot Be Value-Free

There are various points to consider concerning the role of values in political science. The first relates to the inevitable place of values in the study of politics. The criticism runs along the following lines. Although behaviouralists may self-consciously eschew 'ought' questions and try to avoid value judgements, their work in fact is not value-free. A researcher's values and personal experience inevitably influence his selection and definition of an area for study, and even his research methods and his interpretation of data. The study of politics, far from being value-free, is actually impregnated with values, as Weber appreciated. The fund of the researcher's personal experience, which stands outside the behaviouralist's methodology, makes a major contribution to the research. In other words, all researchers either have explicit preferences or pedal their values under the guise of neutrality. I agree: a value-free study is not possible, though the researcher can and should try to separate his biases from analysis.

A second argument is that the value premises of most behaviouralists are conservative, however implicit and unstated they may be.[1] There are different aspects to this charge: that the personal values of behaviouralists are conservative, or their research procedures are, or the substance and consequences of their work are. The objection from the political left is not against bias *per se*. A large literature on the sociology of knowledge casts doubt on the objectivity of any knowledge and points out how the influence of culture, time, or social class acts as a conditioning element upon any work. What critics on the left prefer is a more radical orientation instead of the dominant liberal pluralist one. It is fair to comment that much of the work 'unwittingly purveys an ideology of social conservatism tempered by modest incremental change' (Easton, 1969, p. 1052). The bulk of the American work on voting behaviour, socialisation, public opinion and political development has certainly been supportive of that country's socio-political status quo and its version of a liberal and pluralist democracy (see Chapter 9 above).

One example of alleged 'conservatism' has been the tendency to rewrite normative theories, particularly of democracy and representative government, in the light of empirical research. The new theory was brought into line with behavioural reality; if people fell short of the standards laid down in the theory, then the latter was revised accordingly. But, counter the critics, normative theory always contains an element of the potential, and its validity is not in any way vitiated by people behaving differently from the pattern laid down in the theory. Many of these new interpretations have ended up as elitist statements of democracy, pointing to the usefulness of apathy and low political participation, and either recommending a severe qualification to the rational-activist model of citizenship or suggesting the positive consequences which may follow shortfalls from the ideal (see Chapter 9). There are, therefore, generous amounts of speculation and values laced among the tables and scientific jargon.

We might contrast this approach with that of many classic theorists of democracy who developed their ideas partly in relation to the question 'What is the good society and which set of political arrangements best supports it?'. For this reason it is difficult for the above studies to test or confute the classic theorists, as they claim to do (cf. Duncan and Lukes, 1963). Rousseau and J. S. Mill were not primarily concerned to describe people as they actually behaved; they saw democracy as an ideal to be pursued and were more concerned with the 'developmental' consequences for the individual and society which would stem from membership in a participatory democracy. Many behaviouralists, by contrast, have been more concerned with incremental change and political stability, and the working of political institutions and levels of political participation have been evaluated according to how they serve these twin goals.

But in accepting the partial truth of this criticism one does not have to accept the usually accompanying either-or complaint that is made about much of the political behaviour work – that the willingness of pluralist behaviouralists to describe and not criticise the status quo is implicitly to underwrite it. While the commitment to scientific procedures and the principle of operationalisation certainly discourages speculative and visionary thinking, it is not immediately obvious that empirical research supports the conditions it describes, e.g. analyses of social and economic inequality, political apathy, poverty, tyranny, and so on. As in the case of the early poverty surveys by Booth and Rowntree in England, accurate description of a condition may be a stimulus and tool for its reform. Indeed, from the outset the scientific temper in the United States was joined to a liberal reformist outlook. The hope was that a more exact political science, which would be value-free because scientific, would be used to promote 'better' government and 'good' citizenship.

A third and separate issue is whether the attempted exclusion of value theory impoverishes the study of politics. Some critics complain that modern political science has lost contact with its historical roots. Defenders of political theory note that originally the study of politics was as much concerned with questions of what ought to be – what is the best society, or the appropriate relationship between a citizen and government? – as with empirical matters. The great works of Hobbes, Locke, Rousseau, Marx, Hegel, and so on, are 'philosophies of man' (Plamenatz, 1963, p. xv), dealing with such fundamental questions as law, consent, the nature of authority and obligation. Obviously, how people ought to behave is not a question which can be framed in the form of a hypothesis and tested. But a close study of the adequacy of the assumptions and ideas of these theorists is a useful exercise for the student and, perhaps more important, a means of advancing knowledge about ourselves. To acknowledge this, however, is not also to imply agreement that politics should be studied exclusively through commonsense, *Verstehen*, philosophy, or historical approaches. An accurate account of how people behave in politics is an important datum for theorists.

In so far as the scientific approach relies upon rigour and setting aside personal preferences, then Hobbes and Machiavelli could be recognised as political scientists. With their deductive approaches and their reliance on direct observation, they were clearly of this school, though they were primarily concerned to advance a particular viewpoint. Marxists also claim that they have a scientific view of society, derived from their understanding that the mode of production and economic structure determines the nature of society. They would claim to be able, ultimately, to predict the future course of history.

## The Study of Political Behaviour Is Not Amenable to Generalisation

The above issues connect with the larger debate about whether or not a science of politics, a scientific study of politics and society, is actually possible. Is there a fundamental difference between natural and social science? A pristine *scientific* view is that there is no essential difference between natural and social phenomena, that the latter are in principle amenable to the techniques and methods of natural science. A typical statement of this outlook is: 'the principal tasks of the discipline of political science are to describe, explain and evaluate political behaviour' (Moon, 1975, p. 7). It claims that the explanatory logic for the social sciences is the same as that for the hard sciences. Both are interested in arriving at generalisations and both use the same techniques of observation, measurement and quantification, and so forth. In turn this means that we may develop laws and regularities for political phenomena. Claims for the law-like character of our generalisations mean that such statements must apply to all cases and not reflect an 'accidental' concomitance of events (ibid., p. 139).

A contrasting 'interpretive' position is that social phenomena are quite different from natural phenomena and require different strategies of explanation. This line of argument runs as follows. Human actions, in contrast to natural phenomena, express the purposes of the actors themselves. Therefore, our understanding of a particular action (i.e. its meaning to the actor) depends on knowing the actor's intentions, which in turn requires an understanding of the context of the act and the culture of the society. The explanations offered by social scientists are intrinsically different from those of natural scientists. According to Winch (1958), perhaps the most influential spokesman for this view, the understanding of human behaviour calls not for 'causal laws' or generalisations but, instead, interpretations of knowledge of 'rules' about the behaviour which gives it meaning. Social behaviour is about following rules and studying the meaning or the behaviour. Causal analysis of this behaviour, it is suggested, is irrelevant, for the study of meanings is not amenable to generalisation. There are many regularities in social life, such as getting out of bed, going to work, or reading a morning paper, but these are not uniformities or laws.

Critics point to further difficulties with the idea of a social science. Unlike the phenomena of natural science, human beings have purposes of their own. Once they are aware of a generalisation they may so conduct themselves as to confirm or to undermine the validity of the generalisation. In addition, different definitions of a situation among individuals deny the possibility of generalisations. The difficulties in establishing equivalent behaviours across societies become insuperable; apparently similar actions will have different meanings across different countries. Such a critique also calls into question the meaning of much social science data. Surveys, for example, usually reflect categories which the researcher imposes on the respondent. The researcher may have his standardised questionnaires but the crucial problem is whether the respondents have similar frames of reference when they are responding to his questions and whether the interviewer 'correctly' understands the meaning of the respondents' answers. In other words, what is the final validity of the data which have been interpreted across various 'grids' of meaning?

One may find these arguments persuasive up to a point without agreeing wholly with their conclusions. Demands for an understanding of the actor's point of view raise an important point but there are dangers if one claims that this is the sole criterion for validity. Such an approach will not, for example, explain the unintended consequences of a person's actions and a person may be lying, mistaken, or deceiving himself in describing and accounting for his actions and attitudes.

It is difficult to arrive at any 'laws' of political science, that is, statements that are valid for all times and circumstances. What we have, at best, are 'soft' generalisations or tendency statements about such topics as voting behaviour, political recruitment, political socialisation or policy outputs, and so forth. These findings are by no means trivial, amount to something more than statements about unique cases, and certainly provide a general knowledge about politics. It would be unfortunate if the objection that this does not amount to a science, in the sense in which natural scientists use the term, were carried over to saying that this does not increase our knowledge about political phenomena. Our subject matter is probably too 'soft' for the formal scientific method.

Notwithstanding this apology, one might acknowledge three problems with the *corpus* of political science findings considered from a strictly scientific viewpoint. The first is the requirement that statements be falsifiable, that is, they be stated in a form which allows them to be tested and refuted. Yet the problem posed by probabilistic statements is that such statements allow for a limited number of exceptions without their ceasing to be probabilistic. A second problem is that our generalisations are usually stated more in terms of statistical correlations between factors than explanations. Many of the propositions advanced about voting behaviour (Chapter 5), conditions of stable democracy (Chapter 7) and policy outputs (Chapter 8) are of this kind. That is, they find an association between factors, but do not establish the causal linkages between them.

The third problem is that so much of the research conducted in the 1970s has severely undermined the validity of 'generalisations' or 'tendency statements' about political behaviour made even as recently as the 1960s. One can point to the studies of voting behaviour, political socialisation, public opinion and policy outputs to support the point. Clearly, the changes are compatible with our claims that we have limited generalisations. Political actors may change their behaviour in reaction to a new situation, to new demands and pressures, or even to academic knowledge! Yet if one has to revise the findings about these areas of political behaviour over so short a span of time, then one may be more doubtful about our capacity to generalise over a wider range of time and space. The sheer number of possible partial causes of a phenomenon and the difficulty of completely isolating any one factor weakens our ability to generalise.

Many careful comparative studies have found that the more one looks at specific cases in detail, the more one has to qualify the generalisations. There are so many factors and sub-factors that it becomes extremely difficult to make worthwhile generalisations. Sidney Verba has noted this dilemma in comparative research (1968, p. 113):

> Generalisations fade when we look at particular cases. We add intervening variable after intervening variable. Since the cases are few in number, we end with an explanation tailored to each case. The result begins to sound quite idiographic or configurative.

If there is to be a way out of this impasse it probably lies in a compromise between the two positions. The scientific approach assumes, mistakenly, that the universe is clock-like and that its parts behave predictably. We do not need to be reminded that clocks and clouds have different degrees of determinacy (Popper, 1972; Almond and Genco, 1977) and that the political world we deal with is more cloud-like and unpredictable. Yet one can generalise within limits and establish correlations or regularities, again within limits. In this book I have presented many examples of limited generalisations, but generalisations which fall short of being universal across time and space (cf. Beer, 1970).

## Political Science Should Be More Relevant and Problem-Oriented

Political studies, it is claimed should have a 'pay-off' in the sense of providing applied knowledge. One critic, for example, has called for 'a basic scientific knowledge and a continuing inventory, update and refinement of that knowledge' (Paige, 1977, p. 211). Easton's 'credo of relevance' complains that many major problems – war, pollution, race, urban blight, and so on – have been ignored in research. According to Easton, engagement in policy matters is a social responsibility of the academic: 'reform becomes inseparable from knowledge' (1969, p. 1066). The demand seems to be that relevant knowledge should be developed and then be applied, for example, to the solution of practical problems or the evaluation or selection of political methods and leaders. Before looking at the difficulties in the way of carrying out the recommendations, however, it is worth noting that many studies do deal with serious political issues, that the field of policy analysis is perhaps the fastest growth area in the discipline, that the apparently burning issue of today may not be so vital in five years' time, and that nowhere have the criteria of 'importance' or 'relevance' been actually spelt out. An important question is whether the selection of problems or the grounds of either social concern or relevance advance our understanding of political life? The major goal of political science, surely, is the latter.

This concern is found in recent demands for applied social science. It is also seen in the demands, for example, for the promotion and selection of psychologically healthy political leaders (Rogow, 1963) or the incorporation of measures of personal development and rationality into our theories of political development (Bay, 1965). The recommendation touches on the old question about the appropriate relations between the academic and practitioner, between the pursuit of knowledge for its own sake and the accumulation of knowledge which is relevant for policy. The two domains, however, are subject to different role pressures, time-horizons and incentives, and apply different evaluative criteria to knowledge. The concern to be 'relevant' and 'useful' has echoes of Plato's search for the men of 'gold' and is in line with the calls for a 'new' political science, or a policy science (by, for example, Merriam, Lasswell and, more recently, Easton). The claims assume that (*a*) such knowledge in the form of cross-cultural generalisations is available and (*b*) it can be readily applied to the real world. These are, of course, two crucial and highly debatable assumptions. The experiences of the 1960s – the disaster of the 'Great Society' programme in the USA, the failure of so many 'tech-fix' solutions such as PPBS, and the growing awareness of the sheer intractability of the problems and difficulties of social engineering – have recently induced a new modesty about policy science.

One has only to consider the record in two areas in which numerous American political scientists have diagnosed and prescribed. In 1950 a prestigious group of scholars issued a famous report which itemised the shortcomings of the American parties and proposed reforms which would bring about a 'responsible' two-party system. As is now recognised, the report was not only poor political science in terms of understanding the forces shaping a party system and the probable consequences of different types of party systems, but also peddled value judgements under the academically respectable imprimatur of the American Political Science Association (Kirkpatrick, 1971). Idealisation of F. D. Roosevelt's New Deal presidency led to his successors being judged according to how interventionist and activist they were. 'Strong' presidents were admired, 'weak' ones found wanting. Again, much of the literature is highly normative, is pervaded by a 'liberal' ethos and support for an interventionist federal government, and evinces little concern to discriminate between the use and abuse of power. The disillusioning experience of the Nixon presidency has encouraged a revival of interest in the benefits of limited power (compare Neustadt, 1960, and Hargrove, 1974). While one may point to many other cautionary experiences, these two cases are interesting because they are so well researched. Rather than scholarship being joined to a sense of social responsibility (as policy scientists advocate), it appears that poor political science complemented inadequate policy science.

The academic and the activist are subject to different pressures and role demands in judging a body of knowledge or approaching a problem. The academic's knowledge, even when applied, is specialised and tentative, whereas the problem-solver wants some certainty and, because his problems transcend disciplines, a holistic approach. The scholar's problems are usually too 'undisciplined' for the perspective of the social sciences. To be 'useful' to the policy-maker, a 'discipline' needs a body of verified knowledge, of the 'if . . . then . . .' kind, a consensus on its objectives and a technology which is capable of applying findings to real-world phenomena. Where all these conditions are met, then we may speak of a relevant policy knowledge (Rose, 1976b).

Yet it is worth repeating that the outstanding feature of political science, and other social sciences, is that most of our verified findings are rather low level, for example, about the effects of different electoral systems on party fortunes, budgeting, decision-making on committees, recruitment, and so on. There is no scholarly consensus on many major issues and much of our work may not be directly applicable to the problems facing politicians anyway. In contrast, while economics may not have a scholarly consensus about its objectives (on, for example, the causes of inflation), its knowledge can be applied through the tools of public expenditure, taxation, money supply and budgeting. What political science needs primarily at present is a better and more rigorous explanation of political phenomena before applying the knowledge.

## The Apolitical Study of Politics

To what extent have behavioural studies neglected or de-emphasised political factors? There is some truth in the claim that many early (and even contemporary) advocates of a scientific study of politics saw (see) it as a means of solving problems, developing a more 'rational' society and resolving disagreements. Yet politics, after all, arises from disagreement and, like the nineteenth-century positivists before them, behaviouralists have laid themselves open to the charge of being apolitical (Crick, 1959; Wolin, 1969). Other charges include:

(1) *Explanations are often reductionist*, i.e. political phenomena are explained in terms of a narrow range of personal, cultural, social, or economic causes. Critics object that political phenomena have too frequently been relegated to the status of dependent variables: what they term the fallacy of 'inputism'. To some degree this is a consequence of the interdisciplinary focus on social behaviour, though the impact of Marxism has also resulted in a debate on the ultimate importance of social and economic factors. The competition between the social sciences in strategies of explanation arises from the fact that the political is only one aspect of a person's activity or personality and may indeed be linked to other aspects of his behaviour. A person who is apathetic in politics, for example, tends not to participate in other areas. But too often political sociology is presented as a sociological reduction of politics, rather than a genuine hybrid (Sartori, 1969). Party systems and voting behaviour are seen as reflecting socio-economic factors or cleavages (cf. Lipset and Rokkan, 1963), and the undoubted impact of constitutions or electoral system on the policies and even the system of parties is ignored or regarded as secondary. Yet there are many cases of this political or constitutional 'engineering', and of parties and political rules translating social and economic forces into political processes.

(2) *There is inadequate definition of the political.* Is it activity relating to power, the state, the act of governing, or what? Or should we consider it as an activity exclusively directed to satisfying human needs and wants? Christian Bay has expressed the view that much of our present research deals with what he calls *pseudo-politics,* that is, activity concerned with the satisfaction of private interests. He argues that politics should study, instead, the largely psychological wants and needs of individuals, activity which is 'aimed at improving or protecting conditions for the satisfaction of human needs and demands'. Yet it is fair to ask if Bay's

personal preference for a new agenda amounts to more than definitional dogmatism and the hope that 'correct' policies will emerge from such a standpoint. Should the study of politics be solely or mainly a task-oriented or a humanistic discipline?

(3) *There is a need for the speculative spirit and other forms of knowledge and verification apart from statistical procedures.* It is claimed that phenomena which are observable, measurable, and occur with regularity are not necessarily the most significant.[2] According to Hugh Stretton (1969) the behaviouralists' methods provide us with knowledge that is tentative, at best, though the data may establish relationships between variables and invalidate generalisations. But for the acquisition of tacit knowledge, we have to rely on the exercise of intuition, imagination and tradition. This line of argument may be elaborated. Although some social theory is too abstract for empirical verification, this does not mean that we should discount the activity of theorising. Speculation must go beyond the limits imposed by its amenability to testing. A theory may not be verifiable *at present,* although it may be so at some later date and premature closure of our speculation might lose us many insights.

It is also clear that some important areas of the field are not so susceptible to the 'hard-nosed' rigorous, quantitative approach. In political culture, to take an example, how does one get at the latent, symbolic and subconscious by empirical methods? Finally, we must acknowledge that the sense of imagination and the speculative spirit have been crucial for the emergence of the major orienting concepts of the social sciences. An eloquent protest against undue reliance on the logic-empirical methods and problem-solving outlook has been expressed by Nisbet. He notes that the major concepts in sociology such as *anomie* (Durkheim), *charisma* and *rationalisation* (Weber), or *Gemeinschaft* and *Gesellschaft* (Tönnies) were 'reached in ways more akin to those of the artist than those of the data processor, the logician, or the technologist' (1966, p. 19). None of this means, however, that we should abandon empirical research and retreat into mere subjectivism. The major social science thinkers were also keenly aware of the need to discipline their intuition and to meet tests of inter-subjective validity. The tensions between the hard-nosed data-based school and the intuitive school are common to all the social sciences (Bendix and Roth, 1971).

## Conclusion

A coherent viewpoint is not immediately apparent in the post-behaviouralist critique. There is an implication – rarely stated – that one should return to traditional approaches. Some of the demands and criticisms are, if not self-contradictory, at least difficult to integrate. Satisfying demands for more relevance, in the form of more policy-oriented or problem-related studies, will presumably still require a large empirical and scientific component. On the other hand, demands for a more speculative, visionary spirit or a greater normative concern may encourage a sense of distance from the problems of here and now.

The legacy of the behavioural revolution in political science has resulted in a number of changes and these have been reflected in the preceding pages of this volume. They include: more topics of research, greater cross-disciplinary study, concern for operationalisation of concepts, 'testing' relationships between variables, and quantification and diffusion of particular techniques of data-gathering and analysis, such as sample surveys, game theory and content analysis. In these respects, Dahl was correct to write an 'Epitaph to a Successful Protest' (Dahl, 1961b). Yet one may still be impressed by the tenacity with which political theory, institutional studies and comparative history have held their place and enjoyed a revival. Above all, there has been no emerging consensus on what the foundations of the discipline are. We have cases of scholars studying similar problems but coming up with different conclusions (cf. Sartori, 1976) and different theories and explanations for similar findings. Much of the new political science has been more to do with methods and research styles than with substantive findings about political behaviour. There has been no cumulation but, instead, continuing philosophy of science disputes about what we are doing and should be doing. Most of the goals set out by Easton in 1953, particularly in grand theory, remain unachieved.

## Notes: Chapter 10

1 'Conservative' not in the Burkeian sense of viewing society as an organic unity, favouring hierarchy, and so on, but in the sense of favouring or accepting the status quo. If the status quo is liberal pluralist, or socialist, and one supports it, then one is 'conservative' in this sense.

2 See the discussion on 'the mobilisation of bias' or the 'hidden face of power' and how, if at all, it may be studied (pp. 152–3 above).

# Bibliography

The following abbreviations are used for journals:

| | |
|---|---|
| *AJS* | *American Journal of Sociology* |
| *APSR* | *American Political Science Review* |
| *ASR* | *American Sociological Review* |
| *BJPS* | *British Journal of Political Science* |
| *BJS* | *British Journal of Sociology* |
| *CJEPS* | *Canadian Journal of Economic and Political Science* |
| *CP* | *Comparative Politics* |
| *CPS* | *Comparative Political Studies* |
| *EJ* | *Economic Journal* |
| *EJPR* | *European Journal of Political Research* |
| *G & O* | *Government and Opposition* |
| *ISQ* | *International Studies Quarterly* |
| *ISSJ* | *International Social Science Journal* |
| *JP* | *Journal of Politics* |
| *JSI* | *Journal of Social Issues* |
| *MJPS* | *Midwest Journal of Political Science* |
| *NLR* | *New Left Review* |
| *PAR* | *Public Administration Review* |
| *POQ* | *Public Opinion Quarterly* |
| *PS* | *Political Studies* |
| *PSQ* | *Political Science Quarterly* |
| *RES* | *Review of Economic Studies* |
| *SR* | *Sociological Review* |
| *SSQ* | *Social Science Quarterly* |
| *WP* | *World Politics* |


Adelman, I., and Morris, C. (1967), *Economic Growth and Social Equity in Developing Countries* (Stanford, Calif.: Stanford University Press).

Adorno, T., Frenkel-Brunswick, E., Sanford, N., and Levinson, D. (1950), *The Authoritarian Personality* (New York: Harper & Row).

Almond, G. (1956), 'Comparative political systems', *JP*, vol. 18, no. 3, pp. 391–409.

Almond, G. (1967), 'Political theory and political science', in I. de Sola Pool (ed.), *Contemporary Political Science* (New York: McGraw-Hill), pp. 1–21.

Almond, G. (1980), 'The intellectual history of the civic culture concept', in G. Almond and S. Verba (eds), *The Civic Culture Revisited* (Boston, Mass.: Little, Brown), pp. 1–36.

Almond, G., Flanagan, S., and Mundt, R. (1973), *Crisis, Choice and Change* (Boston, Mass.: Little, Brown).

Almond, G., and Genco, S. (1977), 'Clouds, clocks and the study of politics', *WP*, vol. 29, no. 4, pp. 489–522.

Almond, G., and Powell, B. (1966), *Comparative Politics* (Boston, Mass.: Little, Brown).

Almond, G., and Verba, S. (1963), *The Civic Culture* (Princeton, NJ: Princeton University Press).

Alt, J. (1971), 'Some social and political correlates of county borough expenditure', *BJPS*, vol. 1, pt 1, pp. 49–62.

Alt, J. (1978), *The Politics of Economic Decline* (Cambridge: Cambridge University Press).

Alt, J., Crewe, T., and Sarlvick, B. (1976), 'Partisanship and policy choice: issue preferences in the British electorate February 1974', *BJPS*, vol. 6, pt 3, pp. 273–90.

Anderson, p. (1965), 'Origins of the present crisis', *NLR*, vol. 23, pp. 26–53.

Asher, H. (1976), *Presidential Elections and American Politics* (Homewood, Ill.: Dorsey Press).

Axelrod, R. (1974), 'Communication', *APSR*, vol. 68, no. 2, pp. 718–19.

Bachrach, P. (1967), *The Theory of Democratic Elitism* (Boston, Mass.: Little, Brown).

Bachrach, P., and Baratz, M. (1962), 'The two faces of power', *APSR*, vol. 56, no. 4, pp. 947–52.

Bachrach, P., and Baratz, M. (1963), 'Decisions and nondecisions: an analytical framework', *APSR*, vol. 57, no. 3, pp. 641–51.

Banfield, E. (1961), *Political Influence* (New York: The Free Press).

Barber, J. (1965), *The Lawmakers* (New Haven, Conn.: Yale University Press).

Barber, J. (1972), *The Presidential Character* (Englewood Cliffs, NJ: Prentice-Hall).

Barnes, S., and Kaase, M. (1979), *Political Action: Mass Participation in Five Western Democracies* (London: Sage).

Barry, B. (1970), *Sociologists, Economists and Democracy* (London: Collier Macmillan).

Bay, C. (1965), 'Politics and pseudo-politics', *APSR*, vol. 57, no. 1, pp. 39–51.

Beck, P. (1976), 'A socialization theory of partisan alignment', in R. Niemi and H. Weisberg (eds), *Controversies in American Voting Behaviour* (San Francisco: Freeman), pp. 396–411.

Beer, S. (1970), 'Political science and history', in M. Richter (ed.), *Essays in Theory and History* (Cambridge, Mass.: Harvard University Press), pp. 41–3.

Bell, D. (1960), *The End of Ideology* (Glencoe, Ill.: The Free Press).

Bendix, R., and Roth, G. (1971), *Scholarship and Partisanship* (Berkeley, Calif.: University of California Press).

Bentley, A. (1908), *The Process of Government* (Chicago: University of Chicago Press).

Berelson, B., Lazarsfeld, P., and McPhee, W. (1954), *Voting* (Chicago: University of Chicago Press).

Bloom, H., and Price, D. (1975), 'Voter response to short-run economic conditions', *APSR*, vol. 69, no. 4, pp. 1240-54.

Blumler, J., and McQuail, D. (1968), *Television in Politics* (London: Faber).

Boaden, N. (1971), *Urban Policy-Making* (Cambridge: Cambridge University Press).

Bottomore, T. (1965), *Elites and Society* (London: Watts).

Bramson, L. (1960), *The Political Context of Sociology* (Princeton, NJ: Princeton University Press).

Brittan, S. (1968), *Left or Right: The Bogus Dilemma* (London: Secker & Warburg).

Brittan, S. (1975), 'The economic consequences of democracy', *BJPS*, vol. 5, no. 2, pp. 129–59.

Brody, R., and Page, B. (1972), 'Comment: the assessment of policy voting', *APSR*, vol. 66, no. 2, pp. 450–8.

Brody, R., and Page, B. (1973), 'Indifference, alienation and rational decisions', *Public Choice*, vol. 15, no. 1, pp. 1–17.

Brown, A. (1977), *Soviet Politics and Political Science* (London: Macmillan).

Brown, A., and Gray, J. (eds) (1977), *Political Culture and Political Change in Communist States* (London: Macmillan).

Budge, I. (1979), *Agreement and the Stability of Democracy* (Chicago: Markham).

Burnham, W. D. (1965), 'The changing shape of the American political universe', *APSR*, vol. 59, no. 1, pp. 7–28.

Burnham, W. D. (1970), *Critical Elections and the Mainsprings of American Politics* (New York: Norton).

Burnham, W. D. (1974), 'Theory and voting research: some reflections on Converse's "Change in the American electorate" ', *APSR*, vol. 68, no. 3, pp. 1002–23.

Burns, J. M. (1975), *Leadership* (New York: Harper & Row).

Butler, D., and Stokes, D. (1975), *Political Change in Britain* (London: Macmillan; 1st edn 1969).

Caldeira, C., and Greenstein, F. (1978), 'Partisan identification and political socialisation in Britain, France and the United States', *PSQ*, vol. 93, no. 1, pp. 35–50.

Cameron, D. (1978), 'The expansion of the public economy: a comparative analysis', *APSR*, vol. 72, no. 4, pp. 1243–61.

Campbell, A., Converse, P., Miller, W., and Stokes, D. (1960), *The American Voter* (New York: Wiley).

Castles, F. (1978), *The Social Democratic Image of Society* (London: Routledge & Kegan Paul).

Castles, F. (1979), 'Public welfare provision, Scandinavia and the sheer futility of the sociological approach to politics', *BJPS*, vol. 9, pt 2, pp. 157–71.

Castles, F., and McKinlay, R. (1979), 'Does politics matter?: An analysis of the public welfare commitment in advanced democratic states', *EJPR*, vol. 7, no. 2, pp. 169–86.

Citrin, J. (1974), 'Comment on "Political issues and trust in government, 1964–70" ', *APSR*, vol. 68, no. 3, pp. 973–88.

Cnudde, C., and Neubauer, D. (eds) (1969), *Empirical Democratic Theory* (Chicago: Markham).

Conradt, D. (1980), 'Changing German political culture', in G. Almond and S. Verba (eds), *The Civic Culture Revisited* (Boston, Mass.: Little, Brown), pp. 212–72.

Converse, P. (1964), 'The nature of belief systems in mass publics', in D. Apter (ed.), *Ideology and Discontent* (New York: The Free Press), pp. 206–61.

Converse, P. (1966), 'The concept of the normal vote', in A. Campbell, P. Converse, W. Miller and D. Stokes (eds), *Elections and the Political Order* (New York: Wiley), pp. 9–39.

Converse, P., Clausen, A., and Miller, W. (1965), 'Electoral myth and reality: the 1964 election', *APSR*, vol. 59, no. 2, pp. 321–36.

Converse, P., Miller, W., Rusk, J., and Wolfe, A. (1969), 'Continuity and change in American politics: parties and issues in the 1968 election', *APSR*, vol. 63, no. 4, pp. 1083–1105.

Coser, L. (1956), *The Functions of Social Conflict* (Glencoe, Ill.: The Free Press).

Cowart, A. (1978), 'The economic policies of European governments', parts I and II, *BJPS*, vol. 9, pt II, pp. 285–311, and pt III, pp. 425–39.

Crenson, M. (1971), *The Un-Politics of Air Pollution: A Study of Non-Decision Making in the Cities* (Baltimore, Md, and London: Johns Hopkins University Press).

Crewe, I. (1981), 'Electoral participation', in D. Butler *et al.* (eds), *Democracy at the Polls* (Washington, DC: American Enterprise Institute), pp. 216–43.

Crewe, I. (1982), 'The Labour Party and the electorate', in D. Kavanagh (ed.), *The Politics of the Labour Party* (London: Allen & Unwin), pp. 9–49.

Crewe, I., Fox, T., and Alt, J. (1976), 'Non-voting in British general elections, 1964–October 1974', in C. Crouch (ed.), *The British Political Sociology Yearbook*, Vol. 3 (London: Croom Helm), pp. 38–109.

Crewe, I., and Payne, C. (1976), 'Another game with nature: an ecological regression model of the British two-party vote ratio in 1970', *BJPS,* vol. 6, pt 1, pp. 43–82.

Crewe, I., Sarlvik, B., and Robertson, D. (1977), 'Partisan dealignment in Britain 1964–74', *BJPS,* vol. 7, no. 2, pp. 129–90.

Crick, B. (1959), *The American Science of Politics* (London: Routledge & Kegan Paul).

Crick, B. (1966), *In Defence of Politics* (Harmondsworth: Penguin).

Cutright, P. (1963), 'National political development: measurement and analysis', *ASR*, vol. 28, no. 2, pp. 253–64.

Cutright, P. (1965), 'Political structure, economic development and national security programmes', *AJS*, vol. 70, no. 3, pp. 537–50.

Dahl, R. (1958), 'A critique of the ruling elite model', *APSR*, vol. 52, no. 2, pp. 463–9.

Dahl, R. (1961a), *Who Governs?* (New Haven, Conn.: Yale University Press).

Dahl, R. (1961b), 'The Behavioural Approach in Political Science: Epitaph for a Monument to a Successful Protest', *APSR*, vol. 55, no. 4, pp. 763–772.

Dahl, R. (ed.) (1966), *Political Oppositions in Western Democracies* (New Haven, Conn.: Yale University Press).

Dahl, R. (1967), 'The evaluation of political systems', in I. de Sola Pool (ed.), *Contemporary Political Science* (New York: McGraw-Hill), pp. 166–81.

Dahl, R. (1970), *After the Revolution* (New Haven, Conn.: Yale University Press).

Dahl, R. (1971), *Polyarchy* (New Haven, Conn.: Yale University Press).

Dahrendorf, R. (1957), *Class and Class Conflict in Industrial Society* (Stanford, Calif.: Stanford University Press).

Davies, J. (1970), 'The J-curve of rising and declining satisfactions as a cause of some great revolutions and a contained revolution', in H. Graham and T. Gurr (eds), *The History of Violence in America* (New York: Bantam Books), pp. 690–730.

Dawson, R., and Prewitt, K. (1967), *Political Socialization* (Boston, Mass.: Little, Brown).

Dawson, R., and Robinson, J. (1963), 'Inter-party competition, economic variables, and welfare policies in the American states', *JP*, vol. 25, no. 2, pp. 265–89.

Dennis, J. (1975), 'Trends in public support for the American party system', *BJPS*, vol. 5, pt 1, pp. 187–230.

Deutsch, K. (1961), 'Social mobilisation and political development', *APSR*, vol. 55, no. 3, pp. 493–514.

Downs, A. (1957), *An Economic Theory of Democracy* (New York: Harper & Row).

Dowse, R., and Hughes, J. (1971a), 'The family, the school and the political socialisation process', *Sociology*, vol. 5, no. 1, pp. 21–45.

Dowse, R., and Hughes, J. (1971b), 'Girls, boys and politics', *BJS*, vol. 22, no. 1, pp. 53–67.

Duncan, G., and Lukes, S. (1963), 'The new democracy', *PS*, vol. 11, no. 2, pp. 156–77.

Dye, T. (1966), *Politics, Economics and the Public* (Chicago: Rand McNally).

Dye, T. (1969), 'Income inequality and American state politics', *APSR*, vol. 63, no. 2, pp. 157–62.

Dye, T. (1972), *Understanding Public Policy* (Englewood Cliffs, NJ: Prentice-Hall).

Dye, T. (1976), *Who's Running America?* (Englewood Cliffs, NJ: Prentice-Hall).

Easton, E. (1953), *The Political System* (New York: Knopf; 2nd edn 1971).

Easton, D. (1957), 'An approach to the analysis of political systems', *WP*, vol. 9, no. 3, pp. 383–400.

Easton, D. (1965), *A Systems Analysis of Political Life* (New York: Wiley).

Easton, D. (1967), 'The current meaning of behavioralism', in J. Charlesworth (ed.), *Contemporary Political Analysis* (New York: The Free Press), pp. 11–31.

Easton, D. (1969), 'The new revolution in political science', *APSR*, vol. 63, no. 4, pp. 1051–61.

Easton, D. (1975), 'The concept of political support', *BJPS*, vol. 5, pt 4, pp. 438–59.

Easton, D., and Dennis, J. (1969), *Children and the Political System* (New York: McGraw-Hill).
Eckstein, H. (1963), 'A perspective on comparative politics, past and present', in H. Eckstein and D. Apter (eds), *Comparative Politics* (New York: The Free Press), pp. 3–34.
Eckstein, H. (1966), *Division and Cohesion in Democracy: A Study of Norway* (Princeton, NJ: Princeton University Press).
Eckstein, H., and Gurr, E. (1975), *Patterns of Authority* (New York: Wiley).
Edelman, M. (1964), *The Symbolic Uses of Politics* (Urbana, Ill.: University of Illinois Press).
Edinger, L. (1965), *Kurt Schumacher: A Study in Personality and Political Behaviour* (Stanford, Calif.: Stanford University Press).
Edinger, L. (ed.) (1967), *Political Leadership in Industrialized Societies* (New York: Wiley).
Edinger, L. (1975), 'Where are the political superstars?', *PSQ*, no. 2, pp. 249–68.
Edinger, L., and Searing, D. (1967), 'Social background in elite analysis', *APSR*, vol. 61, no. 2, pp. 428–45.
Erikson, E. (1958), *Young Man Luther* (New York: Norton).
Erikson, E. (1969), *Gandhi's Truth. On the Origins of Militant Nonviolence* (New York: Norton).
Eulau, H. (1963), *The Behavioral Persuasion in Politics* (New York: Random House).
Eulau, H. (1967), 'Segments of political science most susceptible to behavioristic treatment', in J. Charlesworth (ed.), *Contemporary Political Analysis* (New York: The Free Press), pp. 32–50.
Eulau, H. (ed.) (1969), *Behavioralism in Political Science* (New York: Atherton Press).
Eysenck, H. (1951), 'Primary social attitudes', *BJS*, vol. 2, no. 3, pp. 198–209.
Fabricant, S. (1952), *The Trend of Government Activity in the United States since 1900* (New York: Bureau of Economic Research).
Fagen, R. (1969), *The Transformation of Political Culture in Cuba* (Stanford, Calif.: Stanford University Press).
Femia, J. (1979), 'Elites, participation and the democratic creed', *PS*, vol. 27, no. 1, pp. 1–20.
Festinger, I. (1957), *A Theory of Cognitive Dissonance* (New York: Harper & Row).
Field, J., and Anderson, R. (1969), 'Ideology in the public's conceptualisation of the 1964 election', *POQ*, vol. 33, no. 3, pp. 380–93.
Finer, S. (1962), *Man on Horseback* (London: Pall Mall).
Finer, S. (1969), 'Almond's concept of political system', *G & O*, vol. 4, no. 1, pp. 5–21.
Finer, S. (1975), *Adversary Politics and Electoral Reform* (London: Wigram).
Free, L., and Cantril, H. (1968), *The Political Beliefs of Americans* (New Brunswick, NJ: Rutgers University Press).
Frey, B., and Schneider, F. (1978), 'A politico-economic model of the United Kingdom', *EJ*, vol. 88 (June), pp. 243–53.
Fried, R. (1971), 'Communism, urbanism and the two Italies', *JP*, vol. 33, no. 4, pp. 1008–51.

Fried, R. (1975), 'Comparative urban policy and performance', in Greenstein and Polsby (eds), op. cit., Vol. 6, ch. 16.
Fry, R., and Winters, R. (1970), 'The politics of redistribution', *APSR*, vol. 64, no. 2, pp. 5–22.
Gamson, W. (1968), *Power and Discontent* (Homewood, Ill.: Dorsey Press).
George, A. (1968), 'Power as a compensatory value for political leaders', *JSI*, vol. 24, no. 3, pp. 29–50.
George, A. (1969), 'The "operational code": a neglected approach to the study of political leaders and decision-making', *ISQ*, vol. 13, no. 2, pp. 190–222.
George, A., and George, J. (1956), *Woodrow Wilson and Colonel House* (New York: John Day).
Goodhart, C., and Bhansali, R. (1970), 'Political economy', *PS*, vol. 18, no. 1, pp. 43–106.
Goodin, R., and Dryzek, J. (1980), 'Rational participation: the politics of relative power', *BJPS*, vol. 10, pt 3, pp. 273–92.
Gough, I. (1979), *The Political Economy of the Welfare State* (London: Macmillan).
Greenberg, E. (1970), 'Children and government: a comparison across racial lines', *MJPS*, vol. 14, no. 2, pp. 249–75.
Greenstein, F. (1969), 'The benevolent leader: children's images of political authority', *APSR*, vol. 54, no. 4, pp. 934–43.
Greenstein, F. (1960), *Personality and Politics* (Chicago: Markham).
Greenstein, F., Herman, U., Stradling, R., and Zureik, E. (1974), 'The child's conception of the Queen and the Prime Minister', *BJPS*, vol. 4, pt 3, pp. 257–88.
Greenstein, F., and Polsby, N. (eds) (1975), *Handbook of Political Science,* 8 vols (Boston, Mass.: Addison-Wesley).
Greenstein, F., and Tarrow, S. (1969), 'The study of French political socialisation', *WP*, vol. 22, no. 1, pp. 95–138.
Grofman, B., and Muller, E. (1973), 'The strange case of relative gratification and potential for political violence: the V-curve hypothesis', *APSR*, vol. 67, no. 2, pp. 514–39.
Grossholtz, J. (1964), *Politics in the Philippines* (Boston, Mass.: Little, Brown).
Groth, A., Schutz, E., and Blakely, E. (1977), 'Affluence and mass society; some Californian data', *BJPS*, vol. 7, pt 4, pp. 541–9.
Gurr, E. (1970), *Why Men Rebel* (Princeton, NJ: Princeton University Press).
Guttsman, W. L. (1963), *The British Political Elite* (London: Heinemann).
Halsey, A., and Crewe, I. (1968), 'Social survey of the civil service', in *The Civil Service: Surveys and Investigations* (London: HMSO), vol. 3, no. 1, pp. 1–441.
Hamilton, R. (1972), *Class and Politics in the United States* (London: Wiley).
Hargrove, E. (1974), *The Power of the Modern Presidency* (New York: Knopf).
Heclo, H. (1974), *Modern Social Policy in Britain and Sweden* (New Haven, Conn.: Yale University Press).
Heidenheimer, A. (1973), 'The politics of public education, health and

welfare in the USA and Western Europe: how growth and reform potentials have differed', *BJPS*, vol. 3, pt 3, pp. 315–40.

Heidenheimer, A., Heclo, H., and Adams, C. (1975), *Comparative Public Policy* (New York: St Martin's Press).

Hermet, G., Rose, R., and Rouquie, A. (eds) (1978), *Elections without Choice* (London: Macmillan).

Hewitt, C. (1974), 'Policy-making in post-war Britain', *BJPS*, vol. 4, pt 2, pp. 187–216.

Hewitt, C. (1977), 'The effect of political democracy and social democracy on equality in industrial societies: a cross-national comparison', *ASR*, vol. 42, no. 1, pp. 45–64.

Hibbs, D. (1977), 'Political parties and macro-economic policy', *APSR*, vol. 71, no. 4, pp. 1467–87.

Hibbs, D. (1978), 'On the political economy of long-run trends in strike activity', *BJPS*, vol. 8, pt 2, pp. 153–76.

Hofferbert, R. (1966), 'The relationship between public policy and some structural and environmental variables in the American states', *APSR*, vol. 60, no. 1, pp. 73–82.

Hofferbert, R. (1974), *The Study of Public Policy* (Indianapolis, Ind., and New York: Bobbs-Merrill).

Hoffmann, S. (1967), 'Heroic leadership: the case of modern France', in Edinger (ed.), op. cit., pp. 108–54.

Hook, S. (1943), *The Hero in History* (New York: John Day).

Hunter, F. (1953), *Community Power Structure* (Chapel Hill, NC: University of North Carolina Press).

Huntington, S. (1968), *Political Order in Changing Societies* (New Haven, Conn.: Yale University Press).

Huntington, S. (1974), 'Post-industrial society: how benign will it be?', *CP*, vol. 6, n. 1, pp. 1–15.

Huntington, S., and Nelson, J. (1976), *No Easy Choice: Political Participation in Developing Countries* (Cambridge, Mass.: Harvard University Press).

Hyman, H. (1959), *Political Socialization* (New York: The Free Press).

Inglehart, R. (1971), 'The silent revolution in Europe: intergenerational change in post-industrial societies', *APSR,* vol. 65, no. 4, pp. 991–1017.

Inglehart, R. (1979), *The Silent Revolution: Changing Values and Political Styles among Western Publics* (Princeton, NJ: Princeton University Press).

Inkeles, A. (1969), 'Participant citizenship in six developing countries', *APSR*, vol. 63, no. 4, pp. 1120–41.

Janowitz, M., and Miller, W. (1952), 'The index of political predisposition in the 1948 election', *JP*, vol. 14, no. 4, pp. 710–27.

Jaros, P., Hirsch, H., and Fleron, F. (1968), 'The malevolent leader: political socialization in an American subculture', *APSR*, vol. 62, no. 2, pp. 564–75.

Jennings, E. (1979), 'Competition, constituencies and welfare policies', *APSR*, vol. 73, no. 2, pp. 414–29.

Jennings, M., and Niemi, R. (1974), *The Political Character of Adolescence* (Princeton, NJ: Princeton University Press).

Jennings, M., and Niemi, R. (1981), *Generations and Politics* (Princeton, NJ: Princeton University Press).

Katz, D. (1960), 'The functional approach to the study of attitudes', *POQ*, vol. 24, no. 2, pp. 163–204.

Kavanagh, D. (1971), 'The deferential English: a comparative critique', *G & O*, vol. 6, no. 3, pp. 333–60.

Kavanagh, D. (1972a), *Political Culture* (London: Macmillan).

Kavanagh, D. (1972b), 'Political behaviour and political participation', in G. Parry (ed.), *Political Participation* (Manchester: Manchester University Press), pp. 102–24.

Kavanagh, D. (1974), *Crisis, Charisma and British Political Leadership*, Sage Professional Paper in Contemporary Political Sociology I (London: Sage).

Kavanagh, D. (1980), 'From gentlemen to players', in W. Gwynn and R. Rose (eds), *Britain: Progress and Decline* (London: Macmillan).

Kavanagh, D. (1982), 'Still the workers' party?', in D. Kavanagh (ed.), *The Politics of the Labour Party* (London: Allen & Unwin), pp. 95–110.

Kernell, S. (1977), 'Presidential popularity and negative voting', *APSR*, vol. 71, no. 1, pp. 44–66.

Key, V. O., Jnr (1949), *Southern Politics* (New York: Knopf).

Key, V. O., Jnr (1955), 'A theory of critical elections', *JP*, vol. 17, no. 1, pp. 3–18.

Key, V. O., Jnr (1961), *Public Opinion and American Democracy* (New York: Knopf).

King, A. (1969), 'Political parties in Western democracies', *Polity*, vol. 2, no. 2, pp. 111–41.

King, A. (1973), 'Ideas, institutions, and the policies of governments: a comparative analysis', *BJPS*, vol. 3, pts 3 and 4, pp. 291–313 and 409–23.

King, A. (1976), *Britain Says Yes* (London: American Enterprise Institute).

Kirkpatrick, E. (1971), 'Toward a more responsible two-party system: political science, policy science, or pseudo-science', *APSR*, vol. 70, no. 4, pp. 965–90.

Kirkpatrick, J. (1976), *The New Presidential Elite: Men and Women in National Politics* (New York: Russell Sage/Twentieth Century Fund).

Klapper, J. (1960), *The Effects of Mass Communication* (New York: The Free Press).

Klein, R. (1976), 'The politics of public expenditure: American theory and British practice', *BJPS*, vol. 6, pt 4, pp. 401–32.

Klingeman, H. (1972), 'Dimensions of political belief systems: "levels of conceptualisation as a variable" ', *CPS*, vol. 5, no. 1, pp. 93–106.

Kornhauser, W. (1959), *The Politics of Mass Society* (Glencoe, Ill.: The Free Press).

Kramer, G. (1971), 'Short-term fluctuations in US voting behaviour 1896–1964', *APSR*, vol. 65, no. 1, pp. 131–43.

Ladd, E., and Hadley, C. (1976), *Transformations of the American Party System*, 2nd edn (New York: Norton).

Landau, M. (1972), *Political Theory and Political Science* (New York: Collier Macmillan).

Lane, R. (1962), *Political Ideology: Why the American Man Believes What He Does* (New York: The Free Press).

Lane, R., and Sears, D. (1964), *Public Opinion* (Englewood Cliffs, NJ: Prentice-Hall).

La Palombara, J. (1968), 'Macrotheories and microtheories in comparative politics', *CP*, vol. 1, no. 1, pp. 60–71.

Lasswell, H. (1948), *Power and Personality* (New York: Norton).

Lawrence, D. (1976), 'Procedural norms and tolerance: a reassessment', *APSR*, vol. 70, no. 1, pp. 80–100.

Lazarsfeld, P., Berelson, B., and Gaudet, H. (1948), *The People's Choice* (New York: Columbia University Press).

Leites, N. (1951), *The Operational Code of the Politburo (New York: McGraw-Hill).*

Leites, N. (1953), *A Study of Bolshevism* (Glencoe, Ill.: The Free Press).

Lerner, D. (1958), *The Passing of Traditional Society* (New York: The Free Press).

Lewis, J. (1966), 'The study of Chinese political culture', *WP*, vol. 18, no. 3, pp. 503–24.

Lijphart, A. (1968a), *The Politics of Accommodation* (Berkeley, Calif.: University of California Press).

Lijphart, A. (1968b), 'Typologies of democratic systems', *CPS*, vol. 1, no. 1, pp. 3–44.

Lijphart, A. (1980), 'The structure of inference', in G. Almond and S. Verba (eds), *The Civic Culture Revisited* (Boston, Mass.: Little, Brown), pp. 37–56.

Lijphart, A. (1981), 'Political parties, ideologies and programmes', in D. Butler *et al.* (eds), *Democracy at the Polls* (Washington, DC: American Enterprise Institute), ch. 3.

Lindblom, E. (1959), 'The science of muddling through', *PAR*, vol. 19 (Spring), pp. 79–88.

Lippmann, W. (1922), *Public Opinion* (New York: Harcourt Brace).

Lipset, S. (1959), *Political Man* (London: Heinemann).

Lipset, S. (1964), *The First New Nation* (London: Heinemann).

Lipset, S., and Raab, E. (1970), *The Politics of Unreason* (London: Heinemann).

Lipset, S., and Rokkan, S. (1967), *Party Systems and Voter Alignments* (New York: The Free Press).

Lukes, S. (1974), *Power* (London: Macmillan).

Lynd, R., and Lynd, H. (1937), *Middletown in Transition* (New York: Harcourt Brace).

McClelland, D. (1961), *The Achieving Society* (Princeton, NJ: Princeton University Press).

McClosky, H., Hoffmann, P., and O'Hara, R. (1960), 'Issue conflict and consensus among party leaders and followers', *APSR*, vol. 54, no. 2, pp. 406–27.

McConnaughy, J. (1950), 'Certain personality factors of state legislators in South Carolina', *APSR*, vol. 44, no. 4, pp. 897–903.

McFarland, A. (1969), *Power and Leadership in Pluralist Systems* (Stanford, Calif.: Stanford University Press).

Mackenzie, W. (1958), *Free Elections* (London: Allen & Unwin).

Mackenzie, W. (1970), *The Study of Political Science Today* (London: Macmillan).

Mann, M. (1970), 'The social cohesion of liberal democracy', *ASR*, vol. 35, no. 3, pp. 423–39.
Marsh, A. (1977), *Protest and Political Consciousness* (London: Sage).
Marsh, D. (1971), 'Political socialisation: the implicit assumptions questioned', *BJPS*, vol. 1, pt 4, pp. 453–65.
Massey, J. (1975), 'The missing leader: Japanese youths' view of political authority', *APSR*, vol. 69, no. 1, pp. 31–48.
Mayhew, D. (1974), *Congress: The Electoral Connection* (New Haven, Conn.: Yale University Press).
Melnik, C., and Leites, N. (1958), *The House Without Windows: France Selects a President* (Evanston, Ill.: Row, Peterson).
Merelman, R. (1968), 'On the neo-elitist critique of community power', *APSR*, vol. 62, no. 2, pp. 451–60.
Merriam, C. (1925), *New Aspects of Politics* (Chicago: University of Chicago Press).
Milbrath. L. (1965), *Political Participation* (Chicago: Rand McNally).
Miliband, R. (1969), *The State in Capitalist Society* (London: Weidenfeld & Nicolson).
Miller, A. (1974), 'Political issues and trust in government, 1964–1970', *APSR*, vol. 68, no. 3, pp. 951–72.
Miller, A., Bolce, L., and Halligan, M. (1977), 'The J-curve theory and the black urban riots', *APSR*, vol. 71, no. 3, pp. 964–82.
Miller, A., Miller, W., Raine, A., and Brown, T. (1976), 'A majority party in disarray: policy polarisation in the 1972 election', *APSR*, vol. 70, no. 3, pp. 753–78.
Miller, W., and Mackie, M. (1973), 'The electoral cycle and the asymmetry of government and opposition popularity', *PS*, vol. 21, no. 3, pp. 263–79.
Miller, W., and Stokes, D. (1963), 'Constituency influence in Congress', *APSR*, vol. 57, no. 1, pp. 55–65.
Mills, C. W. (1956), *The Power Elite* (New York: Oxford University Press).
Mitchell, W. (1962), *The American Polity* (Glencoe, Ill.: The Free Press).
Moon, J. (1975), 'The logic of political inquiry; a synthesis of opposed perspectives', in Greenstein and Polsby (eds), op. cit., Vol. 1, ch. 1.
Moore, B., Jnr (1966), *Social Origins of Dictatorship and Democracy* (Boston, Mass.: Beacon Press).
Mosca, G. (1939), *The Ruling Class* (New York: McGraw-Hill).
Moyser, G. (1980), 'Political participation in Britain', unpublished paper, Manchester University.
Mueller, E. (1973), *War, Presidents and Public Opinion* (London: Wiley).
Munns, J. (1975), 'The environment, politics and policy literature: a critique and reformulation', *WPQ*, vol. 38, no. 4, pp. 646–67.
Nagle, J. (1977), *System and Succession* (Austin, Texas: University of Texas Press).
Neubauer, D. (1967), 'Some conditions of democracy', *APSR*, vol. 61, no. 4, pp. 1002–9.
Neustadt, R. (1960), *Presidential Power* (New York: Wiley).
Newcomb, T. (1943), *Personality and Social Change* (New York: Holt).

Newcomb, T. (1967), *Persistence and Change: Bennington College and Its Students After Twenty-Five Years* (New York: Wiley).

Nie, N., and Anderson, K. (1974), 'Mass belief systems revisited: political change and attitude structure', *JP*, vol. 36, no. 4, pp. 541–91.

Nie, N., Powell, G., and Prewitt, K. (1969), 'Social structure and political participation: developmental relationships', *APSR*, vol. 63, no. 2, pp. 361–78, and no. 4, pp. 808–32.

Nie, N., and Verba, S. (1975), 'Political participation', in Greenstein and Polsby (eds), op. cit., Vol. 4, pp. 1–74.

Nie, N., Verba, S., and Petrocik, J. (1976), *The Changing American Voter* (Cambridge, Mass.: Harvard University Press).

Nisbet, R. (1966), *The Sociological Tradition* (New York: Basic Books).

Nordhaus, C. W. (1975), 'The political business cycle', *RES*, vol. 42, no. 2, pp. 169–90.

Nordlinger, E. (1968), 'Time sequences and rates of change', *WP*, vol. 20, no. 3, pp. 494–520.

Oakeshott, M. (1951), *Political Education* (Cambridge: Bowes & Bowes).

O'Connor, J. (1973), *The Fiscal Crisis of the State* (New York: St Martin's Press).

Page, B. (1978), *Choices and Echoes in Presidential Elections: Rational Man and Electoral Democracy* (Chicago: University of Chicago Press).

Paige, G. (1977), *The Scientific Study of Political Leadership* (New York: The Free Press).

Parkin, F. (1967), 'Working class conservatives: a theory of political deviance', *BJS*, vol. 18, no. 2, pp. 280–90.

Parkin, F. (1971), *Class Inequality and Political Order* (London: MacGibbon & Kee).

Parry, G. (1969), *Political Elites* (London: Allen & Unwin).

Parry, G., and Morris, P. (1973), 'When is a Decision Not a Decision?' in I. Crewe (ed.), *Elites in Western Democracy*, British Political Sociology Yearbook, Vol. 1 (London: Croom Helm), pp. 317–36.

Parsons, T. (1951), *The Social System* (New York: The Free Press).

Parsons, T., and Shils, E. (1951), *Toward a General Theory of Action* (Cambridge, Mass.: Harvard University Press).

Pateman, C. (1980), 'The civic culture: a philosophic critique', in G. Almond and S. Verba (eds), *The Civic Culture Revisited* (Boston, Mass.: Little, Brown), pp. 57–102.

Patrick, G. (1976), *The Concept of 'Political Culture'*, International Studies Association Working Paper No. 80.

Peacock, A., and Wiseman, J. (1961), *The Growth of Public Expenditure in the United Kingdom* (London: Oxford University Press).

Pierce, J. (1970), 'The changing role of political ideology in American politics', *MJPS*, vol. 14, no. 1, pp. 25–42.

Plamenatz, J. (1963), *Man and Society*, 2 vols (London: Longman).

Polsby, N. (1980), *Community Power and Political Theory: A Further Look at Problems of Evidence and Inference* (New Haven, Conn.: Yale University Press).

Polsby, N., and Wildavsky, A. (1976), *Presidential Elections*, 4th edn (New York: Scribner).

Pomper, G. (1968), *Elections in America: Control and Influence in Democratic Politics* (New York: Dodd, Mead).

Pomper, G. (1972), 'From confusion to clarity: issues and American voters, 1956–1968', *APSR*, vol. 66, no. 2, pp. 415–28.

Pomper, G., and Lederman, S. (1980), *Elections in America*, 2nd edn (New York: Longman).

Popkin, S., Gorman, J., Phillips, P., and Smith, J. (1976), 'Comment: toward an investment theory of voting', *APSR*, vol. 70, no. 3, pp. 779–805.

Popper, K. (1959), *The Logic of Scientific Discovery* (New York: Basic Books).

Popper, K. (1972), *Objective Knowledge: An Evolutionary Approach* (Oxford: Clarendon Press).

Prewitt, K. (1970), *The Recruitment of Political Leaders: A Study of Citizen-Politicians* (Indianapolis, Ind., and New York: Bobbs-Merrill).

Prothro, J., and Grigg, C. (1960), 'Fundamental principles of democracy', *JP*, vol. 22, no. 2, pp. 276–94.

Pryor, F. (1968), *Public Expenditures in Communist and Capitalist Nations* (London: Allen & Unwin).

Putnam, R. (1973), *The Beliefs of Politicians* (New Haven, Conn.: Yale University Press).

Putnam, R. (1976), *The Comparative Study of Political Elites* (Englewood Cliffs, NJ: Prentice-Hall).

Pye, L. (1962), *Politics, Personality, and Nation-Building* (New Haven, Conn.: Yale University Press).

Pye, L. (1965), 'Introduction', in L. Pye and S. Verba (eds), *Political Culture and Political Development* (Princeton, NJ: Princeton University Press), ch. 1.

Pye, L. (1972), 'Culture and political science: problems in the evaluation of the concept of political culture', *SSQ*, vol. 53, no. 2, pp. 285–96.

Rackman, B. (1969), 'A behavioral evaluation of the critique of behavioralism', paper delivered to American Political Science Association.

Ranney, A. (1972), 'Turnout and representation in presidential primary elections', *APSR*, vol. 66, no. 2, pp. 349–60.

RePass, D. (1971), 'Issue saliency and party choice', *APSR*, vol. 65, no. 2, pp. 389–400.

Robertson, D. (1976), *A Theory of Party Competition* (London: Wiley).

Robinson, M. (1976), 'Public affairs television and the growth of political malaise: the case of the selling of the Pentagon', *APSR*, vol. 70, no. 2, pp. 409–32.

Robinson, W. (1950), 'Ecological correlation and the behaviour of individuals', *ASR*, vol. 15, no. 3, pp. 341–57.

Rogin, M. (1967), *The Intellectuals and McCarthy: The Radical Spectre* (Cambridge, Mass.: MIT Press).

Rogow, A. (1963), *James Forestal: A Study of Personality, Politics and Policy* (New York: Macmillan).

Rokeach, M. (1960), *The Open and Closed Mind* (New York: Basic Books).

Rokkan, S. (1966), 'Numerical democracy and corporate pluralism', in Dahl (ed.), op. cit., pp. 70–115.

Rokkan, S., and Campbell, A. (1960), 'Citizen participation in political life: Norway and the United States', *ISSJ*, vol. 12, no. 1, pp. 69–99.

Rose, R. (1971), *Governing Without Consensus: An Irish Perspective* (London: Faber).

Rose, R. (ed.) (1974a), *Electoral Behaviour: A Comparative Handbook* (New York: The Free Press).

Rose, R. (1974b), *The Problem of Party Government* (London: Macmillan).

Rose, R. (1976a), 'On the priorities of government', *EJPR*, vol. 4, no. 3, pp. 247–89.

Rose, R. (1976b), 'Disciplined research and undisciplined problems', *ISSJ*, vol. 28, no. 1, pp. 99–121.

Rose, R. (1980), *Do Parties Make a Difference?* (London: Macmillan).

Rose, R., and Kavanagh, D. (1976), 'The monarchy in contemporary political culture', *CP*, vol. 8, no. 4, pp. 548–76.

Rose, R., and Mackie, T. (1980), *Incumbency in Government: Asset or Liability?*, Studies in Public Policy No. 54 (Glasgow: University of Strathclyde).

Rose, R., and Mossawir, H. (1967), 'Voting and elections: a functional analysis', *PS*, vol. 15, no. 2, pp. 173–201.

Rose, R., and Peters, G. (1978), *Can Government Go Bankrupt?* (New York: Basic Books).

Rose, R., and Urwin, D. (1969), 'Social cohesion, political parties and strains in regimes', *CP*, vol. 2, no. 1, pp. 7–67.

Rosenau, J. (1961), *Public Opinion and Foreign Policy* 'New York: Random House).

Rosenberg, M. (1968), *The Logic of Survey Analysis* (New York: Basic Books).

Runciman, W. G. (1966), *Relative Deprivation and Social Justice* (Berkeley, Calif.: University of California Press).

Russett, B. (1964), *World Handbook of Social and Economic Indicators* (New Haven, Conn.: Yale University Press).

Rustow, D. (1970), 'Transitions to democracy', *CP*, vol. 2, no. 3, pp. 337–63.

Salisbury, R. (1968), 'The analysis of public policy: a search for theories and roles', in A. Ranney (ed.), *Political Science and Public Policy* (Chicago: Markham), pp. 151–78.

Sarlvik, B., Crewe, I., Alt, S., and Fox, A. (1976), 'Britain's membership of the EEC – a profile of the electorate's opinion in spring 1974', *EJPR*, vol. 4, pt 1, pp. 83–113.

Sartori, G. (1969), 'From the sociology of politics to the sociology of politics', in S. Lipset (ed.), *Politics and the Social Sciences* (New York: Oxford University Press), pp. 65–100.

Sartori, G. (1970), 'Concept misformation in comparative politics', *APSR*, vol. 54, no. 4, pp. 1033–53.

Sartori, G. (1976), *The Cumulation Problem in Political Science: An Essay on Research Strategies*, International Studies Association Working Paper No. 88.

Schattschneider, E. (1960), *The Semisovereign People* (New York: Holt, Rinehart & Winston).

Scheuch, E. (1968), 'Progress in the cross-cultural use of sample surveys', in S. Rokkan (ed.), *Comparative Research Across Cultures and Nations* (Paris: Mouton), pp. 174–209.

Schlessinger, J. (1966), *Ambition and Politics: Political Careers in the United States* (Chicago: Rand McNally).
Schoen, D. (1977), *Enoch Powell and the Powellites* (London: Macmillan).
Schumpeter, J. (1942), *Capitalism, Socialism and Democracy* (London: Allen & Unwin).
Scott, J. (1968), *Political Ideology in Malaysia* (New Haven, Conn.: Yale University Press).
Searing, D. (1972), 'Models and images of man and society in leadership theory', in G. Paige (ed.), *Political Leadership: Readings for an Emerging Field* (New York: The Free Press), ch. 1.
Searing, D., Schwartz, J., and Lind, A. (1973), 'The structuring principle: political socialisation and political belief systems', *APSR*, vol. 68, no. 2, pp. 415–32.
Searing, D., Wright, G., and Rabinowitz, G. (1976), 'The primacy principle: attitude change and political socialisation', *BJPS*, vol. 6, pt 1, pp. 83–114.
Sears, D., and Friedman, J. (1967), 'Selective exposure to information: a critical review', *POQ*, vol. 31, no. 2, pp. 194–213.
Seymour-Ure, C. (1974), *The Political Impact of the Mass Media* (London: Constable).
Sharkansky, I. (1970), *The Routines of Politics* (New York: Van Nostrand Reinhold).
Sharkansky, I., and Hofferbert, R. (1969), 'Dimensions of state politics, economics and public policy', *APSR*, vol. 63, no. 33, pp. 867–80.
Sharpe, L. J. (1981), 'Does politics matter?', in K. Newton (ed.), *Urban Political Economy* (London: Pinter), pp. 1–26.
Shils, E., and Young, M. (1953), 'The meaning of the coronation', *SR*, vol. 1, no. 2, pp. 63–81.
Siegfried, A. (1913), *Tableau politique de la France de l'Ouest dans la Troisième République* (Paris: A. Colin).
Simeon, R. (1976), 'Studying public policy', *CJEPS*, vol. 9, no. 4, pp. 548–80.
Solomon, R. (1971), *Mao's Revolution and the Chinese Political Culture* (Berkeley, Calif.: University of California Press).
Somit, A., and Tanenhaus, J. (1967), *The Development of American Political Science: From Burgess to Behavioralism* (Boston, Mass.: Allyn & Bacon).
Stokes, D. (1966), 'Some dynamic elements of contests for the presidency', *APSR*, vol. 60, no. 1, pp. 19–28.
Storr, A. (1969), 'Churchill the man', in A. Taylor (ed.), *Churchill: Four Faces and the Man* (London: Allen Lane), pp. 203–46.
Stretton, J. (1969), *The Political Sciences* (London: Routledge & Kegan Paul).
Sullivan, J. (1972), 'A note on redistributive politics', *APSR*, vol. 66, no. 4, pp. 1301–5.
Thompson, D. (1970), *The Democratic Citizen* (Cambridge: Cambridge University Press).
Tilly, C. (1973), 'Does modernisation breed revolution?', *CP*, vol. 5, no. 3, pp. 425–44.
Tilly, C. (ed.) (1975), *The Formation of National States in Western Europe* (Princeton, NJ: Princeton University Press).
Trenaman, J., and McQuail, D. (1961), *Television and the Political Image* (London: Methuen).

Truman, D. (1951), *The Governmental Process* (New York: Knopf).
Tucker, R. (1972), *The Soviet Political Mind* (London: Allen & Unwin).
Tucker, R. (1973), 'Culture, political culture and communist society', *PSQ*, vol. 88, no. 2, pp. 173–90.
Tufte, E. (1978), *Political Control of the Economy* (Princeton, NJ: Princeton University Press).
Verba, S. (1965), 'Organizational membership and democratic consensus', *JP*, vol. 27, no. 3, pp. 647–97.
Verba, S. (1967), 'Some dilemmas in comparative research, *WP*, vol. 20, no. 1, pp. 111–27.
Verba, S. (1980), 'On revisiting the civic culture: a personal postscript', in G. Almond and S. Verba (eds), *The Civic Culture Revisited* (Boston, Mass.: Little, Brown), pp. 394–410.
Verba, S., and Nie, N. (1972), *Participation in America: Political Democracy and Social Equality* (New York: Harper & Row).
Verba, S., Nie, N., and Kim, J. (1978), *Participation and Political Equality* (Cambridge: Cambridge University Press).
Wahlke, J. (1971), 'Policy demands and system support: the role of the represented', *BJPS*, vol. 1, pt 3, pp. 271–90.
Walker, J. (1969), 'The diffusion of innovation among the American states', *APSR*, vol. 63, no. 3, pp. 880–99.
Wallas, G. (1921), *Human Nature in Politics* (New York: Knopf).
Warner, W., and Lunt, P. (1941), *The Social Life of a Modern Community* (New Haven, Conn.: Yale University Press).
White, S. (1979), *Political Culture and Soviet Politics* (London: Macmillan).
Wildavsky, A. (1964), *The Politics of the Budgetary Process* (Boston, Mass.: Little, Brown).
Wilensky, H. (1975), *The Welfare State and Equality* (Berkeley, Calif.: University of California Press).
Wilson, J., and Banfield, E. (1964), 'Public regardingness as a value premise in voting behaviour', *APSR*, vol. 58, no. 3, pp. 876–87.
Winch, P. (1958), *The Idea of a Social Science and its Relation to Philosophy* (London: Routledge & Kegan Paul).
Wolfenstein, E. (1967), *The Revolutionary Personality: Lenin, Trotsky, Gandhi,* (Princeton, NJ: Princeton University Press).
Wolfinger, R. (1971), 'Nondecisions and the study of local politics', *APSR*, vol. 65, no. 4, pp. 1063–80.
Wolin, S. (1969), 'Political Theory as a Vocation', *APSR*, vol. 63, no. 4, pp. 1062–82.
Wylie, L. (1957), *Village in the Vaucluse* (Cambridge, Mass.: Harvard University Press).

# Index